# PROGRESS IN BEHAVIOR MODIFICATION

## Volume 20

# CONTRIBUTORS TO THIS VOLUME

Ron G. Bittle

Patricia A. Cluss

Dennis J. Delprato

June A. Flora

Stephen P. Fortmann

R. M. Foxx

Robert D. Hill

Pauline M. Langeluddecke

F. Dudley McGlynn

Timothy G. Plaska

James F. Sallis

Warren W. Tryon

# PROGRESS IN BEHAVIOR MODIFICATION

EDITED BY

## Michel Hersen

*Department of Psychiatry*
*Western Psychiatric Institute and Clinic*
*University of Pittsburgh School of Medicine*
*Pittsburgh, Pennsylvania*

## Richard M. Eisler

*Department of Psychology*
*Virginia Polytechnic Institute and State University*
*Blacksburg, Virginia*

## Peter M. Miller

*Sea Pines Behavioral Institute*
*Sea Pines Plantation*
*Hilton Head Island, South Carolina*

**Volume 20**

1986

ACADEMIC PRESS, INC.

**Harcourt Brace Jovanovich, Publishers**
Orlando   San Diego   New York   Austin
London   Montreal   Sydney   Tokyo   Toronto

ACADEMIC PRESS, INC.
Orlando, Florida 32887

*United Kingdom Edition published by*
ACADEMIC PRESS INC. (LONDON) LTD.
24–28 Oval Road, London NW1 7DX

LIBRARY OF CONGRESS CATALOG CARD NUMBER: 74-5697

ISBN 0–12–535620–X
ISBN 0–12–531955–X (paperback)

PRINTED IN THE UNITED STATES OF AMERICA

86 87 88 89      9 8 7 6 5 4 3 2 1

# CONTENTS

## Innovations in Behavioral Medicine

*Dennis J. Delprato and F. Dudley McGlynn*

## Behavioral Interventions as Adjunctive Treatments for Chronic Asthma

*Patricia A. Cluss*

## Health Behavior Change at the Worksite: Cardiovascular Risk Reduction

*James F. Sallis, Robert D. Hill, Stephen P. Fortmann, and June A. Flora*

## The Role of Behavioral Change Procedures in Multifactorial Coronary Heart Disease Prevention Programs

*Pauline M. Langeluddecke*

# CONTRIBUTORS

*Numbers in parentheses indicate the pages on which the authors' contributions begin.*

**RON G. BITTLE** (1), Anna Mental Health and Developmental Center, Anna, Illinois 62906

**PATRICIA A. CLUSS**[1] (123), University of Pittsburgh School of Medicine, Pittsburgh, Pennsylvania 15213

**DENNIS J. DELPRATO** (67), Department of Psychology, Eastern Michigan University, Ypsilanti, Michigan 48197

**JUNE A. FLORA** (161), Stanford Center for Research in Disease Prevention, Stanford University Medical Center, Stanford, California 94305

**STEPHEN P. FORTMANN** (161), Stanford Center for Research in Disease Prevention, Stanford University Medical Center, Stanford, California 94305

**R. M. FOXX** (1), Anna Mental Health and Developmental Center, Anna, Illinois 62906

**ROBERT D. HILL** (161), Stanford Center for Research in Disease Prevention, Stanford University Medical Center, Stanford, California 94305

**PAULINE M. LANGELUDDECKE** (199), Professorial Psychiatric Unit, The University of Sydney, Royal North Shore Hospital of Sydney, Sydney, Australia

**F. DUDLEY MCGLYNN** (67), Department of Basic Dental Sciences, University of Florida, Gainesville, Florida 32610

**TIMOTHY G. PLASKA** (1), Boulder River School and Hospital, Boulder, Montana 59632

**JAMES F. SALLIS** (161), Division of General Pediatrics, University of California, San Diego, La Jolla, California 92093

**WARREN W. TRYON** (35), Department of Psychology, Fordham University, Bronx, New York 10458

[1]Present address: Staunton Clinic, Sewickley Valley Hospital, Sewickley, Pennsylvania 15143.

# GUIDELINES FOR THE USE OF CONTINGENT ELECTRIC SHOCK TO TREAT ABERRANT BEHAVIOR

R. M. FOXX

*Anna Mental Health and Developmental Center*
*Anna, Illinois*

TIMOTHY G. PLASKA

*Boulder River School and Hospital*
*Boulder, Montana*

RON G. BITTLE

*Anna Mental Health and Developmental Center*
*Anna, Illinois*

**1**

PROGRESS IN BEHAVIOR
MODIFICATION, VOLUME 20

## I.  INTRODUCTION

The purpose of this chapter is to present suggested guidelines to follow in (1) deciding whether it is appropriate to use a contingent electric shock program to treat the very serious maladaptive behavior of a mentally retarded, autistic, or mentally ill individual, and (2) obtaining approval to do so if an affirmative decision is reached.

Our major emphasis will be on how to develop an informed consent document since a properly constructed one addresses all of the issues that are relevant to the use of shock. Accordingly, two sample informed consent documents from real cases are presented. One deals with a self-injurious mentally retarded individual and the other with an aggressive dually diagnosed individual.

We shall not discuss the administrative, legal, and clinical issues related to shock usage in detail because in-depth discussions of these issues already exist (cf. Carr & Lovaas, 1983; Foxx, McMorrow, Bittle, & Bechtel, 1985; Matson & DiLorenzo, 1984).

We begin by discussing contingent electric shock from a number of perspectives, including when to consider its use, the behaviors for which it is appropriate, determining whether a facility is capable of using it, ensuring the development of adaptive behaviors, and informed consent. Then, we present the two informed consent documents described above. We conclude with a set of guidelines for developing and implementing shock programs.

Of all the behavioral reductive procedures, contingent electric shock is generally considered to be the most aversive, intrusive, and/or restrictive (e.g., Favell, Azrin, Baumeister, Carr, *et al.*, 1982). The reasons have been discussed previously by Foxx *et al.* (1985), and include (1) the possibility of adverse public and professional reactions, (2) the nature of the aversive stimulus, (3) "potential" legal and ethical problems, (4) safety factors, (5) the sophisticated accountability system that is required because of the "potential" for abuse, and (6) expertise concerns related to the individual(s) responsible for conducting the program.

Yet, the reasons for not conducting a shock program with certain clients may be outweighed by a more important concern; namely, the issue of right to treatment. This, of course, creates a complex dilemma for those individuals who are responsible for providing treatment. On the one hand there is the desire to avoid controversy, while on the other hand there is the legal obligation to provide treatment. We shall now address this dilemma by discussing the conditions under which it is appropriate to use shock.

## A. The Behaviors for Which Shock Is an Appropriate Treatment

The treatment literature indicates that there are basically three classes of behavior for which shock may be appropriate: self-injurious behavior (SIB) including severe forms of pica (Favell *et al.*, 1982), aggression (Foxx *et al.*, 1985), and life-threatening rumination (Kohlenberg, 1970).

Electric shock has been the most widely researched and effective method of initially suppressing SIB (Favell *et al.*, 1982). The general rule in determining if shock should be considered for SIB is that the SIB must be of such severity as to pose a direct threat to the client's life or an indirect threat through the infections that may occur because of tissue damage. Examples of life-threatening behaviors include head-banging against a wall or sharp pieces of furniture to the point where there is bleeding and tissue swelling, biting various parts of the body such as fingers and shoulders so that large pieces of flesh and bone are removed, chewing off fingers, pulling out fingernails with teeth, gouging the eyes with fingers or objects, violently striking the knee against the face, and eating objects such as nails and glass so that periodic surgical removal is required. These behaviors not only pose an immediate danger to the client's survival, but seriously curtail the opportunity for social, emotional, and intellectual development.

Shock also may be an appropriate procedure for the individual who severely attacks others, thereby endangering their lives or brutalizing their social environment. In cases of life-threatening rumination, the decision to use shock is analogous to emergency surgery since a failure to treat could very well lead to death.

## B. When to Consider the Use of Shock

A number of national services that evaluate client care, e.g., the Accreditation Council for Services for Mentally Retarded and Other Developmentally Disabled Persons (ACMRDD), professional organizations, e.g., the Association for the Advancement of Behavior Therapy (AABT), and advocacy organizations, e.g., the National Association for Retarded Citizens (NARC), have addressed the issue of when it is appropriate to consider the use of aversive stimuli, e.g., shock, to treat a client.

The *Final Interpretive Guidelines for the Application of the Regulations for Institutions for the Mentally Retarded or Persons with Related Conditions 45CFR 249.13,* published by the United States Department of Health, Education and Welfare (1977), allows the use of aversive stimuli, e.g., shock, if certain requirements are met, e.g., obtaining informed consent, and if they are used as a last resort and only when documentation shows that positive reinforcement methods have failed. The *Standards for Services for Developmentally Disabled Individuals,* published by ACMRDD (1981), lists similar requirements; namely, that aversive conditioning should only be used in those extreme, last-resort situations in which withholding it would be contrary to the best interest of the individual because his or her behavior is (1) dangerous to self or others, (2) extremely detrimental to his or her development, and (3) documented to be untreatable by positive reinforcement procedures. Both organizations emphasize that punishment or aversive techniques must represent the least restrictive effective alternatives and that treatment programs should be designed to lead to less restrictive ways of managing and ultimately eliminating the behaviors for which the techniques are used.

The use of contingent electric shock was addressed in 1974 by a Florida task force as part of a report on the philosophy, procedures, and safeguards related to the use of behavioral programs. This effort, entitled *Guidelines for the Use of Behavioral Procedures in State Programs for Retarded Persons* (May, Risley, Twardosz, Friedman, Bijou, & Wexler, 1976), was published as a monograph by the Research Advisory Committee of NARC. Shock and exclusionary timeout (Foxx, 1982) were recommended for those clients who may be so dangerous to themselves or others that they frequently or continuously require heavy sedation, physical restraint, or seclusion in a locked room as emergency procedures. The use of less intrusive methods was encouraged after the SIB or aggression had been successfully suppressed.

In 1980, AABT established a task force of preeminent researchers and clinicians to review the SIB treatment literature. Their report, *The Treatment of Self-Injurious Behavior* (Favell *et al.,* 1982), recommended that shock programs should be (1) reserved for use in the most extreme cases, (2) designed and supervised only by highly qualified behavioral experts with extensive training and experience in treating SIB, and (3) employed in settings that provide the highest standards of professional service and human rights compliance.

Others have provided similar recommendations. Martin (1975) suggested that aversive therapy might be used where other therapy has not worked, where it can be administered to save the individual from immediate and continuing self-injury, when it allows freedom from physical restraints that would otherwise be continued, and when its goal is to make other nonaversive therapy possible. Carr and Lovaas (1983) described how nonaversive or mildly aversive procedures should typically be tried before strong aversive procedures such as shock are used to treat severe behavior problems. Horner and Barton (1980) suggested that contingent electric shock should be considered only after less intrusive treatments have failed and used only after a program to promote maintenance and generalization of the therapeutic effect has been carefully planned. Richmond and Martin (1977) have perhaps said it best:

> At times there is a need for punishment procedures, regardless of the numerical adequacy of staffing or the availability of less effective alternatives. The magnitude of the injustice in failing to apply appropriate punishment procedures is especially great when the usual regime of nursing–custodial alternatives is employed. In an effort to prevent harm to the client or others, chemical restraint is usually used. That is, the resident's physician prescribes high doses of behaviorally active drugs to keep him out of harm's way or to prevent harm to others. While the prescription may provide security, the resident may be essentially immobilized. He may be asleep, grossly ataxic, or extremely lethargic most of the time. He may be awake but incapable of participating in training experiences because of the drug. Furthermore, chemical restraint may have to be supplemented. When medication is only partially effective, the client may be exposed to other forms of containment, i.e., he may be placed in a seclusion room.
>
> In summary, some of the accepted alternatives to the use of punishment procedures can destine some clients to a life of deprivation which will insure their continued status as severe behavior problems and drastically curtail any chance of enhancing their humanity. (pp. 470, 471)

To summarize, there appear to be four major concerns that dictate that a shock program be considered for certain individuals (cf. Foxx *et al.*, 1985). First, their maladaptive behaviors are so serious that they may cause self-harm, injuries to others, or even loss of life. Second, their maladaptive behavior often has been exhibited for years and has withstood all less restrictive programming attempts. Third, they often receive virtually no programming for appropriate behavior because of their extremely serious maladaptive behavior. Fourth, custodial "treatments" are likely to be in force (e.g., custodial restraint, medical restraint via large doses of tranquilizers, 1:1 staffing, etc.) in an attempt to limit the occurrence of the maladaptive behavior (cf. Foxx & Dufrense, 1984). Of course, such "treatments" typically fail to have any long-term influence on the maladaptive behavior and are associated with iatrogenic outcomes (e.g., skill deterioration, social isolation, physical side effects from high drug dosages, muscular atrophy from physical restraint, etc.).

Given these concerns, the failure to consider a treatment alternative that may produce a more favorable outcome, i.e., contingent electric shock, could quite reasonably be construed as a violation of the individual's right to treatment or education (Martin, 1975; Richmond & Martin, 1977) and hence an unethical and inhumane act.

Yet, the blanket rejection of punishment techniques that have been repeatedly demonstrated to reduce or eliminate maladaptive behavior is frequently an accepted policy in institutions. Clearly, such facilities are abrogating their responsibility to provide treatment when they fail to consider that the judicious use of punishment techniques is warranted when circumstances suggest that a client will benefit more from receiving such treatment than from not receiving it.

Thus, the guiding principle in the decision to use contingent electric shock is that it involves a *small* amount of pain and discomfort relative to the *large* amount of pain and discomfort that the individual or others will experience if the maladaptive behavior is not treated. Analogous principles can be found in dentistry and medicine (cf. May *et al.*, 1976).

## C.  Determining Whether a Facility Is Capable of Using Shock

In their excellent chapter on the use of electric shock to treat severe behavior problems, Carr and Lovaas (1982) discussed the issue of who should be accountable for implementing and conducting the procedure. Clearly, a facility's decision to employ a shock program depends on a satisfactory answer to two questions. One, does the facility have a good accountability system? Two, is there someone available who possesses sufficient behavioral expertise to conduct the program?

The necessary type of accountability system is demonstrated in the two sample informed consent documents that are presented later. Regarding the necessary behavioral expertise, Carr and Lovaas suggested (and we concur) that the professional chosen to conduct the program and supervise and train staff have the following qualifications:

1.  A thorough familiarity with child and adult psychopathology.
2.  Academic and/or supervised experience in applying learning principles.
3.  A thorough knowledge of the research literature on punishment with humans and lower organisms.
4.  Skill in experimental design and program evaluation.
5.  "Hands-on experience" in using shock under the tutelage of an expert.
6.  Experience in educational planning and curriculum development so that the suppressed behavior can be replaced by appropriate behaviors.

They stated that the professional most likely to have these qualifications is a clinical or educational psychologist. Perhaps even more importantly, they concluded that this individual must have exceptional clinical judgment and sensitivity and his/her personal limitations must be examined. The reason is quite simple: There will be a myriad of pressures brought to bear on this person and he/she must be able to withstand them while still effectively treating the client. Similar considerations should be made regarding the on-line staff who are selected to serve as therapists.

To summarize, if a facility does not have a good accountability system, *it must not consider* implementing a shock program until such a system is in place and functioning. Similarly, if a facility does not have a resident "expert" who possesses the qualifications listed above, *it must not consider* implementing a shock program until such an individual is either hired or an outside consultant is retained to design and initially conduct the program. The real key is having someone with the necessary clinical and behavioral expertise. Unfortunately, such individuals are in short supply.

Even if an outside consultant is hired to design and initially conduct the program, a facility must have at least two employees who possess a sufficient amount of behavioral expertise to successfully carry out the "expert's" program and train treatment staff. The best way to determine whether such employees are available is to rely on the expert's judgment.

### D.  Ensuring the Development of Adaptive Behavior

Special attention must be paid to assuring the protection of the rights of the individual receiving a shock program by enhancing his/her development in accordance with the developmental model. To do so, the individual's program must emphasize the acquisition and maintenance of desirable and adaptive behaviors, rather than merely the elimination or suppression of undesirable ones. This is important because it is unlikely that the maladaptive behavior would be eliminated with shock unless there were alternative behaviors that could be naturally reinforced in the client's environment (cf. Schroeder, Schroeder, Rojahn, & Mulick, 1981). Thus, a reliance on shock as the primary means of behavior control is *unacceptable*.

### E.  Informed Consent

Once the decision has been made to pursue the use of shock, a comprehensive informed consent document must be prepared. It should outline the case history, previous treatment procedures and their results, a description of treatment alternatives, a justification for the use of contingent electric shock, a detailed description of the treatment procedure, a description of possible side effects, special precautions to be taken, the data recording procedures, the expected behavioral outcome, long-term planning considerations, a list of persons who will implement the procedure and their qualifications, and documentation of informed consent from all pertinent individuals.

### II.  PREPARING AN INFORMED CONSENT DOCUMENT FOR THE TREATMENT OF SELF-INJURIOUS BEHAVIOR

The following abbreviated example of an informed consent document is based on one that was used for a self-injurious individual in a state facility for the developmentally disabled. It illustrates the type of self-injurious client for whom contingent electric shock may be necessary and appropriate. The extensive documentation and rigorous preparations completed by the program administrators who were involved in this case provide an example of how to properly justify the use of contingent electric shock and obtain approval for its use. The client's name is fictitious and information regarding the facility and the state have been omitted in the interest of preserving the client's anonymity.

## INFORMED CONSENT FOR THE USE OF CONTINGENT ELECTRIC SHOCK

Name: Carol _____
Birthdate:

Diagnoses: Moderate Mental Retardation due to Unknown Cause Associated with Severe Self-Abusive Behavior Disorder

Date:
Therapist: _____ Ph.D.

Carol _____ is a 24-year-old female who has resided at _____ since November, 1969. She has a long history of engaging in severe self-injurious behavior (SIB) that has frequently resulted in her being seriously injured and hospitalized.

Numerous behavioral treatment procedures have been used in an attempt to decrease her SIB. Some resulted in short-term improvements but all eventually failed to maintain a therapeutic effect.

Various drugs have also been used in an attempt to treat Carol's SIB including Thorazine, Haldol, Serentil, Dalmane, Navane, and lithium carbonate. All failed to eliminate or control her SIB.

Carol's records show that she has been evaluated by numerous physicians, psychiatrists, and neurologists including Drs. _____, _____, _____, _____, and _____. Following these evaluations her SIB has continued to be a problem.

Dr. _____ was hired by the facility on _____ to evaluate Carol and review her treatment history. His recommendation was to pursue the use of contingent electric shock to treat her SIB. This recommendation had previously been made by Drs. _____, _____, _____, _____, _____, and Carol's Habilitation Planning Committee, which included her court-appointed guardian.

Dr. _____ recommended at the last Human Rights Committee Meeting that a neurological evaluation be done including a CAT scan and an EEG. These were completed and copies of the results are attached.

The purpose of this document is to describe a proposed treatment program in which each of Carol's self-injurious behaviors will be punished by a brief electric shock and to obtain permission to implement this program from the State Mental Disabilities Board, _____'s Human Rights Committee, Carol's parents, her court-appointed guardian, the Superintendent of the facility and the Director of the State Department of Mental Retardation Services.

　　　Dr. _____ will be the therapist conducting the initial treatment sessions. Dr. _____ is a licensed psychologist in the State of _____ and Director of Research at _____ in _____. He was a member of the Association for the Advancement of Behavior Therapy Task Force on Self-Injurious Behavior. He is a Fellow in the American Psychological Association in the Divisions of Clinical Psychology, Mental Retardation, Children and Youth Services, and the Experimental Analysis of Behavior. He is also a Fellow in the American Association on Mental Deficiency. He has conducted a number of shock treatment programs in the past at the request of various states. A copy of his vita is attached.

## A.　Description of Previous Treatment Procedures and Reported Outcome

　　　History prior to institutionalization at this facility. (Unless indicated, there was no outcome information on file.)

_____ State Hospital

1965—Appropriate behavior was reinforced, SIB was physically blocked.

1966—Wore foam protective devices around hands and arms; placed in a padded room contingent on SIB. Outcome: SIB ceased in the room but occurred outside the room.

1967–November 1969—Spent 12 to 24 hours per day in mechanical restraints.

November 1969—Transferred out of state to this facility.

_____ Hospital

November 1969–June 1971—Records indicate no use of any treatment procedures.

1971—Compliance program. Outcome: "Improved".

1972—Various types of brief timeout procedures used in combination with Differential Reinforcement of Other Behavior (DRO) schedules. Reportedly enjoyed timeout.

1973—Extinction for head-banging, staff physically blocked SIB attempts, various brief timeout procedures used, DRO and extinction used in a padded dining area, wore full length air splints on arms to prevent head-hitting.

1974—Because Carol enjoyed walking, it was stopped for 30 minutes following SIB.

1975—Wore a helmet; SIB ignored. Received various psychotropics including

Serentil, Thorazine, and Haldol. Five-minute overcorrection arm movement program. SIB increased. Various timeout procedures used.

1976—Restrained much of the time in the facility's hospital; proposed program to use aromatic ammonia disapproved by the Medical Director.

1977—Overcorrection program reinstated. Contingent walking program used that required Carol to walk rapidly up and down a hallway 10 times with no SIB on the last trial. Contingent walking effectively reduced SIB for approximately 8 months; then SIB rapidly increased and procedure discontinued. Hospitalized on grounds and given psychotropics.

1978—Transferred to an intensive training unit that housed three residents. Protective devices used and baseline data collected during various table-top activities. SIB ranged from 35 to 76 responses per minute. SIB rates obtained while Carol wore protective devices during the following procedures were (1) Differential Reinforcement of Incompatible Behavior (DRI) and Extinction, 35 SIBs per minute, (2) DRO and Extinction, 45 SIBs per minute, (3) DRO and Timeout, 50 SIBs per minute, and (4) DRO and overcorrection (arm positioning), 102 SIBs per minute. Restraints removed and contingent walking program reinstated. Arms held to prevent SIB. SIB eventually suppressed for $2\frac{1}{2}$ weeks. Procedure discontinued because Carol resisted walking by biting staff, dragging her feet, dropping to her knees, lifting her feet off the ground, and severely injuring herself with SIB.

1979—Habilitation Planning Committee recommended that (1) a search be undertaken to locate a treatment facility willing to accept Carol, (2) lithium carbonate be considered, and (3) a treatment program using more aversive procedures be pursued. Restraints used to prevent SIB. Noncontingent restraint in a chair when not involved in structured activities. Restraints removed for structured activities such as meals, baths, toileting, and extended walks.

1980—Use of restraints continued. Additional psychiatric and medical consultations completed. Lithium carbonate tried and found to be ineffective. Search for an alternative treatment facility was unsuccessful. Habilitation Planning Committee recommended that contingent electric shock be tried and initiated a search for a consultant to review Carol's case.

1981—DRO program; allowed to engage in preferred activities if unrestrained and no SIB. Restrained in a padded chair in her bedroom for 30 minutes following SIB. Outcome: Spent most of her time restrained in the chair. The following programmatic modifications were made: (1) required to remain in programming situations and finish tasks regardless of SIB; (2) SIB attempts during nonprogramming times physically blocked by staff; (3) only hands restrained to prevent her from spending long periods of time in restraint chair. Restrained in chair for severe SIB.

January 1982—DRO and 30-minute restraint chair programs continued. Left unrestrained and allowed to work independently during scheduled activities, e.g., dressing. SIB attempts blocked and required to complete task before returned to bedroom. Outcome: Spent most of her unscheduled time in chair restraint. Direct care staff were surveyed and reported that Carol would at different times (1) ask to be restrained, (2) ask for restraints to be removed, and (3) engage in SIB following demands, no demands, when alone, when with staff, during preferred activities, when unrestrained, and while restrained.

March 1982—Dr. _____ consulted on Carol's case. He directly observed and interacted with her, conducted a behavioral assessment, observed staff interacting with her, and reviewed her treatment records. His direct observations revealed that Carol must be restrained in a padded chair except when a staff member worked with her and during this time the staff member spent most of the time preventing SIB. His recommendation was that there were two options. (1) Continue the present program which in effect was a denial of Carol's right to treatment, or (2) institute a contingent electric shock program to treat her SIB. He stated that the records and his observations revealed that every reasonable behavioral reductive procedure except contingent electric shock had been tried, as well as every reasonable medical treatment.

September 1982–June 20, 1983—Thorazine discontinued and Carol became more alert and more verbal. SIB during unscheduled activities resulted in 30-minute chair restraint. SIB during scheduled activities blocked by staff unless restraint necessary to prevent injury. SIB occurred if hands were not held or staff did not maintain physical contact. Continued to be restrained in bed at night. In November, SIB again increased and more time spent in restraints (see attached graph). Staff turnover also increased in cottage. Cottage closed and Carol transferred to a cottage containing six other residents on June 21, 1983.

June 21, 1983—Time in restraints increasing. SIB still occurs and is very serious. Not receiving any psychotropics and the January 1982 program is still in effect. Two significant changes have occurred: (1) Carol has become more aggressive toward staff and other residents since she frequently attempts to tear their clothing, pinch, kick, head-butt, scratch, and bite. (2) She attempts SIB most of the time when not restrained, even if her hands are held.

## B.   Description of Other Treatment Alternatives

1. *Remove all restraints and extraordinary treatment.* This is not acceptable since Carol would certainly severely injure herself were she permitted to be unrestrained.

2. *Chemical restraint.* Large doses of psychotropic drugs could be tried but Carol continued to engage in SIB even when she received large doses in the past (e.g., 1600 mg Thorazine). Furthermore, Chapter 20, Section _____, of the _____ State Codes Annotated states that "Medications shall not be used as punishment, for the convenience of staff, as a substitute for a program, or in quantities that interfere with the resident's treatment program." In addition, prolonged exposure to high doses of psychotropics like Thorazine can produce undesirable side effects such as Parkinsonism, involuntary facial movements, dry mouth, constipation, chronic drowsiness, fatigue, hematologic blood dyskrasias (in rare cases), jaundice of the liver, upper abdominal pain, photosensitive skin and eyes, hypotension, fainting, dizziness, prolonged or delayed menstruation, hypothermia, and respiratory depression. For these reasons, chemical restraint is not an acceptable alternative.

3. *Physical restraint.* Chapter 20, Section _____ of the _____ State Codes Annotated states that "Physical restraints shall be employed only when absolutely necessary to protect the resident from injury to himself or to prevent injury to others. Restraint shall not be employed as punishment, for the convenience of staff, or as a substitute for a habilitation program. Restraint shall be employed only if alternative techniques have failed and only if such restraint imposes the least possible restriction consistent with its purpose." When restraint is employed over long periods of time, it can cause physical damage, such as structural changes, demineralization, shortening of tendons, and arrested motor development, as secondary outcomes of the disuse of the limbs. Physical restraint is not an acceptable alternative for these reasons as well as the fact that Carol finds restraint reinforcing.

4. *Water spray mist.* Dr. _____ briefly tried the procedure with Carol and found that it had no effect on her SIB.

5. *Aromatic ammonia capsules.* The adverse side effects of ammonia are well documented in the medical literature. In a letter to the Clinical Director, Dr. _____, dated 11/16/76, Dr. _____ communicated the potential toxic effects of ammonia and discussed some of the harmful side effects. He strongly advised against the use of ammonia in the treatment of SIB.

Since we have not exhausted all the available treatment alternatives, i.e., contingent electric shock, to not attempt a shock program and thereby keep Carol in prolonged restraint would be a violation of her "right to treatment," as mandated by state and federal guidelines.

## C. Justification for the Use of Contingent Shock Procedure

Thus far, none of the procedures described in Carol's treatment history has been effective in eliminating her SIB. Although there are some limitations and problems inherent in the use of shock, it has been shown to be an effective treatment procedure for many cases of SIB.

The Association for Advancement of Behavior Therapy (AABT) assembled a task force to address the treatment of SIB. Its report (Favell *et al.*, 1982) (copy attached) states that

> Aversive electrical stimulation (informally termed shock) is the most widely researched and, with the parameters of shock employed in the research literature, the most generally effective method of initially suppressing self-injury . . . (a long list of references followed). . . .
>
> Although a powerful therapeutic tool with self-injury, shock is considered an extremely *restrictive* procedure: it is painful, very intrusive and highly susceptible to abuse; i.e., it can easily be employed in nontherapeutic and unethical ways. For these reasons, its use is rigorously controlled (May *et al.*, 1976). Specifically, shock programs should be reserved for use in the most extreme cases, designed and supervised only by highly qualified behavioral experts with extensive training and experience in treating self-injury, and employed in settings which provide the highest standards of professional service and human rights compliance. (pp. 540–551)

In a monograph by the Research Advisory Committee of the National Association for Retarded Citizens entitled *Guidelines for the Use of Behavioral Procedures in State Programs for Retarded Persons* (May *et al.*, 1976), shock and exclusionary timeout (see Foxx, 1982) were recommended for those clients who may be so dangerous to themselves or others that they frequently or continuously require heavy sedation, physical restraints, or seclusion in a locked room as emergency procedures. The use of less intrusive methods was encouraged after the SIB or aggression had been successfully suppressed.

THE RIGHT TO EFFECTIVE TREATMENT

Individuals have the right to effective treatment and, when alternative procedures have failed, the use of shock may be both appropriate and necessary. Failure to do so when the behavior is chronic and debilitating may in fact be unethical, inhumane, and a violation of the individual's right to treatment.

Several national services that evaluate client care have addressed the issue of when to consider the use of shock to treat a client. For example, the *Standards for Services for Developmentally Disabled Individuals,* published by the Accreditation Council for Services for Mentally Retarded and Other Developmentally Disabled Persons (1981), allows the use of aversive stimuli if certain requirements are met. These basic requirements are that aversive conditioning should only be used in those extreme, last-resort situations in which withholding it would be contrary to the best interest of the individual because his or her behavior is (1) dangerous to self or others, (2) extremely detrimental to his or her development, and (3) documented to be untreatable by positive reinforcement procedures. The *Final Interpretive Guidelines for the Application of the Regula-*

*tions for Institutions for the Mentally Retarded or Persons with Related Conditions 45CFR 249.13,* published by the United States Department of Health, Education and Welfare (1977), has similar standards and requirements.

Carol's right to receive effective treatment necessitates that electric shock be tried, especially since (1) the need for this intervention has been verified by numerous physicians, psychiatrists, and psychologists; (2) all other reasonable methods have failed; (3) there are no acceptable alternative procedures; and (4) she continues to injure herself. In addition, if the shock program was successful in eliminating her SIB over an extended period of time, she would receive a number of benefits: (1) her restraints could be eliminated; (2) psychotropic drugs would be unnecessary; and (3) she could acquire new behaviors, come into contact with more rewarding aspects of her environment, and engage in some of her most preferred activities. Furthermore, Carol may eventually be able to move to a less restrictive living environment, e.g., the community.

## D.   Description of Treatment Program

1.   OVERVIEW

The proposed treatment procedure involves the use of a brief electric shock following each of Carol's self-injurious behaviors. This type of shock should not be confused with electroconvulsive therapy (ECT) which consists of the application of electric currents to the brain to produce convulsions and/or unconsciousness for therapeutic effects. ECT is used by physicians and primarily in the treatment of various forms of psychosis and depression. The type of shock proposed to be used with Carol is a brief (1 to 2 seconds), 15–18 milliamps (ma) shock delivered to the surface of the forearm or upper arm that results in a painful "sting" but that has no other painful side effects.

The two shock apparatuses to be used will be (1) a Tritronics remote control stimulator (Model A1-70, manufactured by Tritronics, Inc., Tucson, Arizona) that consists of a radio-controlled transmitter that the therapist holds, a shock receiver attached to a belt around Carol's waist, and a shock stimulator that consists of two electrodes attached to her upper arm with an elastic athletic band that assures electrode contact. When the therapist activates the switch on the transmitter, a brief electric shock is delivered, and (2) a Hot Shot Power Mite direct stimulator (manufactured by Hot Shot Products, Inc., Savage, Minnesota) that is a small (approximately 5 inches) battery operated device that has two $\frac{3}{8}$-inch electrodes protruding from one of its ends. The therapist delivers a brief shock by gently pressing the two electrodes against the forearm and pushing a button (information on both devices is attached).

Butterfield (1975) provided a comprehensive set of guidelines and criteria related to the use of contingent shock with humans. He discussed the precautions one should take to avoid the possibility of causing fibrillation of the heart, current leakages, and electrolysis burns. He also addressed the range of amperage that is appropriate, the frequency of the current, the duration of exposure to shock, and different types of shock equipment. For more details see the attached article.

The shock procedure would be conducted as follows. As soon as Carol hits herself, the attending therapist would deliver the shock and simultaneously say a loud "No!" The rationale for pairing the auditory stimulus "No" with the shock is so the word "No" can later be used to deter SIB (1) in situations where shock cannot be used, such as bathing and swimming, and (2) after the shock program has been terminated.

Typically, this procedure should cause Carol to delay her next SIB for a few seconds. As soon as her SIB resumes, the therapist reapplies the shock in the same manner as before. The second (or third, fourth . . . tenth) shock should cause increasing delays in responding. It is of course paramount that Carol's SIB be shocked as soon as it occurs.

Each occurrence of SIB (listed and defined in Section 2 below) will be *immediately* followed by a brief electric shock. The shock amperage will be adjusted to a maximum current of 18 ma.

To ensure Carol's safety, the equipment will be independently tested before its use by the Electrical Engineering Department at _____ State University to ensure that it is in accordance with the safety factors discussed by Butterfield (1975). Carol will also be examined by a licensed physician to determine that she has no medical condition (such as heart problems) that precludes the use of shock.

The availability of two shock devices will provide maximum flexibility in treating Carol's SIB. The use of a remote control shock device should facilitate generalization since there are no discriminative stimuli associated with the delivery of the shock other than the electrode band and shock receiver. Thus, it should be difficult for Carol to discriminate when the shock contingency is or is not in effect. Nevertheless, the electrode band and/or shock receiver may develop some conditioned aversive stimulus properties and may deter Carol's SIB when she is wearing them. Therefore, it may be necessary to use a "mock" receiver with electrodes that Carol can wear when bathing, swimming, etc. Carol also may be required to wear this "mock" device following the termination of the shock program to deter future SIB. In fact, even if Carol had to wear such a device for the rest of her life, it would be a preferable alternative to psychotropics and physical restraints.

The use of the direct stimulator offers two advantages: (1) It would ensure that the shock consequence could be delivered if Carol damaged or attempted to remove the remote control device. (2) It would be very useful when Carol was taken on community trips because of its small size, i.e., 5 inches. The remote control device would not be acceptable for such trips because the receiver around Carol's waist would call undue attention to her.

2.  DESCRIPTION AND DEFINITION OF THE SIB BEHAVIORS TO
     BE TREATED

*Head-hitting:* Defined as Carol's hand or fist striking any part of her head or face.

*Head-banging:* Defined as any part of Carol's head or face striking any solid object or surface.

*Hand-hitting:* Defined as any part of Carol's hand or fist striking any solid object.

*Biting self:* Defined as Carol's teeth pressed against any other part of her body including arms, fingers, shoulders, lips, etc.

*Chin-clipping:* Defined as any part of Carol's chin or jaw line striking any part of either shoulder or any other part of her body.

*Elbow-banging:* Defined as Carol's elbow striking any solid object or surface.

*Knee-banging:* Defined as Carol's knees striking together.

*Leg-kicking:* Defined as Carol hitting any part of one leg with her opposite foot.

Should Carol develop new self-injurious behaviors during the course of her treatment, they will be added to the above list.

3.  DATA RECORDING PROCEDURES

Both baseline and treatment sessions will be videotaped. This will enable precise data to be calculated on the rate per minute of each target behavior and the inter-response times (IRTS). Comparisons between the baseline and treatment sessions for each measure will then indicate whether the use of contingent electric shock has any effect on the target behaviors.

Reliability assessments will be conducted by having two independent observers view the videotapes. Interobserver reliability will be calculated for the baseline and an initial treatment session and during every fifth session thereafter.

### E.  Initial Evaluation of the Program's Effectiveness

The treatment sessions will be conducted on _____, and will be conducted in a room that allows for observation and videotaping of the procedures.

During the baseline and treatment sessions Carol will wear the shock receiver and be unrestrained. She will be prompted to engage in appropriate behavior that is incompatible with SIB and that she enjoys. When she does so, she will be heavily reinforced with social praise, physical contact, and preferred edible reinforcers. Carol will wear clothing from her regular wardrobe that would prevent her from removing the remote control equipment.

Prior to beginning the initial treatment session, Carol will be allowed to engage in SIB during a short baseline period to determine her rate of SIB and the inter-response intervals (IRTS). No consequences will be delivered for SIB. The length of the baseline sessions will be determined by the severity of Carol's SIB and it will be terminated by Dr. _____ if her SIB creates a risk of severe injury. After the baseline period the treatment sessions will begin. Each self-injurious target behavior will immediately be followed by a shock administered to Carol's arm. All shocks will be administered by Dr. _____. The output of the shock unit will be tested by Dr. _____ immediately before the treatment session to ensure that the correct intensity is being used. Before administering the shock to Carol, Dr. _____ will administer the shock to himself. During the treatment session the duration of the shock may be increased or the electrode attachment site may be changed by Dr. _____ if he determines it is necessary to do so based on his professional experience and clinical judgment.

Dr. _____ will terminate the shock program if he determines that it is not effective in suppressing Carol's SIB. A decrease in the rate of her SIB or an increase in the IRTS will indicate that the shock is being effective and if this occurs the treatment sessions will be continued. The amount of time Carol is required to spend engaging in behavior other than SIB will be gradually increased so that eventually she will be engaged in appropriate behavior during the entire day and with no restraints used at night. Also, increasing demands will be placed on Carol through the use of 1:1 acquisition programs, informal living skill programs, activity programs, etc. It is through this type of scheduling that Carol should acquire new behaviors and thus learn new ways of earning reinforcers. A variety of staff will be assigned to act as therapists to facilitate generalization of the therapeutic effects across treatment and educational personnel. Attempts will also be made to generalize the suppression of SIB to other settings within the facility where Carol has exhibited SIB.

### F. Description of Possible Side Effects of Shock

Some possible positive side effects are listed as follows.

1. Carol may benefit from not having any more self-inflicted injuries or pain.

2. Carol may develop new positive or appropriate social behaviors.

3. Carol may reach a point where she can become regularly involved in activities she finds rewarding.

4. Carol may be included in more support services such as Education, Recreation, Physical Therapy, and Occupational Therapy.

5.   Carol's other undesirable behaviors may decrease in rate and/or intensity. Those behaviors include screaming, crying, and smearing feces.

6.   Carol may reach a point where she may no longer require mechanical restraints either during the day or at night.

7.   Carol may reach a point where generalization of the program to a less restrictive living environment is possible.

8.   Carol may be able to function without any future need for psychotropic drugs (she is not receiving any now).

Possible negative side effects are listed below.

1.   Carol may develop new self-injurious behaviors.

2.   Carol may substitute other negative behaviors such as property destruction.

3.   The frequency and magnitude of Carol's SIB may temporarily increase.

4.   Carol may develop an intense fear of her environment.

5.   Carol may exhibit aggressive behaviors toward other residents or staff as a result of "pain-elicited aggression."

6.   Carol may withdraw socially.

Regarding side effects, Carr and Lovaas (1983) reported in a chapter entitled Contingent Electric Shock as a Treatment for Severe Behavior Problems (copy attached) that "there is little published evidence that the side effects of shock are harmful. In fact, the ratio of positive to negative side effects is about 5 to 1 in favor of the positive side effects (Lichstein & Schreibman, 1976)" (p. 235). The outcomes reported following treatment with shock include (1) clients being described as happier, calmer, quieter, and/or smiling more, (2) a widespread enhancement of social behavior, (3) no general suppression of desirable behavior, (4) no general fear of the therapist, and (5) no new "symptoms" such as aggression directed against the therapist (cf. Carr & Lovaas, 1983). Furthermore, there have been reports of a decrease in other problem behaviors following contingent shock treatment, e.g., whining, crying, and avoidance behaviors, as well as increases in toy play (Tate & Baroff, 1966). Finally, the suppression of chronic, nonorganically based vomiting by shock has been associated with weight gain in clients who were previously emaciated from repeated vomiting (Kohlenberg, 1970; Lang & Melamed, 1969; Luckey, Watson, & Musick, 1968; White & Taylor, 1967).

## G.   Special Precautions in Implementing the Treatment Procedure

1.   Prior to the treatment sessions Carol will be examined by a licensed physician to verify that she does not have any medical condition (such as heart problems) that precludes the use of contingent electric shock.

2. A licensed physician will be present during the initial treatment sessions.

3. Carol's parents, representatives from the State Mental Disabilities Board, the Human Rights Committee, the State Department of Mental Retardation, her court-appointed Guardian, and the Superintendent of _____ will be invited to attend the initial treatment sessions.

4. The equipment will be tested by a licensed electrical engineer to verify that the shock intensity to be delivered is safe for use with humans.

5. All shocks during the initial evaluation will be administered by Dr. _____. He will experience the shock before each session. Any others present will also experience the shock.

6. All provisions of Section _____, Part 6 of the _____ State Codes Annotated addressing the use of electric shock devices shall be complied with.

7. All staff involved in implementing the program will be trained as described below in Section H.

8. The first 25 sessions will be videotaped for documentation of program success or failure.


## H. Persons Who Will Implement the Procedure and Staff Training

_____ Ph.D., will conduct the initial treatment sessions. Thereafter, trained staff will assume responsibility for conducting the shock program. The administrator of the program will be designated by the facility's superintendent.

Anyone who will be serving as therapist will be trained and tested on the use of shock. Therapists will be allowed to conduct the procedure *only* after they have passed a written training examination at a 100% proficiency level.

The training will cover the following topics: (1) defining the target behaviors to be shocked, (2) collecting appropriate and reliable records, and (3) reinforcing incompatible behaviors. A "dry run" with each therapist will be conducted before he/she is permitted to conduct the actual procedure. During this dry run the therapists will role-play all aspects of the program. Each potential therapist will be required to experience the shock.


## I. Expected Behavioral Outcome

The short-range goal will be to determine whether the contingent shock program has any therapeutic effect on Carol's SIB. Dr. _____'s recommendation is that there should be a fairly immediate increase in the SIB interresponse times if the program is being effective.

## J.  Long-Term Planning

Should the initial treatment sessions show that the shock program is effective in suppressing Carol's SIB, it will be incorporated into Carol's IHP program. Because the long-term suppression of SIB is the real test of the shock procedure, the shock contingency will remain in effect until Carol has not exhibited any SIB for 6 months. If such success is achieved, then a meeting will be held between all responsible persons to consider whether to terminate the shock contingency and seek alternative, less-restrictive living arrangements for Carol.

Should Carol's SIB reoccur following this 6-month period, a meeting will be held between all responsible persons to determine whether to recommend the reimplementation of the shock procedure.

## K.  Conclusions

The alternatives available for Carol if the shock treatment procedure is not implemented include (1) the continued use of restraint and other mechanical devices to control her SIB, (2) the continued use of psychotropic drugs in an attempt to control the intensity of her SIB, and (3) Carol receiving little or no training in self-help and other skills. More importantly, these alternatives are not in keeping with the "right to treatment" and "right to education" laws mandated by _____ state regulations and federal guidelines concerning the protection of the rights of developmentally disabled individuals.

The purpose of this "informed consent" document is to provide those persons involved in this decision with sufficient information to determine whether to approve this proposed treatment program. The conditions of "informed consent" include the right to withhold consent for the use of this proposed program along with the right to withdraw consent *at any time,* including at any time following the program's implementation.

## L.  Review and Approval for Use of the Treatment Program

1. State Mental Disabilities Board

    Name                        Signatures                          Date

_____

2. Informed Consent from Carol's Parents

   a) As the parent(s) of Carol _____, We, _____

_____

   hereby consent to the use of the treatment procedures described on the previous pages in the treatment of Carol _____.

   b) We acknowledge that no guarantees have been made to us regarding the results of this treatment.

    c) We understand that within the scope of this treatment there is no intent to cause detrimental side effects to Carol _____.

    d) We understand that the treatment procedures described will be closely monitored and supervised and that in the event that any detrimental side effects occur that might be injurious to Carol, the treatment procedure will be immediately terminated (see Section E).

    e) This form has been fully explained to us and we certify that we understand its contents.

| | |
|---|---|
| _____ | _____ |
| Signature | Father              Date |
| _____ | _____ |
| Address | City, state, zip |
| _____ | _____ |
| Signature | Mother           Date |
| _____ | _____ |
| Address | City, state, zip |

3. Informed Consent from Carol's Advocate/Court-Appointed Guardian

    a) As advocate/court-appointed guardian of Carol _____, I, _____ hereby consent to the use of treatment procedures described on the previous pages in the treatment of Carol _____.

    Points b through e are the same as listed for Carol's parents.

4. Director, State Department of Mental Health and Developmental Disabilities.

| Name | Signature | Date |
|---|---|---|
| _____ | _____ | _____ |

5. Superintendent, _____

| Name | Signature | Date |
|---|---|---|
| _____ | _____ | _____ |

6. Physician's Statement

I have examined Carol _____ on _____ and find her to be free of any medical condition that would contraindicate the use of contingent electric shock as described in this document.

| | |
|---|---|
| _____ | _____ |
| Signature | Date |
| _____ | _____ |
| Address | City, state, zip |

7. _____ Behavior Management Committee

| Name | Signature | Date |
|---|---|---|
| _____ | _____ | _____ |
| _____ | _____ | _____ |
| _____ | _____ | _____ |

8. Human Rights Committee

| Name | Signatures | Date |
|------|------------|------|
|      |            |      |
|      |            |      |
|      |            |      |
|      |            |      |
|      |            |      |
|      |            |      |

## III.  PREPARING AN INFORMED CONSENT DOCUMENT FOR THE TREATMENT OF AGGRESSION

The following example of an informed consent document was used at the Anna Mental Health Center for an aggressive individual. It illustrates another type of client for whom contingent electric shock may be a necessary and the appropriate course of action to follow in obtaining approval for its use. The client's name is fictitious in the interest of preserving confidentiality. The results of this treatment program can be found in Foxx *et al.* (1985).

### INFORMED CONSENT FOR THE USE OF A CONTINGENT ELECTRIC SHOCK PROCEDURE

Name:  Gary _____
Birthdate:
Case #:
Diagnosis:  Axis I  —(1) 312.34 Intermittent Explosive Disorder (Primary)
                          (2) 317.00 Mild Mental Retardation
Diagnosis:  Axis II —V71.09
                  Axis III—Deafness, Bilateral, Profound
Date:

Gary is a 20-year-old male who has resided at Anna Mental Health and Developmental Center since July, 1982. He has a long history of engaging in severe physically aggressive and extreme noncompliant behavior that has resulted in his being confined in restrictive settings since the age of seven. His aggressive behavior, especially hairpulling, is so injurious that staff and clients move away when he approaches, avoid walking near him, and rarely engage in any form of physical contact with him. Due to the severity of his aggressive behavior, Gary does not attend activities and eats and bathes alone. He requires a great deal of 1 to 1 staff time and refuses to perform his self-help skills (although he has these skills in his repertoire). It is highly doubtful that Gary will ever move to a less restrictive setting if his severely aggressive and noncompliant behavior continues.

Numerous behavioral treatment procedures have been used in an attempt to decrease Gary's aggressive behaviors. Some produced short-term improvements, but all eventually resulted in long-term failure.

Various psychotropic drugs also have been used including Thorazine, Stelazine, Mellaril, Haldol, and Trilafon. All failed to affect Gary's aggressive behavior.

Gary's records show that he has been evaluated by a number of physicians, psychiatrists, and psychologists and that all of their various treatment recommendations were unsuccessful.

Dr. _____ was directed by the Superintendent of this facility on 1-12-84 to evaluate Gary's case and develop this proposal for the use of contingent electric shock to treat Gary's aggressive behavior.

The purpose of this document is to describe a proposed treatment program in which each of Gary's aggressive behaviors will be punished by a brief electric shock and to obtain permission to implement this program from the Anna Mental Health and Developmental Center's Human Rights and Behavior Management Committees, Gary's parents, the facility Superintendent, and the Director of the State Department of Mental Health and Developmental Disabilities.

Dr. _____ is a licensed psychologist in the State of Illinois and Director of the Department of Treatment Development at Anna Mental Health and Developmental Center in Anna, Illinois.

## A.   Description of Previous Treatment Procedures and Reported Outcome

_____ Hospital, 1970–1974

Admitted at age 7 in a special program for the deaf. Reportedly progressed well in language and communication skills. Pinching behavior noted and described as being greatly reduced (no information provided regarding the procedures used).

_____ School for the Deaf, 1974–1980

Reported to have progressed fairly well until he was included in a "pilot" program sometime in 1978. At that point hairpulling began, along with other aggressive behaviors. Staff held his hands to prevent hairpulling and removed his shoes to prevent kicking. Aggressive behaviors escalated to the point where he could no longer be tolerated in this setting.

_____ Hospital, 1980

Reports of "unprovoked and unpredictable aggression." Treatment approaches used included a timeout room, medications, and occasional wrist restraints. None were effective in reducing aggressive behavior.

_____ Hospital, June 1980–September 1980

Placed on an intensive care unit in a deaf treatment program. Aggression escalated. Required to wear boxing gloves because of hitting and hairpulling. Placed in an isolation room with only a mattress on the floor where he remained 24 hours a day. No effect on aggressive behavior; self-help and communication skills deteriorated.

_____ Children's Unit of _____ Mental Health Center, September 1980–July 1982

Placed in adolescent program for deaf. "Gary's unprovoked and unpredictable aggression" continued. Efforts to identify environmental factors precipitating and maintaining his aggressive behavior were unsuccessful. Procedures used included overcorrection, timeout, drugs, differential reinforcement of incompatible behavior (DRI), differential reinforcement of other behavior (DRO), required relaxation, required running following aggression, and restraints. Aggression not reduced.

By July 1982, Gary was approaching his nineteenth birthday and was no longer eligible for services at _____. Transferred to Anna Mental Health and Developmental Center.

Anna Mental Health and Developmental Center, July 1982–present

July 1982—Two-minute DRO program with punch card and timer. Punches given for appropriate behavior and exchangeable for rewards. Program unsuccessful since high rate of aggression continued.

October 1982—Token economy program plus a timeout room program for aggressive behavior. No significant decrease in aggression noted.

December 1982—Program set up that consisted of task periods with frequent rewards for task completion and appropriate behavior. Hairpulling resulted in the requirement that Gary thoroughly wash his hands and then spend 15 minutes in a timeout room. No significant decrease in aggression noted.

September 1983—Contingent aversive stimuli. Aromatic ammonia capsules were administered for hairpulling or attempted hairpulling. Staff instructed to interact with Gary and encourage him to interact with others. There was a significant increase in interaction with others as well as aggressive behavior.

Varying doses of several psychotropics given. None had an effect on aggressive behavior.

## B. Description of Other Treatment Alternatives

1. *Chemical restraint.* The administration of large doses of psychotropic drugs could be used but even when Gary received large doses in the past (e.g., 1600 mg Thorazine daily), he continued to aggress. In addition, prolonged exposure to such high doses of medications like Thorazine can produce . . . (same description as for Carol, see page 12). For these reasons, chemical restraint is not an acceptable alternative.

2. *Physical restraint.* Chapter 2, Section 2-108 of the IUMH&DD Code states that "Restraint may be used only as a therapeutic measure to prevent a recipient from causing harm to himself or others. In no event shall restraint be utilized to punish or discipline a recipient, nor is restraint to be used as a convenience for the staff." When restraint is used over long periods . . . (same description as for Carol, see page 12). For these reasons, physical restraint is not an acceptable alternative.

3. *Seclusion.* Chapter 1, Section 126 of the IUMH&DD Code states that: Seclusion means the sequestration by placement of a patient or client alone in a room which he has no means of leaving. Seclusion (Section 2-109) may be used only as a therapeutic measure to prevent a recipient from causing physical harm to himself or others. Prolonged use of seclusion is not an acceptable alternative.

Since we have not exhausted all of the available treatment alternatives . . . (same description as for Carol, see page 12).

## C. Justification for the Use of a Contingent Shock Procedure

Thus far, none of the procedures described in Gary's treatment history has been effective in eliminating his aggressive behavior. Although there are some limitations and problems inherent in the use of shock, it has been shown to be an effective treatment procedure for many cases of severe maladaptive behaviors, including aggression.

Ludwig, Marx, Hill, and Browning (1969) used faradic stimulation, i.e., shock, to suppress the violent, potentially homicidal behavior of a hospitalized, chronic paranoid schizophrenic patient. Three factors contributed to the decision to attempt a shock treatment program: (1) the danger posed to others, (2) the failure of previous treatment methods to modify aggression, and (3) the *more* drastic nature of other possible treatment alternatives, such as prefrontal lobotomy, shackling the patient in restraints, or isolating the patient through prolonged seclusion (cf. Ludwig *et al.*, 1969). The treatment goals were to eliminate aggressive/assaultive behavior and stimulate appropriate socialized, responsible behavior through positive reinforcement. The shock program was quite successful since aggressive acts were reduced from a baseline average of 81 instances per week to less than 1 per week over a 22-week period.

Birnbrauer (1968) used contingent shock with a 14-year-old, profoundly retarded boy who engaged in aggressive/destructive behavior. The major problem was that this young man bit others and destroyed objects without any apparent provocation. The effects of shock were relatively rapid and powerful, especially during laboratory sessions where target responses were suppressed for 20 sessions and two of the destructive behaviors never reoccurred after 80 sessions. New target behaviors were later suppressed after one shock treatment.

Risley (1968) used contingent shock to eliminate the aggressive behavior of a 6-year-old hyperactive girl diagnosed as having diffuse brain damage. During the baseline, three or four aggressive acts occurred per day. The girl was shocked for 17 instances of hitting over a 20-day period. During this time aggression decreased from 2.3 instances per day during the first 3 days of the shock program to zero. No further aggression occurred during the remaining 70 days of treatment.

Browning (1971) treated five autistic children with high-voltage, low-amperage shock to decrease their aggressive and self-injurious behavior. Total suppression of aggression was achieved with two children and partial suppression with the other three, i.e., aggression occurred periodically. These results lasted until the children were discharged 35 months later.

Ball, Sibbach, Jones, Steele, and Frazier (1975) used electric shock to treat the aggression of two clients: a 13-year-old girl with an IQ of 35 and a profoundly retarded 30-year-old woman. The girl's aggression and property destruction were reduced to a zero level after 7 months of treatment. The woman, who aggressed approximately twice a week prior to treatment, did so by engaging in day-long cycles of violent outbursts involving a series of assaultive attacks on anyone in the vicinity. Although her assaultive behavior was never eliminated, there was a marked reduction in the number of days in which more than three assaultive behaviors were recorded.

Repeat of Information in Carol's Informed Consent document (see pages 8 and 9).

Gary's right to receive effective treatment necessitates that the use of electric shock be tried, especially since (1) the need for this intervention has been verified by numerous professionals; (2) all other reasonable methods have failed; (3) there are no acceptable alternative procedures; (4) Gary continues to injure others; and (5) Gary's social and self-help skills are regressing.

Furthermore, if the shock program is successful in eliminating Gary's aggressive behavior over an extended period of time, he would receive a number of benefits: (1) he would no longer be isolated from his peer group, (2) psychotropic drugs would be unnecessary, and (3) he could acquire new behaviors, come into contact with more rewarding aspects of his environment, and engage in some of his more preferred activities. He also could be moved, eventually, to a less restrictive living environment.

## D.  Description of Treatment Program

### 1.  OVERVIEW

The description is the same as for Carol's SIB. Each occurrence of an aggressive response (listed and defined in Section 2) will be *immediately* followed by a brief electric shock delivered to Gary's arm. The shock amperage will be adjusted to a maximum current of between 15 and 18 ma.

2.  DESCRIPTION AND DEFINITION OF TARGET BEHAVIORS

*Hairpulling:* Defined as Gary grabbing another person's hair with his hand(s).

*Kicking:* Defined as Gary using his foot to strike another individual.

*Pinching:* Defined as Gary squeezing with his fingers a small portion of another individual's skin.

*Biting:* Defined as Gary's teeth making contact with another individual's body.

*Hitting:* Defined as Gary's hand or fist making quick and hard contact with another individual's body.

*Property destruction:* Defined as Gary throwing, breaking, tearing, or kicking inanimate objects.

*Pushing, shoving:* Defined as Gary's hands or body coming into contact with another individual with intent to cause them to be off-balance.

*Scratching:* Defined as Gary's fingernails coming into contact with another individual's skin.

*Slinging:* Defined as Gary taking hold of another's body or clothing and throwing them.

Should Gary develop new aggressive behaviors during the course of the treatment, they will be added to the above list.

3.  TRAINING OF APPROPRIATE BEHAVIORS

Because Gary resides in a living unit that has a unit-wide token economy program, he will be awarded points for appropriate (social) behaviors and the correct performance of daily living skills (i.e., dining etiquette, grooming and hygiene, room maintenance, etc.). The points earned can be exchanged later (at specific intervals) for preferred rewards (activities, special time with staff, snacks, etc.). A reinforcement menu will be developed based on direct observations of Gary's behavior and input from his direct care staff.

Increasing demands will be placed on Gary through the gradual use of intensive training programs. Hence, the shock program will be employed in a few training areas at first with new training situations gradually added after his aggression has been successfully treated in the old training situations. The training situations will include, but not be limited to, dressing, grooming, bathing, clothing maintenance, room maintenance, dining etiquette, recreational activities, leisure time activities, and socializing in groups. Ongoing training of appropriate social behavior will also occur at other times through the use of points and staff attention and praise.

4.  DATA RECORDING PROCEDURES

Data will be collected on both adaptive skills and aggression. Adaptive skills will be measured by (1) recording Gary's attendance at recreational activities, (2) calculating the percentage of available points earned for task performance, and (3) time sampling social interactions with peers and staff during nonstructured situations.

Aggressive behaviors will be coded and recorded as they occur.

Parts 1 through 4 above comprise Gary's proposed treatment program. He will be treated 24 hours a day.

## E.  Description of Possible Side Effects of Shock

One important concern is whether undesirable side effects follow the use of shock. Most articles dealing with this question have described favorable behavioral side effects including clients seeking more attention, displaying better eye contact, and socializing more (Harris & Ersner-Hershfield, 1978). Ludwig *et al.* (1969) reported that their adult schizophrenic patient showed some temporary adverse behaviors including "pseudo-catatonic sitdown," mild aggression, and SIB, although none proved to be an enduring problem. Some possible positive side effects are listed as follows.

1.  Gary may benefit from not having any more peer-inflicted injuries or pain as a reaction to his initial attack.
2.  Gary may develop new appropriate social behaviors.
3.  Gary may reach a point where he can become regularly involved in activities he finds rewarding.
4.  Gary may be included in more support services such as Recreation, Physical Therapy, and Occupational Therapy.
5.  Gary's other undesirable behaviors may decrease in rate and/or intensity. These behaviors include incontinence, public masturbation, and non-organically vomiting as a means of being noncompliant.
6.  Gary may reach a point where he could leave the institution to live in a less restrictive environment.
7.  Gary may be able to function without any need in the future for psychotropic drugs.

Possible negative side effects are listed below.

1.  Gary may develop self-injurious behaviors.
2.  Gary may substitute other negative behaviors such as smearing feces and public disrobing.
3.  The frequency and magnitude of Gary's aggression may increase.
4.  Gary may develop a fear of his environment.

5. Gary may exhibit new aggressive behaviors toward other residents or staff as a result of "pain-elicited aggression."

6. Gary may withdraw socially.

### F. Special Precautions to Be Used in Implementing the Treatment Procedure

Same as described for Carol's SIB except for citation of relevant state code.

### G. Persons Who Will Implement the Treatment Procedures and Staff Training

_____, Ph.D., will conduct the initial treatment sessions. Thereafter, trained staff will assume responsibility for conducting the shock program on the living unit and at Gary's school.

(Staff training same as described for Carol's SIB, see page 19.)

The program will be monitored by Dr. _____, _____, a Psychologist III from the Department of Treatment Development, the psychologists from Gary's living unit, and the school principal.

### H. Expected Behavioral Outcome

The short-range goal will be to determine if the contingent shock program has any therapeutic effect on Gary's aggression. It is anticipated that there may be an increase in Gary's aggressive behaviors when treatment is begun because of the increased demands that will be placed on him to perform his daily living activities and participate in the unit token economy program.

The initial effectiveness of the shock program will be determined by the following criterion: The shock program will reduce Gary's aggression by 70% of his baseline average after one month. The baseline will represent the number of daily aggressive episodes or instances during a month period prior to the implementation of the shock program. If Gary's aggression is not reduced by 70% of baseline after one month, a meeting will be held with all responsible parties to determine the next course of action. Should the shock program meet the criterion for treatment success, it will be incorporated into Gary's individual program and used until 6 months have passed in which Gary has displayed no aggression in any setting or situation, e.g., home visits.

### I. Long-Term Planning

Should the initial evaluation indicate that the shock program is effective in suppressing Gary's aggression, it will be continued and Gary will receive increased demands to participate in unit routines and programs. Evaluation of treatment effectiveness will be ongoing. Overall success of the treatment program will be defined as a significant increase in Gary's adaptive behaviors (i.e., daily participation in unit programming and recreational/leisure time activities, independent performance of self-help skills, and interacting with staff and peers on a regular basis) concomitant with a significant decrease in aggression.

Maintenance of the therapeutic gains may be a problem. Although the effects of shock can be quite durable, lasting from several months to several years (Corte, Wolf, & Locke, 1971; Griffin, Locke, & Landers, 1975; Merbaum, 1973; Whaley & Tough, 1970), there have been reports of a failure to produce maintenance (Birnbrauer, 1968; Romanczyk & Goren, 1975) with periodic reapplications of shock being necessary to maintain the therapeutic effect (Lovaas & Simmons, 1969). Birnbrauer (1968) suggested that punishment not be discontinued until there is complete and prolonged suppression of the target behaviors.

If such success is achieved, a meeting will be held among all involved parties to consider alternative, less restrictive living arrangements for Gary.

## J.  Conclusions

Same as described for Carol's SIB (see page 20).

## K.  Review and Approval for Use of the Treatment Program

Same as described for Carol's SIB.

## IV.  GUIDELINES FOR DEVELOPING AND IMPLEMENTING A SHOCK PROGRAM

Once the decision has been made to pursue the use of shock, the following guidelines should be followed:

1.   Become thoroughly familiar with the issues related to the therapeutic use of punishment (Romanczyk, Colletti, & Plotkin, 1980; Harris & Ersner-Hershfield, 1978; Matson & DiLorenzo, 1984), procedural and ethical issues surrounding the use of shock and its side effects (Carr & Lovaas, 1983; Lichstein & Schreibman, 1976), safety factors associated with shock usage (Butterfield, 1975; Bernstein, 1975; Tursky, 1975), administrative guidelines for using aversive procedures in state facilities (Nolley, Boelkins, Kocur, Moore, Goncalves, & Lewis, 1980; Ray & Shelton, 1975), and obtaining informed consent (Cook, Altman, & Haavik, 1978; Turnbull, 1977).

2.  Ensure that the proposed treatment program is in compliance with applicable state and federal regulations. Also consider being in compliance with applicable voluntary standards and guidelines such as the *Standards for Services for Developmentally Disabled Individuals* (Accreditation Council for Services for Mentally Retarded and Other Developmentally Disabled Persons, 1981).

3.  Allow everyone concerned about the client's treatment (e.g., administrators, parents) to participate in the initial decision that electric shock be considered. Doing so will guarantee everyone's commitment to the program and may help reduce the various pressures on the therapist who will be responsible for conducting the program (cf. Carr & Lovaas, 1983).

4.  Create a detailed informed consent document similar to the ones described earlier (both were based on the model suggested by Cook *et al.* (1978). Anticipated programmatic alterations or treatment options that may be needed should be covered in the document (e.g., the use of multiple devices). This will eliminate delays if/when these changes are necessary. The informed consent document should prove very useful in demonstrating administrative, committee, and parental support for the program. The document's ultimate message is simply that a failure to consider the use of contingent shock for the client could constitute a violation of the individual's right to an effective treatment.

5.  Conduct a meeting to discuss the proposed treatment program with all concerned parties *before* it is implemented. Doing so will allow administrators and/or parents to communicate their support for the program and ask questions. Have the shock equipment present and encourage everyone to experience it. The meeting's primary purposes are to unify all parties in the pursuit of a common therapeutic goal and further ensure that everyone understands the treatment program.

6.  Keep the program public. Doing so (1) limits the possibility that the shock procedure would be used unethically, arbitrarily, or inappropriately, (2) spreads the responsibility for program implementation and accountability so that everyone has a stake in the program, and (3) permits the immediate use of multiple trainers which should enhance generalization and maintenance (cf. Foxx & Livesay, 1984).

7.  Ensure that everyone who will conduct the shock program is well trained in its implementation by (1) conducting the program publicly, (2) having them witness the program before they are responsible for it, (3) testing them before they are allowed to function as therapists, and (4) having them experience the shock prior to using it.

8.  Maintain daily contact with treatment personnel after they have been given responsibility for conducting the program.

9.  Provide program data regularly to all concerned parties. This can be accomplished by providing periodic written summaries to administrators at all levels and meeting daily with school and living unit personnel, etc., to review the

day's progress and solve any problems that may have arisen. Overall progress should be reviewed on both a weekly and monthly basis.

10. Adhere to specific criteria for treatment success and/or program continuation. To do so, continually compare treatment records to the baseline period in order to evaluate treatment success. Always be prepared to terminate the program if it is ineffective or has lost its effectiveness.

## V. CONCLUDING COMMENTS

We have attempted to demonstrate that the decision to pursue and then implement a contingent shock program is a complex process that involves many issues. Although all of these issues are important, three are particularly important. First, the use of shock should be limited to those cases where the client's maladaptive behaviors are so serious that they may cause self-harm, injuries to others, or even loss of life. Second, clients with such severe behavior problems have a right to treatment and facilities have the responsibility to provide it. Thus, a facility is abrogating its responsibility to provide treatment if it chooses to use custodial measures rather than ones that might benefit the client. Third, the treatment facility must provide the necessary overall environmental support for the shock program. This means that the facility must have the expertise, accountability system, administrative commitment, and quality programming to conduct the program successfully. The availability of someone with the appropriate level of behavioral expertise is especially important.

Once the decision has been made to pursue the use of shock, a comprehensive informed consent document must be prepared. Doing so will help ensure that all relevant administrative, legal, and clinical issues have been addressed.

## REFERENCES

Accreditation Council for Services for Mentally Retarded and Other Developmentally Disabled Persons (1981). *Standards for services for developmentally disabled individuals.* 5101 Wisconsin Avenue, N. W., Washington, D.C.

Ball, T. S., Sibbach, L., Jones, R., Steele, B., & Frazier, L. (1975). An accelerometer-activated device to control assaultive and self-destructive behaviors in retardates. *Journal of Behavior Therapy and Experimental Psychiatry,* **6,** 223–228.

Bernstein, T. (1975). Electrical safety in aversive conditioning of humans. *Behavioral Engineering,* **2,** 31–34.

Birnbrauer, J. S. (1968). Generalization of punishment effects: A case study. *Journal of Applied Behavior Analysis,* **1,** 201–211.

Browning, R. M. (1971). Treatment effects of a total behavior modification program with five autistic children. *Behaviour Research and Therapy,* **9,** 319–327.

Butterfield, W. H. (1975). Electric shock—Safety factors when used for the aversive conditioning of humans. *Behavior Therapy*, **6**, 98–110.

Carr, E. G., & Lovaas, O. I. (1983). Contingent electric shock as a treatment for severe behavior problems. In S. Axelrod & J. Apsche (Eds.), *The effects of punishment on human behavior*. New York: Academic Press.

Cook, J. W., Altman, K., & Haavik, S. (1978). Consent for aversive treatment: A model form. *Mental Retardation*, **16**, 47–51.

Corte, H. E., Wolf, M. M., & Locke, B. J. (1971). A comparison of procedures for eliminating self-injurious behavior of retarded adolescents. *Journal of Applied Behavior Analysis*, **4**, 201–213.

Favell, J. E., Azrin, N. H., Baumeister, A. A., Carr, E. G., Dorsey, M. F., Forehand, R., Foxx, R. M., Lovaas, O. I., Rincover, A., Risley, T. R., Romanczyk, R. G., Russo, D. C., Schroeder, S. R., & Solnick, J. V. (1982). The treatment of self-injurious behavior. *Behavior Therapy*, **13**, 529–554.

Foxx, R. M. (1982). *Decreasing the behaviors of retarded and autistic persons*. Champaign, Il: Research Press.

Foxx, R. M., & Dufrense, D. (1984). "Harry": The use of physical restraint as a reinforcer, timeout from restraint and fading restraint in treating a self-injurious man. *Analysis and Intervention in Developmental Disabilities*, **4**, 1–13.

Foxx, R. M., & Livesay, J. (1984). Maintenance of response suppression following overcorrection: A ten year retrospective examination of eight cases. *Analysis and Intervention in Developmental Disabilities*, **4**, 65–80.

Foxx, R. M., McMorrow, M. J., Bittle, R. G., & Bechtel, D. R. (1985). The successful treatment of a dually diagnosed deaf man's aggression with a contingent electric shock program. *Behavior Therapy*, in press.

Griffin, J. C., Locke, B. J., & Landers, W. F. (1975). Manipulation of potential punishment parameters in the treatment of self-injury. *Journal of Applied Behavior Analysis*, **8**, 458.

Harris, S. L., & Ersner-Hershfield, R. (1978). Behavioral suppression of seriously disruptive behavior in psychotic and retarded patients: A review of punishment and its alternatives. *Psychological Bulletin*, **85**, 1352–1375.

Horner, R. D., & Barton, E. S. (1980). Operant techniques in the analysis and modification of self-injurious behavior: A review. *Behavior Research of Severe Developmental Disabilities*, **4**, 61–91.

Kohlenberg, R. J. (1970). The punishment of persistent vomiting: A case study. *Journal of Applied Behavior Analysis*, **3**, 241–245.

Lang, P. J., & Melamed, B. G. (1969). Avoidance conditioning therapy of an infant with chronic ruminative vomiting: Case report. *Journal of Abnormal Psychology*, **74**, 1–8.

Lichstein, K. L., & Schreibman, L. (1976). Employing electric shock with autistic children: A review of the side effects. *Journal of Autism and Childhood Schizophrenia*, **6**, 163–173.

Lovaas, O. I., & Simmons, J. Q. (1969). Manipulation of self-destruction in three retarded children. *Journal of Applied Behavior Analysis*, **2**, 143–157.

Luckey, R. E., Watson, C. M., & Musick, J. K. (1968). Aversive conditioning as a means of inhibiting vomiting and rumination. *American Journal of Mental Deficiency*, **73**, 139–142.

Ludwig, A. M., Marx, A. J., Hill, P. A., & Browning, R. M. (1969). The control of violent behavior through faradic shock: A case study. *The Journal of Nervous and Mental Disease*, **148**, 624–637.

Martin, R. (1975). *Legal challenges to behavior modification: Trends in schools, corrections and mental health*. Champaign, IL: Research Press.

Matson, J. L., & DiLorenzo, T. M. (1984). *Punishment and its alternatives. A new perspective for behavior modification*. New York: Springer.

May, J. G., Risley, T. R., Twardosz, S., Friedman, P., Bijou, S., & Wexler, O. (1976). *Guidelines for the use of behavioral procedures in state programs for retarded persons.* NARC Monograph. Arlington, TX: MR Research.

Merbaum, M. (1973). The modification of self-destructive behavior by a mother-therapist using aversive stimulation. *Behavior Therapy,* **4,** 442–447.

Nolley, D., Boelkins, D., Kocur, L., Moore, M. K., Goncalves, S., & Lewis, M. (1980). Aversive conditioning within laws and guidelines in a state facility for mentally retarded individuals. *Mental Retardation,* **18,** 295–298.

Ray, E. T., & Shelton, J. T. (1975). A brief note on administrative management of aversive conditioning at Porterville State Hospital. *Behavioral Engineering,* **2,** 68–69.

Richmond, R. G., & Martin, P. (1977). Punishment as a therapeutic method with institutionalized retarded persons. In T. Thompson & J. Grabowski (Eds.), *Behavior modification of the mentally retarded* (2nd ed.). New York: Oxford Univ. Press.

Risley, T. R. (1968). The effects and side effects of punishing the autistic behaviors of a deviant child. *Journal of Applied Behavior Analysis,* **1,** 21–34.

Romanczyk, R. G., Colletti, G., & Plotkin, R. (1980). Punishment of self-injurious behavior: Issues of behavior analysis, generalization, and the right to treatment. *Child Behavior Therapy,* **2,** 37–54.

Romanczyk, R. G., & Goren, E. R. (1975). Severe self-injurious behavior: The problem of clinical control. *Journal of Consulting and Clinical Psychology,* **43,** 730–739.

Schroeder, S. R., Schroeder, C. S., Rojahn, J., & Mulick, J. A. (1981). Self-injurious behavior: An analysis of behavior management techniques. In J. L. Matson & J. R. McCartney (Eds.), *Handbook of behavior modification with the mentally retarded.* New York: Plenum.

Tate, B. G., & Baroff, G. S. (1966). Aversive control of self-injurious behavior in a psychotic boy. *Behaviour Research and Therapy,* **4,** 281–287.

Turnbull, H. R. (Ed.). (1977). *Consent Handbook.* Washington, D.C.: American Association on Mental Deficiency.

Tursky, B. (1975). Factors that can affect the use of electric shock in behavior therapy. *Behavioral Engineering,* **2,** 31–34.

United States Department of Health, Education, and Welfare: Health Care Financing Administration: Health Standards and Quality Bureau (1977). *Final interpretive guidelines for the application of the regulations for institutions for mentally retarded or persons with related conditions* (45 CFR 249.13). Washington, D.C.: U.S. Government Printing Office.

Whaley, D. L., & Tough, J. (1970). Treatment of a self-injuring mongoloid with shock-induced suppression and avoidance. In R. Ulrich, T. Stachnik, & J. Mabry (Eds.), *Control of human behavior.* Glenview, IL: Scott, Foresman.

White, J. C., & Taylor, D. (1967). Noxious conditioning as a treatment for rumination. *Mental Retardation,* **5,** 30–33.

# MOTOR ACTIVITY MEASUREMENTS AND DSM-III

WARREN W. TRYON

*Department of Psychology*
*Fordham University*
*Bronx, New York*

PROGRESS IN BEHAVIOR
MODIFICATION, VOLUME 20

# I.  INTRODUCTION

The intent of this chapter is to review the role that activity measurements play in reaching a diagnosis using the first (APA, 1952), second (APA, 1968), and particularly third (APA, 1980) editions of the Diagnostic and Statistical Manual known as DSM-I, DSM-II, and DSM-III, respectively. The first two editions are reviewed primarily for their historical importance. The major focus is upon DSM-III. A further goal of this presentation is to indicate ways in which future activity research can advance both the diagnosis of selected disorders and the differential diagnosis among these disorders. It is hoped that a clear description of the potential diagnostic benefits of future activity research will be heuristic.

# II.  ACTIVITY

The term activity is used in this discussion to refer to the overt movements of human body parts such as the arms, legs, trunk, and head. That is, we are concerned with publicly observable behavior that can be videotaped. Activity refers to a continuum ranging from the absence or omission of activity to the emission of low, moderate, or high levels of various behaviors. The fact that activity refers to the emission of a broad range of otherwise unidentified behaviors deserves special mention. Human activity is typically discussed as a singular entity in and of itself rather than as an aspect of the full range of all behaviors that people emit. One cannot display activity in and of itself. Rather, one must emit some type of behavior. The frequency, intensity, and duration of the behavior determine the degree of activity present. All behaviors do not involve the same degree of movement by all body parts. Some behaviors involve mainly arm movements, such as desk work. Other behaviors involve mainly leg movements, such as riding an exercycle. Still other behaviors involve both arm and leg movements, such as walking and running. In sum, activity is not a monolithic entity when viewed from a behavioral perspective. Activity is a quantitative description of the movements involved in various body sites as the person behaves.

## A.  Levels of Assessment

Tryon (1976, 1985a) discussed three levels of behavioral assessment that pertain to the assessment of activity. This discussion will be briefly recapitulated here.

### 1. BEHAVIORAL INFERENCE

This level of assessment requires clinicians, parents, teachers, and/or staff members to make global inferences about someone's activity level and to register their judgment using either a quantitative or a qualitative rating scale. It assumes that all the judges share a common definition of activity. It further assumes that the judges have adequately sampled the subject's behavior. Moreover, it additionally assumes that the subject's sex, age, race, religion, and all other sources of bias do not materially affect the judges' behavior. Ratings of activity are requested because they are the easiest assessments to obtain. This matter of convenience appears to outweigh the many methodological problems associated with such assessments that have been recognized for some time.

## 2. BEHAVIORAL OBSERVATION

The position that the behavior of a person can be monitored by one or more people in real time using a structured assessment procedure is a substantial improvement over the method of behavioral inference just discussed. Observers are trained with the aid of a manual to reliably count the frequencies with which predefined behavioral categories are represented in a sample of behavior. The structure provided by this approach and the fact that it pertains to present (real-time) behaviors are the key features responsible for the enhanced reliability and validity of behavioral observation over behavioral inference. Initial enthusiasm for this procedure has given way to greater discussion of its shortcomings.

One problem with behavioral observation is that considerable disagreement exists regarding the best method for calculating reliability. Birkimer and Brown (1979) stated that "Interval by interval reliability has been criticized for 'inflating' observer agreement when target behavior rates are very low or very high. Scored interval reliability and its converse, unscored interval reliability, however, vary as target behavior rates vary when observer disagreement rates are constant. These problems, along with the existence of 'chance' values for each reliability which also vary as a function of response rate, may cause researchers and consumers difficulty in interpreting observer agreement measures" (p. 523). Hartmann and Gardner (1979) indicated that Fisher's Exact Probability Test and a chi-square test of independence are appropriate for evaluating observer reliability. Hopkins (1979) offered additional proposals for evaluating observer reliability. Mitchell (1979) indicated that the standard methods for calculating reliability are based upon interobserver agreement and therefore we can only generalize our data across observers. She indicated that we often wish to generalize our observations over different target behaviors, different settings, and over time. Demonstrating that one's observational system is stable over time, that it pertains to various settings, that it is relevant to the various target responses, and that it can be used by more than one observer requires a generalizability research design. Few investigators have attempted to provide such difficult to obtain information. Cone (1979) noted that the "I've got a better agreement measure" literature continues to grow for two reasons. First, the arguments are purely rational and therefore depend entirely upon how persuasive they appear. Second, each article advocates its own position without indicating how its proposal is superior to the other proposals that have already been put forward. Cone (1979) suggests that we adopt a more empirical attitude by requiring future authors of such articles to compare empirically their proposed methods with previously published methods in order to demonstrate the merits of their proposed alternatives.

A second problem with behavioral observation is that establishing the reliability of observers does not establish their validity. It is clearly possible that both observers are making the same mistakes or share the same biases. Efforts by Cone (1977, 1981) and others to ensure the validity of behavioral observations are laudable but difficult to implement even on a research basis let alone on a clinical basis.

A third problem with behavioral observation is the problem of observer drift. Reid (1970) demonstrated that observer reliability rapidly diminishes subsequent to the end of the training period. This effect is particularly pronounced if the observers are told that they are on their own. One important consequence of observer drift is that the expensive process of observer training must occur periodically. Another important consequence of observer drift is that the reliability of the observer must be checked periodically throughout the duration of the study or clinical intervention.

A fourth problem with behavioral observation is the issue of behavioral sampling. Behavioral observations are usually restricted to relatively brief time periods because it is impractical, even in research settings, to follow subjects about as they travel through the variety of settings that constitute a typical day.

A fifth problem with behavioral observation concerns both the invasion of privacy and the reactivity associated with having an outsider present at intimate times.

All of the above assessment problems associated with behavioral observation and classification exist primarily because a person is being used as a data collection device or instrument. The behavior of the observer interacts with the behavior of the observee in a dynamic fashion that is unstable over time resulting in observer drift. Observer fatigue, expense, and issues of privacy prevent investigators from obtaining extended records, particularly as the person behaves in his or her natural environment. These problems are inherent shortcomings associated with using people to perform the work of scientific instruments.

## 3. BEHAVIORAL MEASUREMENT

The term measurement is used here to indicate that data are collected via an instrument rather than a human observer. This approach has several advantages over behavioral observation. First, the age-old problem of the proper unit of behavior is solved. We simply adopt either the standard centimeter-gram-second (CGS) or the meter-kilogram-second (MKS) units that have long characterized scientific inquiry. Behavior is approached like any other natural science phenomenon and is characterized by the same units of analysis. Second, the reliability, validity, and more importantly the accuracy (cf. Tryon, 1985a) of instruments can be verified in the laboratory. Third, the operating characteristics of electromechanical devices drift far less than those of human observers. This means that instruments (e.g., clocks, voltmeters, etc.) do not require recalibration as often as do human observers. Hence, one does not need to double-check measurements during every segment of the study. Fourth, much more extensive behavioral samples can be obtained with instruments than with human observers.

Portable instruments can be attached to people (cf. Tryon, 1985a) for the purpose of measuring activity while the person behaves in his/her natural environment. Complete records of activity during all waking and sleeping hours can be obtained for days or weeks at a time as is necessary to accurately sample the person's behavior. We typically think of waking behavior when we discuss activity. However, we move during our sleep as well. Johns (1971) pointed out that "Measuring body motility was one of the first objective methods used in sleep research" (p. 489). Cox and Marley (1959), Foster and Kupfer (1975), Hobson, Spagna, and Malenka (1978), Kleitman (1963), Monroe (1967), Oswald, Berger, Jaramillo, Keddie, Olley, and Plunkett (1963), Reich, Kupfer, Weiss, McPartland, Foster, Detre, and Delgado (1974), and Stonehill and Crisp (1971) have studied sleep activity.

## B.   Conceptual Shift

Prior to Laennec, disease was mainly conceptualized in terms of humors that were out of proportion. The altered chest sounds Laennec heard through his stethoscope made sense only after he hypothesized that disease resulted in structural or physiological changes (cf. Reiser, 1979). It is this latter view which dominates current medical theories. Laennec's stethoscope revolutionized the clinical practice of medicine in addition to revolutionizing medical science. Its use introduced the physical examination, which is fundamental to the practice of modern medicine. Prior to Laennec, medical diagnosis was accomplished by interviewing the patient. Subsequent to Laennec, the physician depended upon his or her physical examination to confirm and/or extend the patient's report. ". . . the stethoscope became the first instrument of any kind to be widely used by physicians to diagnose illness" (Reiser, 1979, p. 148). Another example of how instrumentation advanced both medical theory and practice concerns the microscope. The cellular theory of life was a direct result of being able to observe distinct cells in many preparations. Medical practice was altered in that disease was increasingly diagnosed on the basis of microscopic analysis of specimens collected during the physical exam. It is my strong personal opinion that naturalistic measurements will provide for theoretical advances in the understanding and diagnosis of behavior disorders and will substantially alter the nature of clinical practice for treating these disorders.

The methodological shift from either behavioral inference or observation to behavioral measurement requires an associated conceptual shift. Normal and abnormal behavior can no longer be discussed in terms of the old familiar categories. The data obtained using behavioral measurement are in terms of the physical forces measured at one or more sites of attachment. Walking, sitting, running, etc., are no longer treated as distinct categories whose frequency can be counted. Rather, the forces of acceleration on the ankle, waist, and/or wrist are recorded over time as the person emits various behaviors. The challenge is for behavioral researchers to reconceptualize normal and abnormal behavior in terms of these new measurements just as Laennec reconceptualized the nature of disease in terms of the sounds he heard through his newly invented stethoscope and biology was reconceptualized in terms of the cellular structure seen through the microscope.

A subsequent section of this chapter demonstrates that DSM-III prompts present day behavioral researchers to ask a variety of quantitative questions regarding normal and abnormal activity measurements. These are concerned with the diagnosis of various disorders from the normal condition and with differential diagnoses among these entities. We will see that some of the questions that arise are very different from previous behavioral questions. One such question concerns the temporal resolution of behavioral measurements that is sufficient to accomplish the goals of diagnosis and differential diagnosis. This question concerns the number of data points per unit time that must be obtained. Pedomoter readings are typically collected once per day. The present question is whether once-daily measurements are sufficient or whether we need to measure twice a day, once every 4 or 2 hours, once per hour, or whether measurements need to be taken once each minute or once every 15 seconds. Undoubtedly, the temporal resolution required will depend upon the type of behavioral disorder under consideration and its clinical characteristics. A chronic condition may require many fewer points to diagnose from the normal condition than does a transient condition. However, differentially diagnosing between two chronic conditions may require a much greater temporal resolution than was necessary to diagnose either disorder from the normal condition.

A second novel question concerns the duration of measurement necessary before firm conclusions can be reached. This question concerns whether it is sufficient to obtain half-hour or hour-long measurements or whether one should collect data during the person's entire waking day. Should data be collected over more than a single day? If so, how many days, weeks, or months of data should be collected? Should data be collected on consecutive days or on some other basis?

A third novel question concerns whether data should be collected only while the person is awake or should data also be collected while the person is asleep? Perhaps it will be best to obtain data during both periods. All of these issues are empirical questions to be answered by future research.

## III.  DSM-I

Perhaps the best way to describe some of the history of activity data in making diagnoses and to communicate the advances of DSM-III over both DSM-I and DSM-II is to review the relatively few disorders cited in both DSM-I and DSM-II that make explicit reference to motor activity.

Section II,B of DSM-I indicates that "This nomenclature permits the modification of any of the primary diagnoses by the qualifying phrases, .x1 with psychotic reaction, .x2 with neurotic reaction, and .x3 with behavioral reaction" (p. 12). This stipulation suggests the possibility of attaching the .x3 extension to every diagnostic category given abnormal activity data. In this sense, DSM-I was more inclusive than DSM-III regarding the potential role of activity measurements in achieving a diagnosis. I shall confine my remarks to those DSM-I categories that make direct reference to activity.

### A.   Psychotic Disorders: Affective Reactions

Perhaps the largest role for activity measurements relative to DSM-I diagnoses concerns the affective reactions. We will later see that both DSM-II and DSM-III reiterate the importance of activity measurements when diagnosing affective disorders.

1.  MANIC DEPRESSIVE REACTION, MANIC TYPE (000-x11)

"This group is characterized by elation or irritability, with overtalkativeness, flight of ideas, and increased motor activity. Transitory, often momentary, episodes of depression may occur, but will not change the classification from the manic type of reaction" (p. 25). The first point of interest here is that the explicit statement "increased motor activity" is listed among the formal inclusion criteria for the manic reaction. This criterion implies the existence of a premorbid activity measurement or profile to which the present behavior can be compared in order to demonstrate that the person's activity has actually increased. It would not be sufficient to demonstrate that the person in question was significantly more active than a normative group, since he/she may have been unusually active prior to the onset of their disorder. Hence, we have a relative rather than an absolute reference to activity. A second point of interest is that no quantitative guidelines are expressed regarding either the intensity or duration of activity increase necessary to assign this diagnostic label.

2.  MANIC DEPRESSIVE REACTION, DEPRESSED TYPE (000-x12)

"Here will be classified as those cases with outstanding depression of mood and with mental and motor retardation and inhibition; in some cases there is much uneasiness and apprehension. Perplexity, stupor or agitation may be prominent symptoms, and may be added to the diagnosis as manifestations" (p. 25).

The phrase "motor retardation and inhibition" cited in the above inclusion criteria strongly implies decreased activity. Again we notice the lack of any empirical guidelines regarding either the intensity or duration of the activity disturbance that would warrant assigning the diagnosis of manic depressive reaction, depressed type.

The phrase "motor retardation and inhibition" refers to an absolute decrement in activity that is below normal limits. This language stands in contrast to the phrase "increased motor activity" used to describe the *changes* in activity from a premorbid state which define the manic depressive reaction, manic type. It is unclear why one disorder should be defined in relative terms while the very next entry should be defined in absolute terms.

3. MANIC DEPRESSIVE REACTION, OTHER (000-x13)

"Here will be classified only those cases with marked mixtures of the cardinal manifestations of the above two phases (mixed type), or those cases where continuous alternation of the two phases occur (circular type). Other specified varieties of manic depressive reaction (manic stupor or unproductive mania) will also be included here" (p. 25).

This category depends upon the definitions of the prior two categories. Hence, we have a mixture of both relative and absolute criteria for determining the presence of this diagnosis.

The term "manic stupor" appears to be somewhat of a contradiction from the perspective of activity measurement. The manic reaction was defined by "increased motor activity" and stupor is defined by profound inactivity. Hence, it is unclear whether one is looking for abnormally high or low activity levels when attempting to document the existence of "manic stupor." Perhaps the term refers to periods of stupor in persons who are otherwise manic. Such a condition would result in a series of very high activity measurements followed by a series of very low activity measurements. It is unclear whether the transition period is short or long. Nor is it clear what the rate of activity decrease is as stupor begins and what the rate of activity increase is as mania returns.

## B.  Schizophrenic Reactions

Activity disorders were recognized by DSM-I, as they were by DSM-II and are by DSM-III, as characteristic of certain psychotic disorders.

1. SCHIZOPHRENIC REACTION, SCHIZO-AFFECTIVE TYPE
   (000-x27)

"This category is intended for those cases showing significant admixtures of schizophrenic and affective reactions" (p. 27). This diagnosis is reserved for persons who have some or all of the aforementioned characteristics of affective disorders in addition to being schizophrenic. A major problem here is that we are not told what the minimum affective disturbance must be in order to assign the present diagnosis rather than some other category of schizophrenic reaction. Said otherwise, what is the cutoff point below which activity levels or changes in levels are an insufficient basis for assigning the diagnostic extension of schizo-affective type?

2.  SCHIZOPHRENIC REACTION, CATATONIC TYPE (000-x23)

"These reactions are characterized by conspicuous motor behavior, exhibiting either marked generalized inhibition (stupor, mutism, negativism and waxy flexibility) or excessive motor activity and excitement. The individual may regress to a state of vegetation" ( p. 26).

The above statement indicates that this disorder is characterized by excessively high or low activity levels. The emphasis here is upon the word "or," indicating that either condition may be evident. It remains unclear if the person can sometimes show high activity levels and sometimes show low activity levels for when one or the other condition prevails. If the latter alternative is correct, then perhaps a basis exists for creating a subclassification of catatonia depending upon whether the person displays hyper- or hypoactivity. Such a subdivision was adopted by DSM-II.

3.  SCHIZOPHRENIC REACTION, ACUTE UNDIFFERENTIATED
    TYPE (000-x25)

This diagnosis was typically assigned to individuals undergoing an initial psychotic break where the symptoms were not sufficiently characteristic of any of the other types of schizophrenic reactions to be so classified. "Very often the reaction is accompanied by a pronounced affective coloring of either excitement or depression" (p. 27).

We are not told anything about the intensity or the duration of the affective reaction which sometimes accompanies the acute undifferentiated type of schizophrenic reaction. It appears that motor activity increases or decreases can result. Thus, the only diagnostic feature from the perspective of activity measurements is that the data can be abnormal in either direction.

## C.  Psychoneurotic Disorders

DEPRESSIVE REACTION (000-x06)

A synonym for this disorder is reactive depression. DSM-I indicates that this category is distinguished, in part, from a psychotic reaction by the absence of "severe psychomotor retardation" and by "stupor" (p. 34).

It is notable that very little is said about how to recognize the presence of a depressive reaction. DSM-I concentrates mainly upon presenting the psycho-analytic explanation of why people become depressed (object loss). This mistakes explanation for description.

## D.  Summary

One notable feature about the above-mentioned DSM-I diagnoses is that the descriptions of each category are particularly brief. A subsequent section on DSM-III will reveal much more extensive inclusion and, more importantly, exclusion criteria.

A second notable feature of the above-mentioned DSM-I diagnostic categories is the absence of empirical guidelines regarding the minimum intensity and/or duration of the symptoms necessary before the clinician can assign a particular diagnosis to someone.

A final observation is that motor activity measurements were considered relevant to the diagnostic effort by DSM-I and are therefore not novel to DSM-III. This observation indicates that clinicians have taken activity to be an important clinical behavior for some time now. Unfortunately, the technology for obtaining naturalistic activity measurements has lagged behind clinical interest. The unavailability of such devices before 1952 when DSM-I was being developed and published probably explains why more comprehensive activity inclusion and exclusion criteria were not included in DSM-I. Moreover, even the methods of behavioral observation and classification were not included in clinical reports at this time.

## IV.  DSM-II

DSM-II is partly an outgrowth of the World Health Organization's efforts to develop an International Classification of Disease. It was intended to summarize world thought about psychiatric diagnostic classification in 1968. DSM-I was primarily a product of psychiatrists living in the United States of America. DSM-II preserved the role that activity data played in rendering diagnoses with two exceptions. The first exception is that DSM-II no longer clearly implicated activity in the diagnosis of neurosis. The second exception is the addition to DSM-II of a new diagnostic category by the name of Hyperkinetic Reaction of Childhood (or Adolescence).

## A.  Major Affective Disorders

The corresponding heading in DSM-I was Affective Reactions. The present category differs from its DSM-I counterpart in that it does not include the Psychotic Depressive Reaction.

1. MANIC–DEPRESSIVE ILLNESS, MANIC TYPE (296.1)

"This disorder consists exclusively of manic episodes. These episodes are characterized by excessive elation, irritability, talkativeness, flight of ideas, and accelerated speech and motor activity. Brief periods of depression sometimes occur, but they are never true depressive episodes" (p. 36). This definition is in absolute terms, whereas its DSM-I counterpart is in relative terms.

2. MANIC–DEPRESSIVE ILLNESS, DEPRESSED TYPE (296.2)

"This disorder consists exclusively of depressive episodes. These episodes are characterized by severely depressed mood and by mental and motor retardation progressing occasionally to stupor" (p. 36). This definition remains essentially the same as the DSM-I definition from the perspective of activity measurement in that it uses absolute terms.

3. MANIC–DEPRESSIVE ILLNESS, CIRCULAR TYPE (296.3)

"This disorder is distinguished by at least one attack of both a depressive episode and a manic episode. This phenomenon makes clear why manic and depressed types are combined into a single category. (In DSM-I these cases were diagnosed under 'Manic depressive reaction, other.') The current episode should be specified as one of the following:" (p. 37). The two specified subcategories are manic–depressive illness, circular type, manic (296.33) and manic–depressive illiness, circular type, depressed (296.34). The important point here is that the differential diagnosis between these two categories is entirely on the basis of activity level.

4. OTHER MAJOR AFFECTIVE DISORDER (296.8)

"Major affective disorders for which a more specific diagnosis has not been made are included here. It is also for "mixed" manic–depressive illness, in which manic and depressive symptoms appear almost simultaneously. It does not include *Psychotic depressive reaction* (q.v.) or *Depressive neurosis* (q.v.). (In DSM-I this category was included under 'Manic depressive reaction, other.')" (p. 37).

## B. Schizophrenia

1. SCHIZOPHRENIA, SCHIZO-AFFECTIVE TYPE (295.7)

"This category is for patients showing a mixture of schizophrenic symptoms and pronounced elation or depression. Within this category it may be useful to distinguish excited from depressed types as follows:" (p. 35). The two specified subcategories are schizophrenia, schizo-affective type, excited (295.73) and schizophrenia, schizo-affective type, depressed (295.74). Again, it is notable that activity is the sole basis for the differential diagnosis between these two categories.

## 2. SCHIZOPHRENIA, CATATONIC TYPE (295.2)

"It is frequently possible and useful to distinguish two subtypes of catatonic schizophrenia. One is marked by excessive and sometimes violent motor activity and excitement and the other by generalized inhibition by stupor, mutism, or waxy flexibility. In time, some cases deteriorate to a vegetative state" (pp. 33–34). The two specified subcategories are schizophrenia, catatonic type, excited (295.23) and schizophrenia, catatonic type, withdrawn (295.24).

When reviewing catatonic schizophrenia as described by DSM-I, I stated that the diagnostic criteria allowed for high or low activity levels. This is exactly the distinction made in DSM-II. DSM-III no longer makes this same distinction. Like DSM-I, the same diagnosis is given when low or high activity is present. This decision was probably based on the fact that rapid oscillation between the excited and withdrawn states can occur. If so, then perhaps evidence of such oscillation will be reported in the future and can serve as an empirical basis for diagnosing catatonia or for diagnosing a specific form of catatonia.

## 3. ACUTE SCHIZOPHRENIC EPISODE (295.4)

This category was called Schizophrenia, Acute Undifferentiated Type in DSM-I. The definition of this category remains unchanged from the perspective of measuring activity.

## C. Neuroses

### DEPRESSIVE NEUROSIS (300.4)

No specific symptoms are listed by which the clinician can recognize this disorder. Only the psychoanalytic theory of depression (object loss) is described.

## D. Behavior Disorders of Childhood and Adolescence

### HYPERKINETIC REACTION OF CHILDHOOD (OR ADOLESCENCE) (308.0)

"This disorder is characterized by overactivity, restlessness, distractibility, and short attention span, especially in young children; the behavior usually diminishes in adolescence. If this behavior is caused by organic brain damage, it should be diagnosed under the appropriate non-psychotic organic brain syndrome" (p. 50).

This category represents an addition to the DSM-I categories. It clearly indicates that excessive activity level is a major feature of this disorder. The

DSM-II inclusion criteria, like those in DSM-I, lack empirical guidelines regarding the intensity and/or duration of activity that is sufficient for ascribing this diagnosis to someone. The term overactivity implies that activity norms exist for children and adolescents, which is not presently the case.

## V.  DSM-III

DSM-III increased the reliability of diagnostic judgments in two ways. First, the inclusion and exclusion cirteria for each disorder were much more clearly operationalized.

The second method used to increase the reliability of diagnosis is the decision tree procedure for reaching a differential diagnosis. Appendix A (pp. 339–349) presents decision trees for the following differential diagnoses.

1.  Psychotic features.
2.  Irrational anxiety and avoidance behavior.
3.  Mood disturbance.
4.  Antisocial, aggressive, defiant, and oppositional behavior.
5.  Physical complaints and irrational anxiety about physical illness.
6.  Academic and learning difficulties.
7.  Organic brain syndromes.

These decision trees are a series of yes–no questions (whose answers lead either directly to a diagnosis or to other yes–no questions, whose answers lead either directly to a diagnosis or to other yes–no questions, etc.). All of the decision trees result in the making of one diagnosis or another from among a group of related diagnoses. Such decision trees constitute a programmatic method of inquiry leading to a final diagnosis. This structured method of inquiry enhances diagnostic reliability because it indicates both the relevant questions and the proper sequence of questions, thereby removing interclinician variability on both matters. Current efforts at computerized diagnosis are essentially electronic decision trees.

Appendix F of DSM-III reviews the quantative reliability studies conducted using DSM-III categories (cf. pp. 467–472). "Approximately 300 clinicians evaluated a total of 670 adults (18 years and older). Approximately 84 clinicians evaluated a total of 126 child and adolescent patients, approximately half of whom were below the age of eleven" (p. 468). The overall Axis I kappa coefficient for the 339 adults in Phase One was 0.68. The overall Axis I kappa coefficient for the 331 adults in Phase Two was 0.72. The overall Axis I kappa coefficient for the 71 children in Phase One was 0.68. The overall Axis I kappa coefficient for the 55 children in Phase Two was 0.52.

## VI.  DSM-III CATEGORIES INVOLVING ACTIVITY

This section reviews each of the DSM-III disorders that specifically cite activity as an inclusion variable. The general format for reviewing these categories will involve the same two steps as used before. The first step will be to summarize the characteristics of the disorder, with special emphasis upon the role of activity. The second step will be to comment upon the role of activity measurement in light of the preliminary comments made above. It is hoped that this discussion will help clarify and stimulate thinking about abnormal behavior from the behavioral measurement perspective and hopefully generate more research in this area.

### A.  Attention Deficit Disorder

This category refers to what was previously described as "Hyperkinetic Reaction of Childhood, Hyperkinetic Syndrome, Hyperactive Child Syndrome, Minimal Brain Damage, Minimal Brain Dysfunction, Minimal Cerebral Dysfunction, and Minor Cerebral Dysfunction" (DSM-III, p. 41). The overall category of Attention Deficit Disorder is subdivided into two more specific categories depending upon the degree of activity present. Both of these categories are described below.

ATTENTION DEFICIT DISORDER WITH HYPERACTIVITY
(314.01)

The DSM-III inclusion criteria for this disorder include three of five behaviors regarding inattention, three of six behaviors regarding impulsivity, and two of five behaviors regarding hyperactivity. The five hyperactivity behaviors listed on page 44 of the DSM-III are

1. Runs about or climbs on things excessively.
2. Has difficulty sitting still or fidgets excessively.
3. Has difficulty staying seated.
4. Moves about excessively during sleep.
5. Is always "on the go" or acts as if "driven by a motor."

The onset of this disorder must be before the age of seven, have a duration of at least 6 months, and not meet the inclusion criteria for Schizophrenia, Affective Disorder, or Severe or Profound Mental Retardation.

My first observation is that the behavioral criteria are at the level of behavioral inference. Notice the use of subjective terms such as "excessively." How much is too much? What might be normal activity for a playground situation is probably excessive in a classroom setting. All of the items reflect a general clinical impression of hyperactivity without specifying the frequency, intensity, or duration of any behaviors or specifying the overall magnitude of any measurable quantity. Perhaps future research using portable instruments could establish normative distributions for hyperactive and control subjects during their waking and sleep periods. Such information could provide a quantitative basis for inferring the presence of hyperactivity.

My second observation is that the DSM-III criteria require that the condition exist for at least 6 months before a positive diagnosis can be reached. A strict interpretation of this point would require a minimum of 6 months of data before it could be determined if the person in question is hyperactive. A positive diagnosis of hyperactivity would be supported by at least 6 consecutive months where the quantitative criteria for hyperactivity were continuously met. But what conclusion would be reached if one day of normoactive behavior were interspersed in the temporal profile? Strictly speaking, one would have to extend data recording until at least 6 consecutive months of hyperactivity had been recorded. Practically, this would not be done. Perhaps it is also not theoretically necessary. It may be sufficient to diagnose the presence of hyperactivity with considerably less than a 6-month sample when using data from portable instruments that are worn continuously while the subject behaves in his/her natural environment. The continuous nature of these measurements may allow for a differential diagnosis in much less time than is presently required.

A third comment is that the diagnostic inclusion criterion of "Moves about excessively during sleep" requires that activity measures be taken during both sleep and waking periods; i.e., 24 hours per day. This requires that the activity measuring device be one that is comfortable during sleep. Future activity research may indicate that the hyperkinetic reaction is found only during waking periods for some children and only during sleeping periods for some children, and during both sleeping and waking periods for other children. It would be interesting to study the behavioral nature of sleep onset in these children. If excessive nocturnal activity is present, does it occur immediately upon going to bed and then decrease to where sleep begins or does the subject sleep peacefully for a while and then become hyperactive? These considerations would allow a further diagnostic refinement. Perhaps such a diagnostic refinement would also have treatment implications, particularly for chemotherapy.

## 2. ATTENTION DEFICIT DISORDER WITHOUT HYPERACTIVITY (314.00)

The inclusion criteria for this disorder are the same as for the Attention Deficit Disorder with Hyperactivity (314.01), "except that the individual never had signs of hyperactivity" (p. 44). This indicates that data must still be collected for at least 6 months to demonstrate that hyperactivity *is not* present. The child's temporal activity profile (plot of activity as a function of time) must be within normal limits. It is particularly important to note that activity data provide the sole basis for the differential diagnosis between 314.01 and 314.00. It is my opinion that the phrase "never had" should be removed from the inclusion criteria for hyperactivity, since it is impossible to obtain retrospective measurements back to birth which is what this phrase refers to. Perhaps a phrase like "no prior evidence of hyperactivity" would be preferable. It is recognized that neglect can lead to no prior evidence, as can careful longitudinal measurement. But this risk is not as undesirable as being placed in the impossible position of demonstrating that the child in question never exhibited hyperactivity at any time prior to his/her first clinic visit.

### 3.  ATTENTION DEFICIT DISORDER, RESIDUAL TYPE (314.80)

The inclusion criteria here entail (1) having once been diagnosed as having Attention Deficit Disorder with Hyperactivity, (2) not presently hyperactive, (3) still having an attention deficit disorder and/or impulsivity that results in some social and/or occupational impairment, and (4) the present problem cannot be diagnosed as Schizophrenia, Affective Disorder, Severe or Profound Mental Retardation, Schizotypal Personality Disorder, or Borderline Personality Disorder.

My first comment is that the matter of having a prior diagnosis of Attention Deficit Disorder with Hyperactivity is a matter of record which can be verified. One can always wonder whether the previous diagnosis was made accurately. This is important because once the diagnosis exists, rightly or wrongly, then the basis for a later diagnosis of Attention Deficit Disorder Residual Type also exists.

The clinician must demonstrate that hyperactivity is not currently present but the criteria for such a demonstration are not defined. Is the clinician to measure for at least 6 months as indicated in the previous two diagnostic categories? Or does the clinician need only demonstrate that the child is not hyperactive during the clinical examination? Perhaps future activity research will yield a measurement protocol that will provide a basis for determining the presence or absence of a hyperkinetic reaction that could be referred to here when attempting to make the diagnosis of Attention Deficit Disorder, Residual Type.

### B.  Affective Disorders

The DSM-III discussion of affective disorders begins by describing inclusion criteria for a Manic Episode and then for a Major Depressive Episode. This allows reference to these criteria when discussing various official diagnostic categories.

1.  MANIC EPISODE

The first inclusion criterion given by DSM-III for a manic episode is that the person show ''One or more distinct periods with a predominantly elevated, expansive, or irritable mood'' (p. 208). The second inclusion criterion for a manic episode is that three of the following seven criteria must be present if the person's mood is expansive or expansive and irritable. But four of these seven criteria must be present if the person's mood is only irritable (cf. p. 208).

1. Increase in activity (either socially, at work or sexually) or physical restlessness.
2. More talkative than usual or pressure to keep talking.
3. Flight of ideas or subjective experience that thoughts are racing.
4. Inflated self-esteem (grandiosity which may be delusional).
5. Decreased need for sleep.
6. Distractibility; i.e., attention is too easily drawn to unimportant or irrelevant external stimuli.
7. Excessive involvement in activities that have a high potential for painful consequences which is not recognized.

The above behaviors must exist for at least 1 week. No minimum duration is required if hospitalization is necessary. Exclusionary criteria are provided on p. 209 that will not be repeated here due to space considerations.

Criterion No. 1 above is an awkward one. The main reference to an increase in activity or physical restlessness clearly indicates that this behavior would be detected by the measuring devices available for monitoring activity in the person's natural environment. It is the parenthetical addition that is somewhat confusing. Does it mean that the person socialized more than before, works more than before, and/or has increased his or her sexual activity from prior levels? If so, then an activity measuring device would sense an increase in activity only if a compensatory decrease in some other aspect of their behavior did not also occur. This latter possibility is probably not very likely.

Criterion No. 5 above refers to the person's need for sleep. Activity monitors cannot directly assess psychological or physiological needs. However, activity monitors can determine if the person is sleeping less than normal or if the person's sleep period is characterized by abnormally high activity. I interpret this criterion to mean that the person does not sleep as often as he/she did before, and that this is the basis for the inference that the person's need for sleep appears diminished. This discussion of sleep activity raises the general need for further sleep activity research on both normal and clinical populations. It is difficult to determine if sleep activity is abnormal in a person suspected of having a manic episode unless one knows more about age appropriate sleep activity behavior in normal people.

DSM-III requires that the criteria listed above last for at least 1 week unless hospitalization is required. This is probably a reasonable time frame given a moderate or greater manic episode.

## 2.   MAJOR DEPRESSIVE EPISODE

The first criterion given by DSM-III for a Major Depressive Episode is "Dysphoric mood or loss of interest or pleasure in all or almost all usual activities and pastimes" (p. 213). *Stedman's Medical Dictionary* (1972) defines dysphoric as "Restlessness; a feeling of being ill at ease" (p. 386). DSM-III further indicates that at least four of the following eight criteria must exist for at least 2 weeks in adults. At least three of the first four criteria must be met in children under 6 years of age before a diagnosis of major depressive episode can be given (cf. pp. 213–124).

1. Poor appetite or significant weight loss when not dieting. Failure to make expected weight gains in children under 6.
2. Insomnia or hypersomnia.
3. Psychomotor agitation or retardation (but not merely subjective feelings of restlessness or being slowed down) (in children under 6, hyperactivity).
4. Loss of interest or pleasure in usual activities or decrease in sexual drive not limited to a period when delusional or hallucinating (in children under 6, signs of apathy).
5. Loss of energy; fatigue.
6. Feelings of worthlessness, self-reproach, or excessive or inappropriate guilt (either may be delusional).
7. Complaints or evidence of diminished ability to think or concentrate such as slowed thinking or indecisiveness not associated with marked loosening of associations or incoherence.
8. Recurrent thoughts of death, suicidal ideation, wishes to be dead, or suicide attempt.

DSM-III discusses several exclusion criteria that will not be repeated here to save space (cf. p. 214).

My first comment is that dysphoric mood is not in and of itself a behavior. Dysphoric mood per se will not show up on a videotape. However, *Stedman's Medical Dictionary* indicates that dysphoria involves restlessness as stated above. Restlessness strongly suggests an increase in activity. Criterion No. 3 refers to psychomotor agitation or retardation, which strongly imply activity increases and decreases, respectively. A major question is whether these varying influences on activity will yield a net increase, decrease, or will cancel each other out and result in no net change. It is important to note that DSM-III explicitly rules out "subjective feelings of restlessness or being slowed down" (p. 213) as a basis for diagnosing a Major Depressive Episode. Such exclusion of verbal report requires the clinician to document psychomotor retardation or agitation by reference to an observable behavioral sample such as naturalistic activity measurements.

The term psychomotor is appropriate when referring to tasks which require the person to respond differentially on the basis of sensory cues. Such information processing tasks involve the coordination of psychological and sensorimotor processes. The term psychomotor is used in Criterion No. 3 to refer to noninformation processing related changes in motor activity. The assumption here is that the activity increases or decreases reflect the presence of depressive psychological processes. DSM-I also used the term "psychomotor retardation" when referring to the activity of depressed people. However, DSM-I speaks of "motor retardation and inhibition," "increased motor activity," and "excessive motor activity" when referring to the abnormal activity associated with other diagnostic categories. DSM-II speaks of "accelerated speech and motor activity," "motor retardation," and "violent motor activity" when referring to various diagnostic categories. I suggest that we limit the term "psychomotor activity" to refer exclusively to information processing tasks requiring a motor response where slowness of reaction has been observed.

The symptoms of insomnia and hypersomnia mentioned in Criterion No. 2 are directly related to activity. People obviously are much less active when they sleep. Hypersomnia involves an excessive amount of sleep. Hence, such people should have considerably lower activity levels than would normal people. Insomnia involves reduced sleep, which is likely to be associated with continued activity such as tossing and turning while awake in bed or getting out of bed and doing various other things when typically the person would have been asleep. A fine grained sleep activity analysis may reveal substantial differences between the sleep activity of insomniacs and normal sleepers.

The loss of interest cited in Criterion No. 4 implies not engaging in various activities that were previously characteristic of the person. This implies a reduction in activity level from the person's premorbid activity level. Whether or not this reduction results in hypoactivity depends upon both the person's initial activity level and the extent of his/her activity reduction. A sample of the person's premorbid activity is the best comparison for diagnosing an activity reduction, just as the person's premorbid EKG is the best comparison for diagnosing heart disease. The same is true for blood pressure and blood level readings. It is better to compare the person with himself/herself than with a normative criterion because of the wide interindividual differences that exist in these phenomena.

The loss of energy and fatigue cited in Criterion No. 5 implies decreased activity. Taking a rest is a common response to feeling tired. A chronic sense of fatigue may give rise to continuous low activity levels.

In sum, a major depressive episode involves disturbances of activity during both the waking and sleep periods. Perhaps future research into the waking and sleep profiles (activity vs time) of normal and depressed persons will clarify how the behavior of depressed people differs from that of nondepressed people.

### 3. MAJOR DEPRESSION, SINGLE EPISODE (296.2x)

The inclusion criteria for this disorder are those discussed above under Major Depressive Episode. The exclusion criterion is that the person has never had a manic episode as described above under the heading Manic Episode. The comments made above about these two headings apply equally well to this section but they will not be repeated here to conserve space.

### 4. MAJOR DEPRESSION, RECURRENT (296.3x)

Inclusion and exclusion criteria are the same here as for the previous diagnosis (296.2x), with the addition that this diagnosis refers to people who have previously had a major depressive episode. Inaccurate activity data may have erroneously produced a previous diagnosis of Major Depression and therefore a current misdiagnosis as a recurrence of such a depression.

### 5. BIPOLAR DISORDER, MANIC (296.4x)

The inclusion criteria for this disorder are those discussed above under the heading of Manic Episode. DSM-III indicates that ''If there has been a previous manic episode, the current episode need not meet the full criteria for a manic episode'' (p. 217).

The implications for activity measurement relative to this diagnosis have been discussed previously. However, it is important to note here that the full criteria for a manic episode need not be met if the person has previously had such an episode. Therefore, how inactive can a person be before he/she can no longer be considered a candidate for the diagnosis of Bipolar Disorder, Manic? This is an empirical question concerning the behavior of normal and hypomanic persons. Naturalistic activity measurements for these two groups would help clarify the diagnostic limits for this category. Perhaps a higher cutoff point could be used when making this diagnosis for the first time and a lower cutoff point could be used when this diagnosis had been given previously.

The parenthetical reference to the most recent manic episode suggests that this diagnosis can be made after the fact when the person's activity has returned to a normal condition. Such a post hoc diagnosis would almost certainly be made in the absence of activity data collected during the prior manic episode while the person behaved in his/her natural environment.

### 6. BIPOLAR DISORDER, DEPRESSED (296.5x)

The major inclusion criterion for this disorder is that the person ''has had one or more manic episodes'' (p. 217). The full inclusion criteria need not be met if the person has previously received this diagnosis. My comments regarding the activity of manic patients are the same as my comments about the partial criteria, but they will not be repeated here for considerations of space.

## 7.  BIPOLAR DISORDER, MIXED (296.6x)

The first DSM-III inclusion criterion is that the "Current (or most recent) episode involves the full symptomatic picture of both manic and major depressive episodes (pp. 208 and 213), intermixed or rapidly alternating every few days" (p. 217). The second inclusion criterion is that the "Depressive symptoms are prominent and last at least a full day" (p. 217).

It is interesting to note that the depressive phase need only last for 1 day when making this diagnosis compared with a minimum of two consecutive weeks when making the diagnosis of Major Depressive Disorder. This, in combination with the statement that the disorder alternates every few days, suggests that continuous monitoring for 1 or 2 consecutive weeks should reveal several complete cycles. Such evidence would likely be very distinctive when contrasted with the normal condition. Several cycles of data would rule out the possibility that particularly low activity levels were simply due to the person spending much of the day relaxing or that particularly high levels of activity were obtained because the person was engaged in an active sport. The diagnosis would be made upon the distinctive oscillation between periods of augmented and diminished activity.

Sleep activity measures may also assist in making the diagnosis of Bipolar Disorder, Mixed. Perhaps the sleep activity of people with a mixed bipolar disorder evidences cycle changes that are similar to those noted above for the waking period. The sleep data may well provide a double check on the waking data, thereby enhancing both the reliability and validity of this diagnostic category.

Another issue is that no lower limit on the duration of the manic episode is indicated. Must the manic period also exist for at least 1 day as was indicated for the depressive period? I doubt if a lesser duration would be advisable. An interesting question for future research would be to compare the duration of the manic and depressive phases in persons thought to have Bipolar Disorder, Mixed. The data from such studies would be very helpful in arriving at empirical guidelines for diagnosing the presence of Bipolar Disorder, Mixed.

## 8.  CYCLOTHYMIC DISORDER (301.13)

The cyclothymic disorder is qualitatively like both the manic and depressive episodes, but is quantitatively less extreme and therefore nonpsychotic. In short, the cyclothymic disorder is a minor bipolar disorder. DSM-III describes the time course of cyclothymic disorders as follows: "During the past two years, numerous periods during which some symptoms characteristic of both the depressive and manic syndromes are present, but were not of sufficient severity and duration to meet the criteria for a major depressive or manic episode" (p. 219). Periods of normal behavior may be interspersed between manic and depressive episodes.

"The depressive periods and hypomanic periods may be separated by periods of normal mood lasting as long as months at a time, they may be intermixed, or they may alternate" (p. 219).

A person must exhibit at least 3 of the 12 behaviors listed on page 220 of DSM-III to qualify as having a depressive episode and 5 of them refer to activity. These five are listed below.

1. Insomnia or hypersomnia.
2. Low energy or chronic fatigue.
3. Decreased effectiveness or productivity at school, work, or home.
4. Restriction of involvement in pleasurable activities.
5. Feeling slowed down.

A person must exhibit at least 3 of the 12 behaviors listed on page 220 of DSM-III to qualify as having a manic episode; 5 of them refer to activity. These five are listed below.

1. Decreased need for sleep.
2. More energy than usual.
3. Increased productivity, often associated with unusual and self-imposed working hours.
4. Excessive involvement in pleasurable activities.
5. Physical restlessness.

The exclusion criteria include "Not due to any other mental disorder such as partial remission of Bipolar Disorder. However, Cyclothymic Disorder may precede Bipolar Disorder" (p. 220).

It is noteworthy that substance abuse is common among persons with cyclothymic disorders. They treat their depressive episodes with alcohol and sedatives. They treat their hypomanic episodes with stimulants and psychedelics (cf. pp. 218–219). Such substance abuse may well augment the activity changes associated with cyclothymic disorders.

The major feature of this disorder is an alternation between hypomanic and hypodepressive episodes over a 2-year period. Hence, it appears that it would take 2 or more years of continuous measurement to diagnose this disorder if no prior records were available. A more likely possibility is that the person would seek help when, for example, he /she experienced a depressive episode. Perhaps a 2-week activity sample was taken at this time and kept on record. Perhaps the person returned for further treatment when he/she experienced a subsequent hypomanic episode and another 2-week activity sample was taken and kept on record. Assume further that the person returned for additional treatment when he/she experienced a subsequent hypodepressive episode and an additional 2-week activity sample was collected. The clinician could now use the activity data recorded in the client's chart along with the present activity data to demonstrate the presence of one complete oscillation (from diminished to augmented back to diminished activity) over a 2-year period. This, then, could substantiate a diagnosis of Cyclothymic Disorder. These longitudinal considerations have two important implications for clinical practice. *First,* activity measurement should be taken to help reach a diagnosis. *Second,* activity data should be carefully entered into the client's chart to assist with any future diagnosis that might need to be made. The present case illustrates a situation where the correct diagnosis of cyclothymic disorder emerges only after repeated clinic visits over at least a 2-year period.

It is unclear as to what frequency of alternation is consistent with the cyclothymic disorder. Would one cycle over a 2-year period be sufficient? What about one cycle over a 5-year period? Some upper bound should be placed on the time allowed for one complete cycle to occur. It appears that the basic issue is that a cyclothymic disorder involves very slow cycling, whereas the mixed bipolar disorder involves rapid cycling. Perhaps future research will more carefully document the dominant frequency of cycling characteristics of at least these two disorders.

The intensity and duration of behavior sufficient to qualify as a hypomanic or hypodepressive episode are also unclear. We know that hypomanic behavior should be greater than normal and less than that characteristic of a full manic episode, but we have no empirical guidelines for determining the magnitude of these three activity categories. The same quantitative problem exists for hypodepressive behaviors. We know that they should involve less than normal activity but not so little activity as is found in people suffering from a major depressive episode. Again, we need empirical guidelines to assist in our diagnostic judgments. This discussion assumes that we are comparing a person's activity data with a norm. Such a procedure may be adequate to correctly diagnose some people but not others depending upon their initial activity level and the degree of activity change involved. It is conceivable that a cyclothymic person could oscillate within the normal range of activity. Such a person might still be diagnosed as cyclothymic if his or her activity involved a dominant oscillation with a 2-year period. Research is needed to determine if periodicities are found in the behavior of normal persons. If not, then the presence of periodicity may well constitute evidence of a cyclothymic disorder, even though all values are strictly within two standard deviations of the normative mean.

## 9. DYSTHYMIC DISORDER (OR DEPRESSIVE NEUROSIS) (300.40)

DSM-III describes the time course of Dysthymic Disorder as follows: "During the past two years (or one year for children and adolescents) the individual has been bothered most or all of the time by symptoms characteristic of the depressive syndrome but that are not of sufficient severity and duration to meet the criteria for a major depressive episode" (p. 222). We are also informed that "The manifestations of the depressive syndrome may be relatively persistent or separated by periods of normal mood lasting a few days to a few weeks, but no more than a few months at a time" (p. 222). "During the depressive periods there is either prominent depressed mood (e.g., sad, blue, down in the dumps, low) or marked loss of interest or pleasure in all, or almost all, usual activities and pastimes" (p. 223).

At least 3 of 13 symptoms must be present during a depressive period for this disorder to be diagnosed. The four symptoms relating to activity are listed below (cf. p. 223).

1. Insomnia or hypersomnia.
2. Low energy level or chronic tiredness.
3. Decreased effectiveness or productivity at school, work, or home.
4. Loss of interest in or enjoyment of pleasurable activities.

The exclusion criteria are an "Absence of psychotic features, such as delusions, hallucinations, or incoherence, or loosening of associations" (p. 223). Plus "If the disturbance is superimposed on a preexisting mental disorder, such as Obsessive Compulsive Disorder or Alcohol Dependence, the depressed mood, by virtue of its intensity or effect on functioning, can be clearly distinguished from the individual's usual mood" (p. 223).

The Dysthymic Disorder appears to be a low-grade activity disorder spanning the previous 2 or more years. It is sort of a mini Major Depressive Disorder. Because it involves behavior over a 2-year period it shares the same measurement problems as does the Cyclothymic Disorder described above.

Perhaps a 2-week or 1-month activity profile (plot of activity as a function of time) would reveal a characteristic signature or pattern that could be used to diagnose the presence of a Dysthymic Disorder without having to collect data over a 2-year period. This promise might also be realized with regard to the Cyclothymic Disorder. Then we would face a problem of the differential diagnosis of these two disorders. Hopefully, their activity profile signatures would be sufficiently different so as to allow for their differential diagnosis.

## 10. ATYPICAL BIPOLAR DISORDER (296.70)

DSM-III describes this as ". . . a residual category for individuals with manic features that cannot be classified as Bipolar Disorder or as Cyclothymic Disorder" (p. 223). For example, the person may have had a previous major depressive episode and currently exhibit a hypomanic episode that is not severe enough to meet the criteria for a manic episode. This type of disorder is sometimes referred to as Bipolar II.

Like all residual categories, this group must be distinguishable from the existing categories and from the normal condition. This is basically a quantitative problem in discriminant analysis. The major point here is that the person fit the criteria for either a major depressive episode or a manic episode but not both. Comprehensive activity measures should be of assistance in determining if this is the case, because they are influenced by both the manic and the depressive aspects of the disorder.

## 11. ATYPICAL DEPRESSION (296.82)

DSM-III describes this as ". . . a residual category for individuals with depressive symptoms who cannot be diagnosed as having a Major or Other Specific Affective Disorder or Adjustment Disorder" (p. 223). Examples of Atypical Depression include: (1) depression in a person with Schizophrenia, Residual Type who is currently psychotic, (2) a person who would be diagnosed as Dysthymic Disorder except that he/she has normal periods lasting more than a few months, and (3) a brief depressive episode not meeting the criteria for a Major Affective Disorder which is also not reactive to a stressor, so it cannot be diagnosed as an Adjustment Disorder.

## 12. SCHIZOPHRENIC DISORDER, CATATONIC TYPE (295.2x)

Any of the following symptoms listed on page 191 of DSM-III are sufficient to reach a diagnosis of Schizophrenic Disorder, Catatonic Type.

1. Catatonic stupor (marked decrease in reactivity to environment and/or reduction of spontaneous movements and activity) or mutism.
2. Catatonic negativism (an apparently motiveless resistance to all instructions or attempts to be moved).
3. Catatonic rigidity (maintenance of a rigid posture against efforts to be moved).
4. Catatonic excitement (excited motor activity, apparently purposeless and not influenced by external stimuli).
5. Catatonic posturing (voluntary assumptions of inappropriate or bizarre posture).

Catatonic excitement very definitely involves excessive activity. It is likely that a high temporal resolution (perhaps four data points per minute) activity profile (activity as a function of time) would show clear differences between catatonic excitement and vigorous behavior by normal people. It may be that vigorous behavior by normal people is evidenced in spurts with brief rest periods in between, such as might occur while playing tennis. Perhaps catatonic excitement is characterized by nearly equivalent activity peaks but without the intervening brief rest periods. The typical sleep periods may contain a great deal of activity for one who exhibits catatonic excitement.

Catatonic stupor is said to be characterized by a reduction in spontaneous movements and activity, indicating a very low level of activity. It would be interesting to compare the activity of persons undergoing a Major Depressive Episode with persons exhibiting catatonic stupor. It seems that persons with catatonic stupor should be considerably less active than persons with a Major Depressive Episode, given the general meaning of the word stupor.

DSM-III (p. 190) indicates that sometimes there is rapid alternation between catatonic excitement and stupor. The frequency range with which such behavioral oscillations occur was not specified. Apparently, catatonia can involve a form of very rapid mixed bipolar disorder. The dominant frequency of behavioral oscillation between excitement and depression may provide a means for differentially diagnosing Bipolar Disorder, mixed from Schizophrenic Disorder, Catatonic Type. This cyclical feature is probably the main reason for not continuing the distinction between the excited and withdrawn forms of catatonia described in DSM-II.

Catatonic negativism, rigidity, and posturing indicate a profound absence of activity. A high-resolution activity profile is likely to show that consecutive activity points are more nearly alike given catatonic negativism, rigidity, and/or posturing than given any other diagnostic category. This would be caused by retaining a single posture for longer than normal and longer than is typical of persons with other disorders.

It is important to note that a major depressive episode can occur after psychotic symptoms appear for any of the schizophrenias. Hence, activity disturbances can appear when depression is superimposed upon a schizophrenic process. This suggests that activity samples might be taken to evaluate whether or not persons diagnosed as schizophrenic should also carry a secondary diagnosis of depression.

## C.  Organic Mental Disorders

The major role for activity data with regard to organic mental disorders is to determine if they are associated with either depression or delirium. An interesting empirical question is whether depression appears the same when it is associated with an organic mental disorder compared to when no organic mental disorder is present. The criteria for delirium specified by DSM-III include (cf. p. 107)

1. Perceptual disturbance: misinterpretations, illusions, or hallucinations.
2. Speech that is at times incoherent.
3. Disturbance of sleep–wakefulness cycle with insomnia or daytime drowsiness.
4. Increased or decreased psychomotor activity.

A positive diagnosis of delirium requires that two of the four above-mentioned symptoms be present. Notice that item No. 4 clearly refers to hyper- or hypoactivity. Item No. 3 also involves abnormal activity levels. Insomnia is almost certainly associated with excessive nighttime activity and daytime drowsiness is likely associated with decreased daytime activity. This means that it is possible to reach a diagnosis of delirium on the basis of activity data alone. The following DSM-III diagnoses involve an assessment for either depression or delirium.

1. Primary Degenerative Dementia, Senile Onset with Delirium (290.03).
2. Primary Degenerative Dementia, Senile Onset with Depression (290.21).
3. Primary Degenerative Dementia, Presenile Onset with Delirium (290.11).
4. Primary Degenerative Dementia, Presenile Onset with Depression (290.13).
5. Multi-infarct Dementia with Delirium (290.41).
6. Multi-infarct Dementia with Depression (290.43).

## D. Substance-Induced Organic Mental Disorders

Many pharmacologically active substances modify behavior. This fact provides the basis for the entire field of behavioral pharmacology (cf. Thompson & Boren, 1977). Pharmaceutical companies regularly make use of the methods of behavioral pharmacology to determine the effects of new compounds on behavior. Many of these substances have mild to moderate behavioral effects when taken as prescribed by a physician. The term substance abuse indicates self-administration of doses in excess, often far in excess, of typically prescribed doses. The diagnostic categories to be discussed below all involve some degree of mental disorder. It is likely that activity level will be altered either before or by the time noticeable mental disorder has resulted from substance abuse. Inclusion criteria for the diagnostic categories listed below share two commonalities. First, they require evidence that the particular drug in question was recently injected, usually within the last hour. Second, "psychomotor agitation" is specified among the inclusion criteria. At an earlier point in this discussion, I discussed my reasons for using the word activity to refer to noninformation processing references to hypo- and hyperactivity. The point here is that all of the substances named in the six diagnostic categories listed below increase activity level.

1. Cocaine Intoxication (305.60).
2. Amphetamine or Similarly Acting Sympathomimetic Intoxication (305.70).
3. Amphetamine or Similarly Acting Sympathomimetic Delusional Disorder (292.11).
4. Phencyclidine or Similarly Acting Arylcyclohexylamine Intoxication (305.90).

5. Caffeine Intoxication (305.90).
6. Phencyclidine (PCP) or Similarly Acting Arycyclohexylamine Delirium (292.81).

The following two diagnostic categories involving substance abuse disorders make reference to activity measurements for the assessment of delirium.

7. Phencyclidine (PCP) or Similarly Acting Arylcyclohexylamine Delirium (292.81).
8. Other or Unspecified Substance Delirium (292.81).

The remaining diagnostic category involves the simulation of an affective disorder, and therefore altered activity levels, through substance abuse.

9. Other or Unspecified Substance Affective Disorder (292.84).

The inclusion criteria for Caffeine Intoxication specify insomnia. It is likely that all of the other substance abuse categories listed above also produce insomnia resulting in increased activity during typical sleep periods. This should be a fruitful area for future research.

The above discussion has focused upon the acute activity changes resulting from a recent excessive dose of a particular drug. Chronic substance abuse may well lead to long-term activity changes. Comparing and contrasting the long- and short-term activity effects of substance abuse is an interesting area for future research.

## VII.  OTHER DISORDERS

The first disorder to be discussed in this section, Anorexia Nervosa, appears in the DSM-III, but activity is not listed as an official inclusion criterion. The remaining disorders to be discussed in this section do not appear in the DSM-III but are of interest to health psychologists, and therefore they will be mentioned briefly.

### A.  Anorexia Nervosa (307.10)

I was surprised to learn that the DSM-III inclusion criteria for Anorexia Nervosa do not include activity level given the popular view that these people are excessively active. Either the popular view is false or insufficient research has been conducted to document an associated activity disturbance to the point where it could be listed among the official inclusion criteria. I am presently unaware of any published studies investigating the activity of anorectics prior to hospitalization. The existing literature pertains to activity during hospitalization and its relationship to weight gains made prior to discharge. Goldberg, Halmi, Casper, Eckert, and Davis (1977) reported that activity increases, as rated by ward nurses, were significantly correlated with greater weight gains during hospitalization [$r(42) = .35, p < .02$]. Halmi, Goldberg, Casper, Eckert, and Davis (1979) replicated this finding using ratings of activity by two ward nurses [$r(79) = .35, p < .01$]. Foster and Kupfer (1975) reported a correlation of $r(83) = .77$, $p < .001$ between nocturnal activity and weight gain during the premedication phase of the patient's treatment. Falk, Halmi, and Tryon (1985) placed actometers on the wrists and ankles of 20 hospitalized female anorectics 24 hours each day during the first 14 consecutive days of hospitalization. The correlation between the average activity and the average percentage target weight over these 14 days was $r(12) = .811, p < .01$ for the wrist measures and $r(12) = .76, p < .01$ for the ankle measures. In sum, it appears that persons admitted to hospitals with the diagnosis of Anorexia Nervosa are hypoactive. My first impression upon seeing these data was that these people were depressed. The fact that these people are often hospitalized against their own wishes or are reluctant volunteers at best is consistent with the hypothesis of depression. However, it is particularly important to note that hospitalization often occurs when the person has become so emaciated that her life is threatened. The greatly weakened condition of these people upon hospitalization is probably the main reason for both their initial low activity levels and the positive correlation with percentage of target body weight. Future research should concentrate upon the prehospitalization activity level of anorectics to determine if they actually accomplish their weight reduction via hyperactivity. A finding of normal activity would strongly suggest that they achieve their weight reduction mainly through restriction of caloric intake.

## B.  Obesity

Straw and Rogers (1985), Goldstein and Stein (1985), and Tryon (1985a) have discussed the role of activity measurement in the assessment of obesity. This vast literature cannot be reviewed here due to space constraints. I mention this topic to alert the reader to its appropriateness to the present discussion.

## C.  Arthritis

Goldstein and Stein (1985) indicate that one of the effects of arthritis is to diminish activity due to the sometimes painful consequences of ambulation for people with this disease. These authors have monitored the clinical progress of arthritic patients using pedometer activity measures.

## D.  Cirrhosis

Goldstein and Stein (1985) indicate that "Ambulation is attenuated in proportion to the advancement of the cirrhosis; weakness, edema and confusion may all contribute to the major motor limitations." Goldstein, Stein, Smolen, and Perlini (1976) reported the results of a 3-year study of 13 persons with Laennec's cirrhosis indicating that activity, as measured by pedometers, was correlated with various aspects of their clinical condition.

## E.  Coronary Heart Disease

Goldstein and Stein (1985) report that angina can occur as infrequently as once a year or as often as 10 times a day. The resulting pain and fear of a subsequent heart attack can lead to decreased activity. These authors have found it possible to monitor the clinical course of heart disease by measuring activity with a pedometer.

## F.  Chronic Obstructive Pulmonary Disease

Goldstein and Stein (1985) indicate that the shortness of breath associated with Chronic Obstructive Pulmonary Disease (COPD) leads to decreased activity. They indicated that it is possible to evaluate the functional status of COPD patients by monitoring their activity with pedometers.

## VIII.   CONCLUSIONS

Motor activity measurements have played an important theoretical role in the diagnosis of behavioral disorders from at least the time that DSM-I was published in 1952, through publication of DSM-II in 1968, up to and including DSM-III, published in 1980. The present review suggests a number of research questions that may well advance our understanding of behavior disorder to the point where additional empirical guidelines may be forthcoming from future research that will enhance both the reliability and validity of diagnostic judgments.

Advances in activity research will occur in direct proportion to two other changes. First, a conceptual reorientation (paradigm shift) of the type disucssed at the beginning of this article is necessary. We need to give up our familiar behavioral categories and think in terms of the physical forces associated with particular sites of attachment. In short, behavioral physics will need to be seen as a subspeciality within the broader area of behavioral assessment. This will happen when journals that publish research in behavioral assessment begin accepting articles reporting activity data on interesting groups for its descriptive value rather than for its ability to test one theoretical hypothesis or position against another. We need bench marks and ultimately norms for patient and normal populations if we are to develop an empirical basis for rendering diagnoses using activity measurements. Tryon (1985b) has comprehensively reviewed the published activity data in an effort to provide a starting point for reaching this goal.

The second collateral area governing the rate with which advances will be made in activity research concerns the availability of suitable devices for measuring human activity over extended period of time as people behave in their natural environment. Tryon (1985a) has reviewed the present technology for obtaining activity measurements both in laboratory and naturalistic settings. It is hoped that both federal and private funding sources will increasingly appreciate the need to develop better instrumentation in order to collect the necessary data to allow the advances in behavioral measurement discussed in this chapter. It is my strong personal opinion that naturalistic measurement will lead to new theoretical developments and clinical practices regarding activity research. I believe there is much to be learned by studying human activity and encourage others to join me in this endeavor.

# REFERENCES

American Psychiatric Association (1952). *Diagnostic and statistical manual of mental disorders.* Washington, D.C.: Author.

American Psychiatric Association (1968). *Diagnostic and statistical manual of mental disorders* (2nd ed.). Washington, D.C.: Author.

American Psychiatric Association (1980). *Diagnostic and statistical manual of mental disorders.* (3rd ed.). Washington, D.C.: Author.

Birkimer, J. C., & Brown, J. H. (1979). A graphical judgmental aid which summarizes obtained and chance reliability data and helps assess the believability of experimental effects. *Journal of Applied Behavior Analysis, 12,* 523–533.

Cone, J. D. (1977). The relevance of reliability and validity for behavioral assessment. *Behavior Therapy, 8,* 411–426.

Cone, J. D. (1979). Why the "I've got a better agreement measure" literature continues to grow: A commentary on two articles by Birkimer and Brown. *Journal of Applied Behavior Analysis, 12,* 571.

Cone, J. D. (1981). "Psychometric" considerations in behavioral assessment. In M. Hersen & A. S. Bellack (Eds.), *Behavioral assessment: A practical handbook* (2nd ed.). Oxford: Pergamon.

Cox, G. H., & Marley, E. (1959). The estimation of motility during rest or sleep. *Journal of Neurology, Neurosurgery, and Psychiatry, 22,* 57–60.

Falk, J. R., Halmi, K. A., & Tryon, W. W. (1985). Activity measures in anorexia nervosa. *Archives of General Psychiatry, 42,* 811–814.

Foster, G. C., & Kupfer, D. J. (1975). Psychomotor activity as a correlate of depression and sleep in acutely disturbed psychiatric inpatients. *American Journal of Psychiatry, 132,* 928–931.

Goldberg, S. C., Halmi, K. A., Casper, R., Eckert, E., & Davis, J. M. (1977). Pretreatment predictors of weight change in anorexia nervosa. In R. A. Vigersky (Ed.), *Anorexia nervosa.* New York: Raven. (pp. 31–41).

Goldstein, M. K., & Stein, G. H. (1985). Ambulatory activity in chronic disease. In W. W. Tryon (Ed.), *Behavioral assessment in behavioral medicine.* New York: Springer. (pp. 148–165).

Goldstein, M. K., Stein, G. H., Smolen, D. M., & Perlini, W. W. (1976). Bio-behavioral monitoring: A method for remote health measurement. *Archives of Physical Medicine and Rehabilitation,* **57,** 253–258.

Halmi, K. A., Goldberg, S. C., Casper, R. C., Eckert, E., & Davis, J. M. (1979). Pretreatment predictors of outcome in anorexia nervosa. *British Journal of Psychiatry,* **134,** 71–78.

Hartmann, D. P., & Gardner, W. (1979). On the not so recent invention of interobserver reliability statistics: A commentary on two articles by Birkimer and Brown. *Journal of Applied Behavior Analysis,* **12,** 559–560.

Hobson, J. A., Spagna, T., & Malenka, R. (1978). Ethology of sleep studied with time-lapse photography: Postural immobility and sleep-cycle phase in humans. *Science,* **201,** 1251–1253.

Hopkins, B. L. (1979). Proposed conventions for evaluating observer reliability: A commentary on two articles by Birkimer and Brown. *Journal of Applied Behavior Analysis,* **12,** 561–564.

Johns, M. W. (1971). Methods for assessing human sleep. *Archives of Internal Medicine,* **127,** 484–492.

Kleitman, N. (1963). *Sleep and wakefulness.* Chicago: Univ. of Chicago Press.

Mitchell, S. K. (1979). Interobserver agreement, reliability and generalizability of data collected in observational settings. *Psychological Bulletin,* **86,** 376–390.

Monroe, L. J. (1967). Psychological and physiological differences between good and poor sleepers. *Journal of Abnormal Psychology,* **72,** 255–264.

Oswald, I., Berger, R. J., Jaramillo, R. A., Keddie, K. M. G., Olley, P. C., & Plunkett, G. B. (1963). Melancholia and barbiturates: A controlled E. E. G., body and eye movement study of sleep. *British Journal of Psychiatry,* **109,** 66–78.

Reich, L. H., Kupfer, D. J., Weiss, B. L., McPartland, R. J., Foster, F. G., Detre, T., & Delgado, J. (1974). Psychomotor activity as a predictor of sleep efficiency. *Biological Psychiatry,* **8,** 253–256.

Reid, J. B. (1970). Reliability assessment of observation data: A possible methodological problem. *Child Development,* **41,** 1143–1150.

Reiser, S. J. (1979). The medical influence of the stethoscope. *Scientific American,* **240,** 148–156.

*Stedman's medical dictionary* (22nd ed.) (1972). Baltimore: Williams & Wilkins.

Stonehill, E., & Crisp, A. H. (1971). Problems in the measurement of sleep with particular reference to the development of a motility bed. *Journal of Psychosomatic Research,* **15,** 495–499.

Straw, M. K., & Rogers, T. (1985). Obesity assessment. In W. W. Tryon (Ed.), *Behavioral assessment in behavioral medicine.* New York: Springer. (pp. 19–65).

Thompson, T., & Boren, J. J. (1977). Operant behavioral pharmacology. In W. K. Honig & J. E. R. Staddon (Eds.), *Handbook of operant behavior.* New York: Prentice Hall. (pp. 540–569).

Tryon, W. W. (1976). A system of behavioral diagnosis. *Professional Psychology,* **7,** 495–506.

Tryon, W. W. (1985a). The measurement of human activity. In W. W. Tryon (Ed.), *Behavioral assessment in behavioral medicine.* New York: Springer. (pp. 200–256).

Tryon, W. W. (1985b). Human activity: A review of quantitative findings. In W. W. Tryon (Ed.), *Behavioral assessment in behavioral medicine.* New York: Springer. (pp. 257–299).

# INNOVATIONS IN BEHAVIORAL MEDICINE

DENNIS J. DELPRATO

*Department of Psychology*
*Eastern Michigan University*
*Ypsilanti, Michigan*

F. DUDLEY McGLYNN

*Department of Basic Dental Sciences*
*University of Florida*
*Gainesville, Florida*

PROGRESS IN BEHAVIOR
MODIFICATION, VOLUME 20

The first section of this chapter contains a brief history of the behavioral medicine movement and an overview of the numerous and diverse activities currently ongoing within the field. The second section contains reviews of recent innovations in the treatment area of behavioral medicine. In the third and fourth sections of the chapter, new behavioral contributions to health care delivery are reviewed along with innovative behavioral technologies in disease and disability prevention. The fifth section begins by addressing the methodological quality of the literature reviewed. It then draws parallels and contrasts between behavioral medicine and both the behavior-therapy and psychosomatic-medicine movements. Finally, it contains a call for conceptual integration along with an outline of how field behaviorism can serve the goal of conceptual integration.


## I.  HISTORICAL OVERVIEW AND CURRENT STATUS

Behavioral medicine exploded on the psychological scene at the end of the 1970s. As of the middle 1980s, its participants are engaged in a massive and variegated research and clinical effort directed toward understanding, treating, managing, and preventing large numbers of problems heretofore seen as strictly medical. Pomerleau (1982) has enumerated significant historical events in the evolution of the new field, and we add a few here. In 1973, the term behavioral medicine first gained prominence in the book *Biofeedback: Behavioral Medicine* (Birk, 1973). In 1974, the Center for Behavioral Medicine was formed at the University of Pennsylvania. At about the same time, the Laboratory for the Study of Behavioral Medicine was formed at Stanford University. In 1977, the Yale Conference on Behavioral Medicine brought various early participants together and, among other things, produced the initial definition for the new field (Schwartz & Weiss, 1978). The late 1970s and early 1980s witnessed the establishment of various special-interest groups, e.g., the Academy of Behavioral Medicine Research, the Society of Behavioral Medicine, and the Division of Health Psychology within the American Psychological Association. Three new journals also were founded during this period—the *Journal of Behavioral Medicine, Behavioral Medicine Abstracts,* and *Health Psychology.* Also, this period saw the establishment of behavioral medicine funding units within several agencies, e.g., the National Heart, Lung, and Blood Institute, the National Cancer Institute, and the National Institute of Dental Research.

Blanchard's (1982) brief but cogent history of why all this happened traces it to the successes of operant technology with health-related problems such as smoking, to the successes of biofeedback technology with problems such as headache, and to the recognition in medical and public health circles that *behaviors* with important roles in catastrophic and chronic diseases were potentially amenable to psychological modification. Agras (1982) adds that the development of behavioral medicine was fostered by runaway health care costs. In any case, the result of these and other historical events is a new and evolving system of communication between several clinical and research disciplines heretofore not well connected, e.g., various behavioral sciences, biomedical sciences, and medical specialities (Agras, 1982). Some specialists continue to work in the areas from which behavioral medicine evolved and in other well-established research/practice areas, e.g., smoking, obesity, hypertension, headache, asthma, insomnia, chronic pain, coronary-prone behavior, peripheral vascular disease, and diabetes. Others are carving out new areas for behavioral medicine research and practice, e.g., arthritis, musculoskeletal disorders, gastrointestinal disorders, and cancer.

A "behavioral dentistry" movement also has emerged within the last decade. As of the middle 1980s, its participants are engaged in a substantial research effort targeted on problems heretofore seen as the purview of the dentist. Sachs, Eigenbrode, and Kruper (1979) and Page (1978) have provided adequate histories of how this occurred. Kleinknecht, Klepac, and Bernstein (1976) delineated the basic scope of the newly emerging behavioral dentistry field (see also Bryant, 1979; Melamed, 1979; Melamed & Bennett, 1985). The major interest areas repeat the dominant themes in behavioral medicine. They are (1) understanding, measuring, and treating dental fear/avoidance, (2) managing the in-operatory behavior of pedodontic patients, (3) promoting adherence to prescribed dental regimens, and (4) assessing and treating patients with disorders of craniomandibular articulation. The a priori desiderata for theory, research, and practice in a behavioral dentistry ought not be expected to differ from corresponding criteria in behavioral medicine. Hence, some innovations in behavioral dentistry are included conveniently in the present chapter.


## II.   TREATMENT


Most of the remainder of the chapter reviews contemporary innovations in clinical behavioral medicine. There is no attempt at systematic criticism in the following sections. The studies reviewed share many of the same methodological shortcomings, thus rendering separate critiques repetitive. As noted, a narrative *is* offered after the "innovations" sections that characterizes the status of the behavioral medicine field methodologically.

The organization of the narrative in the following treatment section is in terms of biological systems. This compartmentalized organization was chosen *solely* for the purpose of expository clarity.

## A.  Neurologic System

### 1.  BRAIN INJURIES

Recent work with brain-injured patients has brought into question the traditional reductionistic account of brain–behavior relations, according to which disorders associated with demonstrable organic impairment are placed into a separate category from those without obvious organic involvement and recovery requires either direct organic intervention or an adventitious "natural healing" process.

Clinicians recently have created new areas of specialization involving the application of psychological principles to therapeutic intervention for neuropsychological problems (Horton, 1979, 1982, 1984; Miller, 1980), and a special interest group ("Behavioral Neuropsychology") now exists within the Association for Advancement of Behavior Therapy. The literature contains several innovative approaches to treating disorders secondary to brain damage resulting from cerebrovascular accident (stroke), trauma, and surgery.

*a.  Neuromuscular and Musculoskeletal Disorders Associated with Brain Injury.* One established area of behavioral neuropsychology is that in which electromyographic (EMG) feedback is used in the rehabilitation of patients with neuromuscular and musculoskeletal disorders due to cerebrovascular accident. Indeed, Fernando and Basmajian (1978) have said that sufficient data exist to warrant the assertion that EMG feedback is no longer an "experimental" treatment for hemiplegic patients. This is not to imply, however, that the application of EMG feedback with stroke patients is not in need of further controlled research (Fernando & Basmajian, 1978; Keefe & Surwit, 1978; Wolf, 1983a,b). The best research in this area has progressed to analytic and controlled clinical experiments. The techniques themselves are not particularly innovative, but the research represents state-of-the-art methodology in an innovative area.

Wolf and Binder-Macleod (1983b) examined EMG feedback with hemiplegic patients in an important study that was the first to use a no-treatment control group of chronic stroke patients. This study also improved upon earlier work with its more quantitative measures of upper extremity functioning. None of the 31 experimental patients nor any of the 9 controls received any form of concurrent treatment during the period of the study (5–9 months). Experimental treatment (EMG feedback) consisted of training patients to relax specific hyperactive muscles (e.g., upper trapezius, pectoralis major, biceps brachii) and attempts to recruit weakened antagonistic muscles. Pretreatment-to-posttreatment comparisons for controls and experimentals were not encouraging for either the neuromuscular or functional measures. Experimental patients exhibited statistically significant improvements on only 21 of the 138 neuromuscular measures analyzed (controls improved on two measures). Experimental patients showed significant improvement on only 4 of the 29 functional measures analyzed (controls improved on no measures). Prompted by these unimpressive results, the authors further examined the experimental group. They found EMG feedback had maximally benefited functional recovery of patients who survived the stroke with relatively greater active range of motion at the major upper extremity joints and with less hyperactivity within muscles that contribute to flexor synergy. These post hoc findings suggest it would be valuable to examine a priori the contribution of EMG feedback to recovery of upper extremity functioning in relation to pretreatment status of the patient and in conjunction with other concurrent neuromuscular reeducation regimens.

Wolf and Binder-Macleod (1983a) provided the first study with chronic stroke patients in which EMG feedback training was the only form of neuromuscular reeducation provided to improve lower extremity status. Control patients received one of three conditions: no treatment, upper extremity treatment, or general relaxation training. The experimental condition showed improvement in active knee and ankle range of motion, apparently in conjunction with increases in synergistic muscle recruitment. In comparison with controls, experimental patients did not show improvements on several quantitative measures of walking; however, EMG feedback was associated with significant reductions in cumbersomeness of assistive devices necessary for ambulation.

Koheil, Reg, and Mandel (1980) observed that when used in gait training, EMG feedback of knee action confused hemiplegic patients because it required the proper phasing of two or three muscle groups during each gait cycle. This led Koheil et al. to build a knee-joint angle detector that provides auditory feedback signaling hyperextension of the knee during the stance phase of gait. They then provided the device to a woman who suffered right hemiplegia associated with a cerebrovascular accident. Baseline phases, consisting of no-feedback walks, were interspersed with some periods of a standard physical therapy regimen and with other periods in which the knee-joint position feedback device was added to physical therapy. Reductions in the proportion of knee hyperextension "errors" per step were obtained with the addition of joint-position feedback to the physical therapy regimen.

*b. Aphasia.* Aphasia research is beginning to turn around the traditional neurologic position that therapy for aphasia is ineffective (Benson, 1979). That aphasics improve is not controversial, but the widely held view has been that improvement represents "spontaneous recovery," presumably resulting from adventitious organic healing processes.

A study that has begun establishing support for aphasia rehabilitation is that of Basso, Capitani, and Vignolo (1979) who studied 162 treated and 119 control aphasic patients. The inevitable problem of obtaining untreated controls was handled by using a self-selected group that did not participate in treatment for a variety of reasons ("family" and "transportation" problems are cited as examples). Experimental patients received at least 5 consecutive months of individual therapy following the "stimulation approach" (Vignolo, 1964). In brief, in the stimulation approach to aphasia therapy the therapist (1) presents prompts for meaningful language responses, (2) verbally praises, disapproves, or ignores the patient's responses, and (3) usually supplements individual training with homework and group meetings. A therapist who had not treated the experimental patients classified the subjects as clinically improved or unchanged on second administrations of several language examinations. Significantly more experimentals than controls were judged improved.

Therapists have used group treatment as well as individual treatment with aphasic patients (Eisenson, 1984). In a cooperative study at five Veterans Administration Medical Center Speech Pathology and Neurology Services, investigators compared group with individual approaches (Wertz, Collins, Weiss, Kurtzke, Friden, Brookshire, Pierce, Holtzapple, Hubbard, Porch, West, Davis, Matovitch, Morley, & Resurreccion, 1981). Their individual therapy apparently was similar to that of Basso et al. (1979), while the nonspecific group therapy was purposefully dissimilar from the individual treatment and functioned mainly as an attention placebo (e.g., Paul, 1965). Rigid selection criteria permitted a high degree of control over potentially confounding patient characteristics. For example, patients were required to enter the program at 4 weeks postonset and continue until 48 weeks postonset. This requirement allowed the researchers to monitor language performance during similar periods of recovery for all patients. Also, the 48-week duration extended beyond the longest estimate (6 months) for "spontaneous recovery" (Eisenson, 1984). Both individual and group therapy showed statistically significant improvements within groups on a battery of language measures that was scored by "blind" judges. Differences between the two groups on various measures always favored individual therapy but were rarely significant statistically. Factors unrelated to the specifics of training could have been a major source of "improvement" for both groups.

In a thoughtful review of the international picture of aphasia rehabilitation, Hilton and Kraetschmer (1983) mentioned several innovative approaches that are in early stages of evaluation. Some of the central features of these treatment methods include (1) utilizing a still-intact linguistic function in the initial phases of treatment (Weigl); (2) preventing the early development of undesirable patterns of speech such as telegraphic style (Beyne); (3) whistling or singing therapy (Baldi, Ustvedt); (4) computer-assisting therapy for aphasic patients with writing disturbances (Seron); and (5) recognizing special considerations in language therapy for bilingual and foreign-speaking aphasic patients (Hilton) (all authors are cited in Hilton & Kraetschmer, 1983). Hilton and Kraetschmer concluded that the aphasiologist must treat the patient holistically because language deficits of aphasic patients are not simply reducible to localized brain damage.

Hilton and Kraetschmer's (1983) perspective led them to redefine the goals of aphasia therapy. Instead of seeking to retrain premorbid *vocal* skills as is commonly done, the therapist should aim for the reacquisition of "communicative proficiency," including nonverbal performances. Researchers have begun to examine systematically the use of nonverbal communication therapy in certain cases. Helm-Estabrooks, Fitzpatrick, and Barresi (1982), for one example, described a new approach to facilitating gestural communication with stroke patients diagnosed as globally aphasic. The hierarchically structured, three-level program was designed to train patients to use symbolic gestures for visually absent stimuli. Patients showed statistically significant pretest-to-posttest improvements on the Porch Index of Communicative Ability (Porch, 1967) subtests that measure pantomimic and auditory comprehension skills. While no untreated controls were tested, the failure of the treated patients to improve on subtests that assess skills on which they were not trained (verbal responses) somewhat overcomes internal validity problems associated with omission of an independent control group.

c. *Cognitive Impairments Associated with Brain Injury.* Brain injury frequently is followed by impairments of those subtle psychological adjustments that historically have been labeled "cognitive." Cognitive behaviors such as attending, perceiving, knowing, and remembering often do not unfold as they did prior to the disruption of brain integrity. Therapeutic neuropsychology is an innovative area in behavioral medicine, and a major trend in this area is the development of rehabilitation programs for defective cognitive behaviors (Diller & Gordon, 1981; Gianutsos, 1980; Horton, 1979, 1982; Satz & Fletcher, 1981).

Brain injury is associated with a variety of deficits in visual perceiving (Gianutsos, Glosser, Elbaum, & Vroman, 1983). Diller and Gordon (1981) estimated that approximately 40% of right-brain damaged patients experience difficulty in responding to stimulus objects on the left side of the body or in the left visual field (referred to as hemi-inattention). Weinberg, Diller, Gordon, Gerstman, Lieberman, Lakin, Hodges, and Ezrachi (1977) reasoned that if patients with deficits in visual responding following right-brain damage could be trained to more completely scan visual space, then general improvements on a variety of visual tasks would result. They designed a visual scanning training procedure to increase the frequency and duration with which patients tracked the left side of the visual field. The critical feature of the program was the systematic presentation of stimuli in the patients' visual field. Although not explicitly stated, the trainers used the operant principle of stimulus control (viz., prompting and fading) to increase left-side responding and maintain left-side responding when the prompt was no longer provided. Twenty-five patients with unilateral brain damage following a cerebrovascular accident were randomly assigned to the experimental (treated) group, and 32 patients served in an untreated control condition. Experimental patients underwent 20 hours of treatment over a 4-week period. All patients were tested prior to treatment and 1 month later with an extensive battery of tests. Although controls did not show statistically significant changes over the two test administrations, the improvements of experimental patients on several measures reached conventional levels of significance. The findings support the notion that training improved scanning and, in turn, that scanning generalized to a variety of tasks involving visual responding.

Weinberg, Diller, Gordon, Gerstman, Lieberman, Lakin, Hodges, and Ezrachi (1979) expanded their earlier treatment to include additional forms of visual scanning training for perceptual responding. One new training procedure required the patient to touch the spot on the back of a manikin that corresponded to a spot on his/her own back touched by the trainer. The other added procedure involved training in visual-size estimation. Prompt feedback regarding performance on training trials was provided in both procedures. The results of the earlier study were reproduced, and it appeared that adding the two procedures enhanced the efficiency and quality of the brain-injured patients' perceptual behavior.

Webster, Jones, Blanton, Gross, Beissel, and Wofford (1984) reported strong findings that nicely support and expand those of Weinberg et al. (1977, 1979). These researchers worked with patients who had suffered a right middle cerebral artery stroke that was followed by left homonymous hemianopsia (half-field blindness) and hemi-attention. The important features of their study include (1) use of intrasubject replication methodology, (2) multiple assessments of target responses, (3) empirical demonstration that visual scanning training was followed by improvements only on tasks requiring visual scanning (letter cancellation and navigation of a wheelchair on an obstacle course), and (4) follow-up evidence that improvements in scanning were maintained for 1 year. Likewise, Gouvier, Cottam, and Webster (unpublished) administered visual scanning training to stroke patients, and the patients' performance on a wheelchair obstacle course improved.

A multiple-component perceptual training regimen also has been used with acquired brain-damage patients who were experiencing deficiencies in driving performance (Sivak, Hill, Henson, Butler, Silber, & Olson, 1984). The program consisted of a variety of tasks tailored to the trainers' evaluations of individual requirements. The tasks were designed to occasion perceptual behaviors such as scanning, directing eye movements, and perceiving figure/ground. Perceptual training was followed by improvements in driving performance on city streets. Although this study did not include a no-treatment control group, the researchers did demonstrate no changes in performance over two pre-training driving tests. Kewman, Seigerman, Henson, Kintner, and Chu (unpublished) also investigated the remediation of brain injured patients' deficient driving performance. Using a specially designed electric wheelchair, patients who underwent 16 hours of training on specific exercises (e.g., S-curve, figure-8 curve, serpentine curve) improved their city driving more than did patients who merely drove the wheelchair. Furthermore, there was a slight tendency for patients who received the driving-related exercises to improve more than controls on certain standardized cognitive/perceptual measures. Taken together, the studies of Sivak *et al.* (1984) and Kewman *et al.* (unpublished) suggest that training (or retraining) of perceiving responding might be an important factor in improving driving performance among brain-injured patients.

Those cognitive responses involving a temporal delay typically are referred to as memorial or remembering behavior. Researchers have begun investigating procedures to overcome memory problems that are associated with brain damage. Lewinsohn, Glasgow, Barrera, Danaher, Alperson, McCarty, Sullivan, Zeiss, Nyland, and Rodrigues (1977b) presented a comprehensive four-stage paradigm for clinical intervention in cases of memory disorders. The first stage consists of a variety of assessment procedures (neuropsychological and behavioral) intended to identify the patient's unique memory difficulties. The second stage involves laboratory-based training of memorial skills using techniques selected from the experimental literature, as well as techniques used by professional mnemonists. The third stage involves naturalistic training of memorial skills; some aspects of this phase include self-monitoring, homework assignments, and involvement of significant others. The fourth main stage consists of assessing changes in the patient's functioning. The model is designed to be flexible in order to meet each patient's unique circumstances. Lewinsohn *et al.* (1977b) presented preliminary data on the effectiveness of their approach; they obtained encouraging results with a number of individual cases. While the most convincing data came from the laboratory measures, patients did report satisfaction with their *in vivo* improvements. There are other reports of improvements in the memorial performances of brain-injured patients on laboratory tasks (e.g., Gianutsos & Gianutsos, 1979; Lewinsohn, Danaher, & Kikel, 1977a; Malec & Questad, 1983; Webster & Scott, 1983).

## B. Musculoskeletal System

### 1. SCOLIOSIS

Idiopathic scoliosis is a condition of lateral spinal curvature that occurs at the onset of puberty predominantly among females (Kane, 1977). In the typical case, scoliosis begins as a single curve that is followed by the appearance of a second, presumably compensatory, curve in the opposite direction. Dworkin (1982) and Dworkin, Miller, Dworkin, Birbaumer, Brines, Jonas, Schwentker, and Graham (unpublished) identified several disadvantages of conventional brace therapy and reported the development, application, and preliminary evaluation of a new therapeutic procedure for adolescent ideopathic scoliosis.

Dworkin and his associates reasoned that corrective posturing could be trained if the patient was supplied with continuous feedback regarding her posture. They developed a Posture-Training Device that can be worn comfortably and inconspicuously day and night. Two transducers are used to detect spinal length (curvature) and to correct for artifacts in measurement attributable to respiration. Criterion curvature can be adjusted, permitting shaping of posturing. The Posture-Training Device contains tonal sources with volumes detectable only by the patient or by others as well. The critical contingencies most recently used have been (1) onset of patient's tone when posture fell below criterion for more than 20 seconds, (2) immediate termination of the tone with occurrence of criterion posture, (3) the requirement that each second of time out from the tone be preceded by 2 seconds of criterion responding, and (4) onset of a louder tone following below-criterion posture for 40 seconds.

B. Dworkin *et al.* (unpublished) conducted a preliminary evaluation of their method with 12 adolescent females whose condition was progressively deteriorating as judged from several orthopedic examinations. Orthopedists followed the patients in the conventional manner; this included measurement of the standard Cobb angle from radiographs. The quantitative Cobb angle measurements indicated that progressive changes in the scoliotic curvature stopped in patients considered as a group. Moreover, 10 of the 12 patients' orthopedists clinically evaluated them as not in need of conventional bracing. This is important, especially in the absence of untreated comparison subjects, because the deteriorating condition of the patients had been comparable to that of patients who do progress to brace therapy.

### 2. BRUXISM

Bruxism denotes a class of oral motor behaviors that includes nonfunctional or parafunctional clenching, grinding, and gnashing of the teeth (cf. Dubner, Sessle, & Storey, 1978). Bruxism is important to health care professionals because it is widespread (Scharer, 1974) and because its associated symptoms frequently prompt help-seeking. Common among these symptoms are abnormal tooth wear, damage to the temporomandibular joint (TMJ), various facial pains, referred pains, and headache (Alling & Mahan, 1985; Ramfjord & Ash, 1983).

Dentists have traditionally treated bruxism with one (or some combination) of three modalities: (1) restoring occlusion with tooth grinding and/or prostheses, (2) a mouthpiece that serves to normalize occlusion and prevent bruxing contacts between maxillary and mandibular teeth, or (3) muscle relaxants such as diazepam. Psychologists have systematically addressed the problem of therapy for bruxism by (1) training patients in progressive muscle relaxation, (2) guiding patients in "negative practice" of the habit, (3) teaching patients to detect the habit and rehearse an incompatible response, (4) exposing patients to mildly aversive stimulation contingent on bruxing, or (5) providing patients with feedback-signal devices for bruxing occurrences. A comprehensive review of both dental and psychological approaches to bruxism has been provided by McGlynn, Cassisi, and Diamond (1985). Therefore, we restrict the following narrative to exemplary efforts that represent major trends in the literature.

*a. Diurnal Bruxism.* Bruxing may occur during the day (diurnal bruxism), during the night (nocturnal bruxism), or during both periods. The etiological factors that participate in diurnal bruxism probably differ systematically from those involved in nocturnal bruxing. The participating muscles usually differ as well. Therefore, different treatment approaches and different means of assessment exist for the two problems.

Patients frequently can overcome diurnal clenching simply by being told it is important not to clench (Ramfjord & Ash, 1983). Many patients, however, do not modify clenching behaviors with such minimal assistance.

Habit reversal (Azrin & Nunn, 1973) is a behavioral technique that focuses on the elimination of "nervous habits" and tics by (1) increasing the efficiency of the patient's attending to the problematic behavior, (2) interrupting the chain of behavioral precursors to it, (3) teaching the patient an incompatible response that involves the muscles of habit expression, and (4) shifting any previously habit-contingent social reinforcers so as to make them contingent upon appropriate behavior.

Azrin, Nunn, and Frantz-Renshaw (1982) compared habit reversal with massed negative practice (Dunlap, 1932; Heller & Forgione, 1975) as a treatment for several parafunctional oral habits among 10 patients who responded to newspaper announcements. Habit-reversal training was used with five of the patients and was tailored to individuals. On the basis of self-monitored reports, habit reversal yielded 99% reduction in parafunctional oral-motor behaviors through a 22-month follow-up; this outcome was far superior to that found with negative practice.

*b. Nocturnal Bruxism.* Progressive relaxation, biofeedback-assisted facial relaxation, and massed negative practice have received attention as treatments for nocturnal bruxing. However, the most innovative body of literature has evolved around the use of EMG-feedback-based nocturnal alarms.

Masseteric EMGs recorded during bruxing are wholly unlike those recorded at other times. Hence, EMG thresholds can be used to signify bruxist activity in sleeping subjects and EMG signals can be used to trigger nocturnal alarms (see Solberg & Rugh, 1972). Research taking advantage of this technology in the treatment of bruxist patients has evolved to single- and comparative-group designs.

In one of two exemplary studies, Clark, Beemsterboer, and Rugh (1981) used a nocturnal EMG-activated tone coupled with an arousal task to treat 10 patients who presented to a TMJ clinic. The tone was triggered by suprathreshold masseter tension and, in turn, served to prompt the patients to get out of bed, cross the room, and record the time and sleep quality theretofore. Patients' chart recordings of nightly recorded suprathreshold EMG durations defined bruxing. Mean bruxing during 7–14 days after nocturnal feedback was significantly less than mean bruxing during 10–12 days before nocturnal feedback. This was true for 9 out of 10 TMJ clinic patients.

In another of two exemplary studies, Casas, Beemsterboer, and Clark (1982) compared stress-reduction behavioral counseling, nocturnal EMG feedback, and a combined counseling-followed-by-feedback procedure among 12 bruxist males and females who presented to a TMJ clinic. Stress-reduction behavioral counseling was based on a faithful adaptation of Goldfried, Decenteceo, and Weinberg (1974) and Meichenbaum (1974). The nocturnal EMG-feedback treatment was the same as that used by Clark et al. (1981). An assessment–wait–reassessment control group of four patients was used for various comparisons. By contrast with the four untreated subjects, those in each of the three treatment conditions reduced significantly their durations of suprathreshold masseter EMG responding from 10 days before to 10 days after treatment.

## C. Digestive System

### 1. BOWEL DISTURBANCES

Fecal incontinence is one of the disturbances secondary to myelomeningocele, a congenital defect in the walls of the spinal canal (Freeman, 1974). Since manometric studies reveal contractile deficiences of the external anal sphincter when the rectum is distended (White, Suzuki, El Shafie, Kumar, Haller, & Schnaufer, 1972), standard treatment relies on the internal anal sphincter alone to prevent incontinence by placing the patient on a regular schedule of suppositories or enemas. Whitehead, Parker, Masek, Cataldo, and Freeman (1981) reported a unique application of biofeedback training in the treatment of eight incontinent children with myelomeningocele. The patients first were trained to contract the external sphincter in the absence of rectal distension while they viewed polygraph feedback and the trainer verbally praised pen deflections indicative of sphincter contractions. The feedback and praise procedure was continued as the patients next were trained to contract the external sphincter when the rectum was distended with progressively larger volumes of air via a balloon. This procedure continued in the final phase of treatment, except visual feedback was discontinued and verbal praise was gradually withdrawn. Five of the eight patients achieved complete or nearly complete continence through follow-up evaluations of 12 months or longer. Another patient's accidents were down to one per day from a pretreatment level of three or four per day. Patients eliminated or greatly reduced their use of enemas and suppositories.

Some authorities have suggested that the term irritable bowel syndrome be used for a nonspecific bowel disorder that has been called the irritable colon syndrome, mucous colitis, spastic colitis, nervous diarrhea, colon neurosis, and dyssynergia of the colon (Drossman, Powell, & Sessions, 1977; "Management of the Irritable Bowel," 1978). Drossman *et al.* (1977) defined the irritable bowel syndrome as "a disturbed state of intestinal motility for which no anatomical cause can be found" (p. 811). This syndrome is characterized by various combinations of diarrhea, constipation, and poorly localized chronic abdominal pain, as well as various nonspecific symptoms, including "gas," "bloating," nausea, dysuria, and complaints of dyspepsia (Drossman *et al.*, 1977). Numerous conventional medical modalities of treatment (e.g., diet and drug therapy) have been used with satisfactory results in individual cases ("Management of the Irritable Bowel," 1978), but without a great deal of general success (Drossman *et al.*, 1977). A few early (Jackson & Yalom, 1966) and recent (Drossman *et al.*, 1977) studies suggest that factors such as untoward family interaction patterns can be involved in the development of the irritable bowel syndrome and, hence, that interdisciplinary approaches to intervention are called for.

One step toward an interdisciplinary approach is afforded by Milby, Beidleman, Welte, Dolce, Slaughter, Triplett, and Gurwitch (unpublished). Prompted by the relevance of everyday life conditions to the irritable bowel syndrome, Milby *et al.* used a stress-management intervention comprising functional analysis, training in relaxation, training to identify and evaluate implicit behaviors related to exacerbations of bowel disturbances, and modeling with practice in performing various "stress-coping" strategies (e.g., problem solving, direct action, assertiveness coping). The program was conducted over 14 weeks with three patients. Assessments were taken weekly or at least at pretreatment, posttreatment, and at 6-month follow-up. The three patients showed reductions in bowel disturbances ("gas," bloating, abdominal pain, cramping, and diarrhea), in frequency and types of medications, and in some self-reported anxiety and depression scores.

## 2.  BULIMIA NERVOSA

Bulimia nervosa is an eating disorder characterized by bouts of overeating followed by self-induced vomiting. One recent hypothesis maintains that eating and thinking about weight gain provoke aversive anxiety responding and vomiting is negatively reinforced by anxiety reduction (Rosen & Leitenberg, 1984). The anxiety reduction hypothesis led to two studies (Leitenberg, Gross, Peterson, & Rosen, 1984; Rosen, 1984; Rosen & Leitenberg, 1982) in which patients ingested targeted foods and subsequent vomiting was prevented. Of the six subjects treated over the two studies, five reduced vomiting frequency at home subsequent to treatment. Lohr, Stauffacher, Lewis, and Sims (unpublished), Mizes and Fleece (unpublished), and Mizes and Lohr (1983) also argued that the binges of eating reduce anxiety. Each trained one patient to use relaxation as a self-management coping technique (Goldfried, 1971) and to practice relaxing whenever she noticed an urge to binge. All three subjects considerably reduced frequencies of binges in association with the experimental treatment.

The data do not justify strong statements regarding anxiety reduction as the reinforcer of vomiting in bulimia nervosa. Indeed, a substantial amount of basic and clinical research brings into question the value of postulating an anxiety reduction construct per se (see especially, Delprato & McGlynn, 1984). However, the *procedures* of exposure, response prevention, and self-managed relaxation training might still prove useful. Encouraging results have been obtained, for example, from treating bulimia nervosa with one innovative program developed without systematic consideration of anxiety (Fairburn, 1981). Fairburn's multiple-component intervention had the following major characteristics: emphasizing direct control of food intake by manipulating food availability, prompting to engage in behavior incompatible with binging, interviewing the patient's friends and relatives concerning the problem, training in behavioral problem-solving techniques, identifying and changing "irrational self-statements," and graduating exposure to targeted foods. The program was accompanied by complete elimination of binges and vomiting with 9 out of 11 cases. An additional subject showed reductions in combined binges and vomiting from 21 to 2 per week.

## D.   Respiratory System

### 1.   CHRONIC OBSTRUCTIVE AIRWAY DISEASES (COAD)

Authorities in chest diseases (e.g., Hodgkin, Balchum, Kass, Glaser, Miller, Haas, Shaw, Kimbel, & Petty, 1975) classify chronic obstructive airway diseases (COAD) into three clinical groups. Asthma entails intermittent attacks of airway obstruction in conjunction with a history of wheezing or dyspnea. Chronic bronchitis is characterized by a sputum-producing cough that occurs for at least 3 months during 2 consecutive years that is not attributable to other diseases. (The airway resistance is reversible in asthma and partially reversible in chronic bronchitis.) Emphysema is defined as nonreversible airway resistance that results from structural damage (enlargement and destruction of the walls of air spaces distal to the terminal bronchioles). Of the respiratory disorders, asthma has received the most attention in behavioral medicine. For excellent reviews see Creer (1982), Epstein, Katz, and Zlutnick (1979), King (1980), and Kotses and

Glaus (1981). Applications of behavioral principles to bronchitis and emphysema have begun only recently.

Much of the work with respiratory ailments has involved biofeedback to augment the functional capacity of the respiratory system (Kotses & Glaus, 1981), although a fair amount of work has been done with exercise regimens (Atkins, Kaplan, Timms, Reinsch, & Lofback, 1984; Bass, Whitcomb, & Forman, 1970; Christie, 1968; Fishman & Petty, 1971). Corson, Grant, Moulton, Green, and Dunkel (1979) reported a unique application of biofeedback to the problem of weaning patients from respirators. Attempts to wean two patients with trial-and-error methods and with the intermittent mandatory ventilation technique (Downs, Klein, Desautels, Modell, & Kirby, 1973) had been unsuccessful. The patients first were continued on mechanical ventilation while being trained to increase tidal volume and decrease respiratory rate with the aid of oscilloscopic feedback. Respiratory feedback was associated with clinically significant increases in tidal volume and vital capacity and with decreased respiratory rate. The increased vital capacity permitted switching to a pressure-limited respirator and ultimately to a respirator-free condition for continued feedback training. Eventually, both patients were removed from respirators completely.

Holliday (1984) overviewed contemporary biofeedback-based pulmonary rehabilitation for emphysema patients and identified four areas in which biofeedback is recommended. First, Holliday suggested biofeedback-assisted relaxation training. This suggestion was based on the finding across several measurement conditions that mean frontalis EMG, upper pectoral EMG, and blood pressure scores of COAD patients were significantly higher than were those of "chronically anxious" patients. Second, Holliday recommended using EMG feedback from the area of the diaphragm to retrain breathing. This is done to strengthen the diaphragm, and, in turn, to reduce the necessary breathing involvement of the upper pectoral muscles. Third, Holliday suggested that unrectified EMG be used in diaphragm-muscle fatigue testing. The fatigue point is construed as an index of muscle strength, and, in turn, as a sign of the diaphragm's respiratory role. Finally, Holliday alluded to biofeedback for weaning patients from respirators, as demonstrated by Corson et al. (1979).

## 2. TRACHEOSTOMY DEPENDENCE

Many tracheostomized children become dependent upon the tracheal tube and do not regain respiration functions with cannular occlusion or closure of the tracheostomy incision (Wright, Schaefer, & Solomons, 1979). During the period of tracheostomization, these patients might acquire breathing responses that replace the normal breathing pattern (Wright, Nunnery, Eichel, & Scott, 1969).

Elliot and Olson (1982) reported a novel modification of a behaviorally based decannulation procedure developed several years earlier by Wright et al.

(1969). The original procedure involved three elements: occluding the cannula for progressively longer trial durations over a standard 21-day period, delivering positive social attention during the occlusion trials, and minimizing social and sensory stimulation between the occlusion trials. While Wright *et al.* (1979) reported virtually 100% success with their procedure, the lengthy period of hospitalization is problematic, as is the required isolation of the child (over 95% of the day in the first week).

Elliot and Olson (1982) addressed the major limitations of the procedure of Wright *et al.*, while maintaining its efficacy (at least as determined from the outcome of four cases). The major variations were increasing the number of occlusion trials per day (up to eight trials vs the standard maximum of three), more rapidly increasing the durations of successive occlusion trials, determining the frequencies and durations of occlusion trials by the patient's response (rather than by a fixed progression), and reducing the level of "social isolation." These modifications reduced the required hospital stay by an average of 7 days. Moreover, there was a much more positive response of parents and nursing staff to the shorter periods of required isolation.

## E.  Metabolic Disorders

### 1.  DIABETES MELLITUS

Diabetes mellitus refers to a variety of disorders affecting intermediary metabolism in which a deficiency of insulin results in abnormally high levels of blood glucose (Boshell & Gomez-Perez, 1974; Mason & Boucher, 1978). Most of the behavioral work has been with juvenile-onset diabetic patients who require daily insulin injections. Some impressive bodies of imaginative research with these patients have accumulated in recent years. Compliance with prescribed home-care regimens is one of them and is discussed later (Section III,A,2,b). Relaxation training with diabetic patients is another of them and is discussed here.

Researchers and clinicians working with diabetics long have discussed the patient-management implications of the notion that blood and urine glucose levels are related to psychobiologic "stress" (Johnson, 1980; Pinkerton, Hughes, & Wenrich, 1982; Rose & Firestone, 1983). However, relaxation training methods have only recently been brought to bear upon the problem of lowering glucose levels. Rose, Firestone, Heick, and Faught (1983) used a multiple-baseline across subjects design to determine whether a variation of Suinn's (1975) "anxiety management training" would reduce urine glucose levels. The power of their methodological approach was augmented further by including a lengthy attention-control condition between baseline and treatment phases. Statistically and clinically significant reductions in mean daily urine glucose values were obtained with five out of six subjects. However, there were concomitant dietary and exercise components in the therapeutic regimen.

Landis, Jovanovic, Landis, Peterson, Groshen, Johnson, and Miller (unpublished) studied six adult diabetics and found that 15 weeks of biofeedback-assisted relaxation was accompanied by improvements in blood glucose control ranging from 9–40%. The measure of "glucose control" was arrived at by dividing each daily range of blood glucose levels by the daily insulin dose. Surwit and Feinglos (1983) used taped relaxation instructions and five sessions of frontalis EMG feedback with each of six adult diabetic patients who were not insulin dependent. The treated group displayed mean pretreatment-to-posttreatment increases in incremental glucose area (calculated from 3-hour oral glucose tolerance tests) that significantly differed from repeated assessments of untreated control patients.

Seeburg and DeBoer (1980) sounded a cautionary note regarding intervention with diabetic patients. They reported that frontalis feedback for relaxation with a juvenile-onset insulin-requiring patient allowed the patient to reduce daily insulin dosages, but that biofeedback training was associated with dangerous instability in the patient's condition. This instability disappeared with withdrawal of the biofeedback condition, returned when biofeedback was reinstituted after a 6-month period, and gradually declined after termination of biofeedback.

## F.  Visual System

Although Bates (1920) long ago advocated a rudimentary version of a behavioral intervention as an alternative to corrective lens and other treatments of myopia, the visual system has been the focus of relatively little systematic clinical behavioral medicine work. However, a modestly sized literature has evolved in which behavioral analytic tools are applied to myopia, and this work recently has been reviewed in Volume 7 (Epstein *et al.*, 1979) and Volume 13 (Collins, Epstein, & Gil, 1982) of this series and elsewhere (Rosen, Schiffman, & Cohen, 1984). Therefore, we briefly consider a few interesting studies involving the visual system that focused on problems other than myopia.

### 1.  BLEPHAROSPASM

Blepharospasm refers to recurrent spasms of eye closure involving orbicular oculi contractions with such frequencies and durations as to sometimes render patients functionally blind (Marsden, 1978). A few researchers have attempted EMG feedback training for this disorder with individual cases and have obtained promising results. To cite one example, Peck (1977) provided auditory EMG feedback from electrodes attached to the left frontalis and lower orbicularis oculi muscles while the patient was instructed to keep her eyes open. Standard baseline sessions and an attention "placebo" treatment preceded EMG feedback training.

Notable reductions in EMG levels and frequency of spasm occurred over 17 training sessions, little change in these measures having been observed during the baseline and "placebo" sessions. The patient and her husband reported virtual elimination of the spasm outside the training setting, and although only one eye was trained, therapeutic effects were bilateral.

## 2. EXTRAOCULAR MOTILITY DISORDERS

Owing to its anatomical and physiological characteristics, the extraocular musculature is highly suitable for EMG biofeedback training, and, in turn, for biofeedback approaches to modifying occulomotor-control disorders (Rotberg, 1983; Rotberg & Surwit, 1981). Fixational unsteadiness of amblyopic eyes is one extraocular motility disorder for which biofeedback has yielded encouraging preliminary results. For example, Flom, Kirschen, and Bedell (1980) used a noninvasive recording method of infrared photoelectrooculography to monitor adult amblyopes' eye position. Training consisted of providing continuous auditory feedback of eye position with the goal of gradually reducing the magnitudes of eye excursions. This procedure amounted to eye-fixation training. All subjects showed increases in foveal fixation that were maintained in the absence of feedback.

Nystagmus (typically horizontal occular oscillations) is another oculomotor movement disorder that has responded to biofeedback in early work with some individual cases. Abadi, Carden, and Simpson (1979, 1980) introduced a treatment for congenital nystagmus that uses photoelectrooculography to monitor nystagmic eye movements and circuitry that produces tonal frequency changes in correspondence with them. Thus, the patient's task is one of keeping the tone constant. The equipment is portable, enabling patients to give themselves training at home. Abadi et al. (1980) reported clinically significant reductions in the frequencies and amplitudes of nystagmic movements and improvements in visual sensitivity for both the horizontal and vertical meridians. The investigators presented results for one subject as representative of those obtained routinely with their procedure.

## G.  Urogenital Tract

Urogenital problems stimulated some of the earliest innovative work in behavioral medicine. Mowrer and Mowrer's (1938) bell-and-pad device for treatment of nocturnal enuresis is outstanding here, as is Jones' (1956) less well known procedure of distorted bladder pressure feedback to decrease frequency of urination. Recent research of note, only some of which is described here, has incorporated both relaxation training and biofeedback.

1.  URINARY RETENTION AND INCONTINENCE

In 1979, researchers reported a pioneering application of EMG feedback in the treatment of urinary retentive and incontinent patients. Maizels, King, and Firlit (1979) studied three children with vesical sphincter dyssynergia, i.e., lack of coordination of the external urethral sphincter/pelvic floor musculature with the detrusor (of the bladder). The investigators assumed it to be a "learned" voiding problem amenable to relaxation training of the urethral sphincter during micturation. After the child was acclimated to frequent voiding into a specialized commode, electrodes were attached to the perianal skin to detect EMG activity in the urethral sphincter/pelvic floor musculature. Concurrent recordings of urethral sphincter EMGs and urinary flow were then taken, and the child observed the charts, permitting visual detection of dyssynergia. The child was instructed to attempt to suppress the dyssynergia during repeated voidings by concurrently maintaining a relaxed pelvic floor musculature. The trainer provided verbal encouragement on an unspecified schedule. One of the three children attained long-standing sphincter synergia, continence, voiding with a full urinary stream, and an improved voiding pattern. Another attained sphincter synergia and improved continence, but did not improve in urinary frequency. Libo, Arnold, Woodside, and Borden (1983) used a biofeedback procedure similar to that of Maizels et al. (1979) to train sphincter–bladder synergia during a child's voiding. In this more recent study, the authors expanded the biofeedback procedure to include self-recording, night waking, parental reinforcement, and general relaxation training. They obtained clinically significant therapeutic gains that were observed at 1-year follow-up. A novel use of biofeedback in the treatment of a single case of chronic urinary retention also was reported by Campbell and Latimer (1980). These researchers installed a catheter in the patient's bladder and connected the balloon to a pressure transducer. The patient was then instructed to void while concurrently observing the stream and a physiograph chart of bladder pressure. Normal micturition was rapidly established.

Urinary incontinence is a common problem among elderly residents of nursing homes (Dufault, 1978). Institutional incontinence programs typically rely upon placing the patient on a bedpan at specified intervals (Dufault, 1978). Unfortunately, this practice brings urination under the stimulus control of staff persons and creates needless demands on them. These considerations, in conjunction with the burgeoning geriatric nursing home industry, make timely a report in which easily implemented behavioral procedures were used to address geriatric incontinence in nursing homes (Schnelle, Traughber, Morgan, Embry, Binion, & Coleman, 1983). The intervention was designed to increase requests for toileting assistance. During a 5-day baseline period aides checked the patient's clothing hourly, recorded whether the patient was wet or dry, and recorded requests for toileting assistance. (Baseline recording conditions continued throughout the study for untreated control subjects.) Intervention required aids to (1) verbally prompt patients at the hourly checks, (2) provide assistance only if the patient replied affirmatively to the request, (3) deliver social approval for dry checks and for requests for toileting assistance, and (4) deliver social disapproval for wet checks. Baseline and intervention conditions were used at two nursing homes and produced comparable results in each. Patients in the intervention groups were judged wet on 29.7% of the checks during baseline and on only 15% of the checks during intervention. Their individual mean daily requests for assistance increased from .31 per day to 2.0 during treatment. In contrast, controls showed virtually no change on these measures over the same intervals.

## 2. GYNECOLOGIC PROBLEMS

Menstrual pain that occurs in the absence of obvious pathology (primary dysmenorrhea) has received the attention of behavior therapists over the years (see Denney & Gerrard, 1981). By and large, "vintage" behavior therapy techniques (e.g., systematic desensitization) have been used with the problem. In addition, success with a self-control version of desensitization (Goldfried, 1971) has been reported (Cox & Meyer, 1978; Quillen & Denney, 1982).

A gynecologic problem that has received only recent attention from behavioral psychologists is menopausal hot flashes. Typically, the hot flash is described as a sudden hot feeling accompanied by facial flushing and sometimes sweating that occurs for up to several minutes. Medical research on flashing mainly has revolved around the propriety of estrogenic treatment.

Wolf-Wilets, Woods, and Betrus (1981) reported perhaps the first attempt to control hot flashes with behavioral techniques. Their abstract indicates that statistically significant reductions in frequency of flashes were obtained in two different groups of subjects who received one of two 12-session interventions. One of these was temperature feedback from a finger and from a site where the particular patient's hot flashes started. The other was an unspecified program referred to as "group systematic relaxation."

Stevenson and Delprato (1983) argued that many of the events surrounding menopausal hot flashes were similar to those associated with what are often referred to as "stress" and "anxiety" response patterns. They designed a multiple component, self-control program that incorporated anxiety-management techniques, temperature biofeedback, and systematic steps to alter problematic conditions in patients' lives. Temperature data from four subjects showed reductions from a baseline phase to a phase of instructed temperature lowering under both the feedback and subsequent nonfeedback-test conditions. All four subjects reported clinically significant reductions in flash frequency relative to a 3–4 week attention "placebo" baseline. Reductions in self-reported frequencies ranged from 48–91% at 6-month follow-up.

Other investigators (Condor, 1983; Wineburg, Kronenberg, Khanukayev,

& Inz, 1983) have also reported promising results in the control of menopausal flashes, especially with temperature feedback. However, the well-documented short-term response of flashes to pharmacological placebos (e.g., Clayden, Bell, & Pollard, 1974) limits the force of available data.

## H. Cardiovascular System

The cardiovascular system has been the focus of important pioneering work in behavioral medicine. Documented relationships between organism–environment transactions and cardiovascular activity (Cohen & Obrist, 1975) and indications that certain patterns of eating, low levels of physical activity, smoking, and "Type A" behavior pattern were risk factors for cardiovascular diseases (Sexton, 1979; Stamler, 1979) provided impetus for research on prevention (see Section IV). In this section, we discuss prototypical developments in the treatment of Raynaud's disease and vascular headache.

### 1. RAYNAUD'S DISEASE

Raynaud's disease is a painful disorder of the peripheral vasculature characterized by vasospastic attacks usually affecting the fingers and toes. Exposure to cold and "emotional stress" are cited as common antecedents to the attacks (Abramson, 1974). Since Raynaud's disease is a vasoconstrictive disorder, clinical researchers have attempted interventions based upon blood volume and temperature feedback, as well as relaxation-related training. Surwit, Pilon, and Fenton (1978) compared two treatments with independent groups of subjects. During each of six biweekly sessions, subjects in an "autogenic training" group were exposed to an audiotape that "suggested" relaxation and prompted thinking of words such as "heavy," "relaxed," and "warm." The same audiotape was presented to subjects in the other group, then they received finger-temperature feedback. Subjects in both groups were instructed to practice hand warming at home and were provided explicit prompts to do so. The two conditions were evaluated before and after treatment by instructing subjects to keep their hands warm during a "stress test" that took place amid successively lowered room temperatures. Significant and equivalent improvements on the laboratory stress test, as well as in the number of reported naturalistic attacks, were obtained for the two treatments. Keefe, Surwit, and Pilon (1980) added a modification of Jacobson's (1938) progressive relaxation training to the autogenic and autogenic-plus-biofeedback conditions used in the earlier experiment. The three treatments were significantly but not differentially effective vis-à-vis both laboratory measures of peripheral temperature and self-reports of naturalistic vasomotor attacks.

A major implication of the behavioral assessor's concept of "situational specificity" is that clinical evaluation and treatment of problematic response patterns should take place in circumstances that at least approximate the concrete conditions in which the naturalistic problem occurs. Raynaud's patients, as noted, display vasomotor attacks when exposed to cold temperatures. Hence, from a specificity point of view, temperature biofeedback training for Raynaud's patients should take place in cool settings. Freedman, Ianni, and Wenig (1983) performed an experiment consistent with this reasoning. It was like those above, but it included finger-temperature feedback *concurrent* with exposure to cold stress. The short-term results of the concurrent treatment were low-temperature scores relative to those of subjects who received feedback without concurrent cooling. However, a 1-year follow-up showed concurrent-training subjects superior to standard-training subjects on both the laboratory finger-warming assessment and self-reports of naturalistic attacks.

Marshall and Gregory (1974) reasoned that Pavlovian procedures could be used to condition a peripheral vasodilation response to cold stimulation. In turn, such a conditioning history could be used to directly counteract vasoconstriction in Raynaud's disease and simple cold hypersensitivity. They reported three cases that were treated by systematically pairing a cold room (conditional stimulus) with warm water applied to the hands (unconditional stimulus for vasodilation). Measures of skin temperature taken before and after treatment and qualitative clinical observations suggested that most of the eight patients improved. Jobe, Sampson, Roberts, and Beetham (1982) randomly assigned Raynaud's patients to a similar conditioning treatment or to a no-treatment control group. Conditioned patients' finger temperatures during cold-temperature assessments significantly increased from before to after treatment and were significantly higher than those of the controls on the posttreatment test. Along with an extensive literature on vasomotor conditioning (Figar, 1965), these findings support use of Pavlovian procedures to enhance vasodilation in cases of Raynaud's disease. On the other hand, Jobe *et al.* did not include a full range of controls, and certain features of their study are difficult to reconcile with the basic research literature. For example, development of conditional vasodilative responses (in normals) is both extremely slow (70–90 pairings) and subject to rapid extinction (Figar, 1965). Yet Jobe *et al.* report presumably stable conditional responses after only 6–27 trials.

## 2.   MIGRAINE HEADACHE

Migraine headache is characterized by severe, throbbing pain thought to result from vasodilation of extracerebral cranial arteries. Temperature feedback for the problem is one of the early and influential success stories in the biofeedback and behavioral medicine movements. Cephalic vasomotor feedback and relaxation training also have been used (Williamson, 1981). A recent innovation has been the application of behavioral treatment to childhood migraine. In what may be the first controlled group experiment, Labbe and Williamson (1984) assigned children suffering from migraine to either a no-treatment, waiting-list control condition or to a treatment consisting of skin-temperature feedback with warming instructions plus structured home practice in temperature-related autogenic training. Subject-supplied records provided separate therapy-outcome indices (such as headache frequency, duration, and intensity) as well as a composite score. Control subjects' scores tended not to change from pretreatment, to posttreatment, to 1-month follow-up, whereas the scores of experimental subjects tended to show statistically reliable improvements over these phases.

## III.  HEALTH CARE DELIVERY

As noted earlier, recognition of the role of behaviors in catastrophic and chronic diseases was one major impetus to the behavioral medicine movement. Over the past several years, research literature has evolved that addresses two behavioral domains: (1) health care delivery and (2) disease and disability prevention (Epstein & Martin, 1977). By and large, research in health care delivery cuts across medical specialities and settings to address issues that are of general importance, e.g., health monitoring, follow-through with referrals, appointment keeping, management of health care avoidance and anxiety behaviors, and adherence to prescribed regimens (Epstein & Cincirpini, 1977; Epstein & Ossip, 1979). In this section we consider innovative work with adherence and with preparation to receive health care services. In the following section, we review contemporary work on disease and disability prevention.

### A.  Adherence to Health Care Regimens

Adherence (also referred to as compliance) refers to the degree to which an individual's concrete responses correspond to those specified in a particular health care recommendation. Assessment of adherence is one problem confronting the clinician. Promoting adherence is another. Portions of the vast amount of research on these problems are reviewed in Haynes, Taylor, and Sackett (1979), Epstein and Cluss (1982), Garfield (1982), and Peck and King (1982).

1.  ASSESSMENT OF ADHERENCE

Muscular relaxation training is, as we have seen, a prevalent component in behavioral medicine treatments. Home practice of relaxation is a frequent recommendation, and there is an evolving literature on assessing adherence to prescribed relaxation regimens. Even though we are not addressing behavioral medicine assessment systematically in the chapter, the relaxation adherence literature is used here as illustrative of work in the assessment area.

Collins, Martin, and Hillenberg (1982b) and Martin, Collins, Hillenberg,

Zabin, and Katell (1981) developed an embedded tone approach to assessing home relaxation practice. On selected tapes, a 1-second tone is embedded near the beginning, middle, or end of the relaxation instructions. The patient is instructed to record the presence or absence of the tone, as well as its location when present. By comparing this record to a master the clinician can obtain a reasonably accurate measure of adherence. In a preliminary study, Collins *et al.* (1982b) compared the relaxation behavior of volunteer subjects asked to monitor the tone with that of subjects relaxed under standard conditions. The task of monitoring the tone did not interfere with relaxation performance. The embedded tone procedure is promising but not without limitations as Collins *et al.* note.

Another group of researchers has developed an automated technique for assessing adherence to taped relaxation training regimens. Hoelscher, Lichstein, and Rosenthal (1984) inserted a digital wristwatch into the battery compartment of a portable cassette tape player. Appropriate circuitry results in activation of the watch only when the PLAY function of the tape player is depressed; thus, cumulative playing time is recorded. The tape player is sealed such that all of its playing time is devoted to the relaxation tape. Hoelscher *et al.* used this method to monitor home practice of volunteer participants in a relaxation training program. Illustrating the need for objective assessment, a comparison of self-reported practice durations with those obtained automatically showed subjects overestimated their practice by 126%.

## 2. PROMOTING ADHERENCE

Most research on promoting adherence to health care regimens has involved medication usage. Among the numerous approaches to promoting medication usage are flavoring the medication, self-regulating the medication dosage, chaining the ingestion of medication onto routine daily activities, self-monitoring of the symptoms targeted by the medicine, self-monitoring of medication ingestion, reinforcement for reductions in the symptom targeted by medication, contingency contracting, provision of discriminable environmental prompts for medication ingestion, and patient education (see Epstein & Cluss, 1982; Garfield, 1982; Haynes *et al.*, 1979; Peck & King, 1982). As research on the assessment of adherence has progressed, attempts to promote adherence other than medication usage have appeared. Among the adherence performances targeted have been exercise (Dishman, 1982), appointment keeping (Rice & Lutzker, 1984; Shepard & Moseley, 1976), special performances required by renal dialysis (Cummings, Becker, Kirscht, & Levin, 1981; Keane, Prue, & Collins, 1981), and parental performances of postscreening follow-up recommendations for their children (Reiss, Piotrowski, & Bailey, 1976).

The dental community has been actively *trying* to promote adherence to oral health care recommendations for well over a half century. A reasonably cohesive literature is evolving and some of the innovative and/or state-of-the-art studies are reviewed in the next section. By far the most impressive literature that exists concerning adherence is that on diabetes self-management approaches. That literature also is highlighted as a special subsection. Finally, an evolving literature on adherence to cancer therapy regimens is noted.

    *a.   Oral Hygiene Adherence.* Toothbrushing, flossing, and fluoride mouth rinsing are the daily behaviors dentists prescribe. Whether they are construed as treatment or prevention depends, to a large extent, upon the patient's oral-health status. The historical precursors to modern community dentists took a public health view of the problem and launched both water fluoridation and mass media educational approaches to address it. The latter approaches did teach people relevant facts and concepts (Boffa & Kugler, 1970), but they failed to influence the rates with which people performed home care behaviors as such (cf. Craig & Montague, 1976). With the advent of classical behavior modification, applications to the domain of oral health care soon were seen. Reports began to appear in which reinforcing contingencies were brought to bear on oral-hygiene performances among moderately (Horner & Keilitz, 1975) and severely (Abramson & Wunderlich, 1972) retarded persons and among normal youths (Lattal, 1969). These contingency management approaches did increase the skill levels and rates of oral hygiene performances as such (cf. Martens, Frazier, Hirt, Maskin, & Prosheck, 1973).

    Contingencies of reinforcement are the foundation of contemporary approaches to oral hygiene adherence as well. In one contemporary strategy, parents are trained to provide tangible reinforcers to their children soon after the children have brushed and/or flossed. Claerhout and Lutzker (1981), for example, trained parents of four particularly recalcitrant children to use feedback, points, and "menus" of reinforcers to increase rates of dentally prescribed home-care behaviors. Their study is state-of-the-art because intrasubject replication design logic was used flexibly as required in individual cases and because biological measures of oral status supplemented chart recordings of behavior as indices of program efficacy. For the 12–15 weeks of the study, reported rates of the children's home-care behaviors increased dramatically and were accompanied by decreased dental plaque and decreased cariogenic bacterial activity. Follow-up interviews with parents between 6 months and 1 year later indicated good maintenance of treatment effects even though the formal reinforcement program was still ongoing in only one household.

    In a second contemporary strategy, personnel in social agencies such as schools or summer camps are taught to provide tangible reinforcers for oral-hygiene performances among the groups they serve. Exemplary work along these lines is seen in reports by Lund and his colleagues (e.g., Lund & Kegeles, 1979) of studies wherein school personnel reinforced home mouth-rinse utilization among pupils. Uniquely, in these studies an experimental mouth-rinse dispenser has been used that dispenses only one rinsing dose per day and, hence, makes possible reinforcement contingencies based on amounts of rinse missing from prefilled bottles at various "turn-in" periods.

The aggregate of work on oral-hygiene adherence is distinctly operant in flavor. Advantage is being taken of the power of well-managed, short-term incentives to influence rates of much practiced psychomotor performances. The history of behavior modification shows the obvious value of a straightforward operant analysis in such circumstances.

*b.   Adherence to Diabetic Management Procedures.* As noted earlier, compliance (adherence) among diabetic patients is the most highly evolved area within the compliance literature and, in many ways, could serve as a model for behavioral medicine workers in other compliance arenas.

Diabetic compliance involves fairly complex perceptual–motor behaviors for urine testing and self-injection. Recently, behavioral clinicians have developed assessment tools with which to characterize individuals' performances on these tasks. An excellent example is Pollak and Johnson's (1979) skills demonstration test for urine sugar testing and for self-injections. An analysis of the micro-details of these tasks enabled the authors to devise an assessment instrument that clinicians can use to identify trouble spots in urine sugar testing and self-injecting performances that could interfere with adherence. Additional advances in assessment with insulin-dependent children and their parents have been made by Johnson, Pollak, Silverstein, Rosenbloom, Spillar, McCallum, and Harkavy (1982). The latter developed a psychometrically satisfactory paper-and-pencil battery that measures general information, diabetes-related problem solving, and skill at urine testing and self-injection.

Researchers also have begun to develop components of skills training packages for comprehensive diabetes management programs. Epstein, Figueroa, Farkas, and Beck (1981b), for example, demonstrated that uncomplicated feedback was more effective than was simple repeated practice for increasing accuracy of juvenile diabetics' self-monitored urine glucose determinations. Gilbert, Johnson, Spillar, McCallum, Silverstein, and Rosenbloom (1982), for another example, obtained indications that a modeling film enhanced the self-injection performance of insulin-dependent children more than did standard self-injection instructions. Carney, Schechter, and Davis (1983), for a third example, trained parents in contingency management skills and obtained large increases in the rates with which insulin-dependent children tested their blood glucose.

Some clinicians (e.g., Pennebaker, Cox, Gonder-Frederick, Wunsch, Evans, & Pohl, 1981) have recently pointed out that diabetes adherence might depend on a patient's response to important physiological changes relevant to his/her condition. For juvenile diabetics, adherence might also importantly depend on parents' response to behavioral concomitants of such physiological changes. A fair amount of recent work has, therefore, addressed self- and parental-monitoring skills as they relate to detecting relevant physiological and behavioral states of affairs. In the absence of specific training, neither patients nor parents accurately predict blood glucose levels (Eastman, Johnson, Silverstein, Spillar, & McCallum, 1983). Patients, parents, and physicians frequently disagree regarding the symptoms of hyperglycemia and hypoglycemia (Eastman *et al.*, 1983). Specific reported symptoms do seem associated with differing blood glucose levels but the associations are idiosyncratic (Freund, 1983; Pennebaker *et al.*, 1981). Insulin-dependent adolescents can improve the accuracy of blood glucose estimates with a training program involving practice, feedback, education, incentives, and aids to estimation (Eastman, Johnson, Rosenbloom, Spillar, & Silverstein, unpublished).

A noteworthy innovation in clinical diabetes adherence research is direct targeting of urine glucose reductions among insulin-dependent children (Epstein, Beck, Figueroa, Farkas, Kazdin, Daneman, & Becker, 1981a). Multiple-baselines across groups were used to evaluate a multiple component intervention in which the children received points and parental praise when urine glucose tests indicated adequate control. The component intervention conditions involved steps in teaching the children and their parents how to accomplish control over glucose levels (e.g., training in urine-glucose testing, diet, exercise, self-injection training). The major finding was that percentages of negative urines increased with introduction of the intervention. This study is of interest also because it adapted the marked-item strategy (Epstein & Masek, 1978) for corroborating adherence so it would fit the context of urine-glucose control.

   *c. Radiation Therapy and Chemotherapy.* Radiation therapy and chemotherapy present unique adherence problems for cancer patients. Both forms of cancer therapy occasion frequent and interrelated iatrogenic effects, including anticipatory (pretreatment) nausea and vomiting (Lazlo, Lucas, & Pharm, 1981), food aversions and appetite loss (Bernstein & Bernstein, 1981; Costa & Donaldson, 1979), and odor aversions (Vickers, Nielsen, & Theologides, 1981). A well-established learned food aversion literature (e.g., Milgram, Krames, & Alloway, 1977) permits the view that these effects relate to respondent and/or operant ontogenies (Bernstein, 1978; Bernstein & Bernstein, 1981; Nesse, Carli, Curtis, & Kleinman, 1980; Redd & Andresen, 1981). The evolutional nature of these aversive reactions and the serious limitations of available antiemetic agents (Penta, Poster, Bruno, & MacDonald, 1981) have stimulated behavioral researchers to investigate techniques for helping cancer patients cope with the aversion problem.

   Systematic desensitization (e.g., Wolpe, 1958) has received some attention as a means of preparing patients for cancer therapy. Hailey and White (1983) reported an innovative application with one patient receiving chemotherapy.

Morrow and Morrell (1982) compared desensitization with nondirective counseling and with no contact in a randomized group experiment. In terms of patient-reported nausea and vomiting, desensitization was superior to the other two conditions. Goldfried's (1971) self-control desensitization format also has been used to treat successfully a patient suffering from gastric pain attacks that had evolved in the context of cobalt radiation therapy (Hamberger, 1982). Lyles, Burish, Krozely, and Oldham (1982) compared a self-control version of desensitization with attention and with no contact in a randomized-group experiment. The experimental treatment was superior to both control conditions on a number of measures, including ratings of anxiety responding and nausea by patients and nurses.

## B. Preparation for Medical Procedures

Medical and dental procedures such as surgery, renal dialysis, and gastrointestinal endoscopy are very aversive. Hence, they occasion patient behaviors that interfere with the procedure and/or with recovery. Anxiety behaviors are major undesirable accompaniments of painful invasive procedures. Research focusing on improving patients' collateral behaviors during aversive procedures began more than 20 years ago, but the early work involved only very primitive behavioral principles (for a review, see Anderson & Masur, 1983). As the modern behavioral movement evolved, clinicians used classical methods such as modeling, relaxation training, and systematic desensitization to alleviate medically and dentally cued anxiety behavior (cf. Melamed & Siegel, 1975). A cohesive literature produced mainly by Melamed and her colleagues exists on preparing children for operative dentistry. Developments in that literature have been reviewed very recently (Melamed & Bennett, 1985). Among the recent developments with invasive medical procedures is preparatory training in self-management of anxiety. That work is noted here as illustrative of contemporary innovation.

Kendall, Williams, Pechacek, Graham, Shisslak, and Herzoff (1979) reported state-of-the-art research on pain management preparatory to cardiac catherization. Two 45-minute interventions administered the day before catheterization were compared with two control conditions in a randomized-group experiment. Patients in an education group received detailed individual instruction concerning the procedure and a demonstration of catheterization using an artificial heart. The other experimental group received stress self-management instruction, including training to identify anxiety-related cues, application of relaxation and other responding in response to such cues, modeling, and behavioral rehearsal. Attending physicians and technicians rated the patients' behavior independently on several variables during the catheterization. Raters agreed that behaviors among patients in both experimental groups were significantly more appropriate than were those of patients assigned to an attention-control or to a current hospital (control) condition. Furthermore, statistical comparison between the two experimental groups showed ratings of the patients in the self-management condition to be reliably higher than were those of patients in the education regimen.

Kaplan, Metzger, and Jablecki (1983) reported a similar application of stress-management training preparatory to a painful EMG exam. Stress-management training much like that of Kendall *et al.* (1979) was done immediately before the painful exam and its effects were compared with those of relaxation training and with those of attention control via a randomized-group experiment. A variety of measures, including self-reports of pain, heart rate, and behavioral ratings by a "blind" rater, indicated that the self-management group behaved more appropriately during the EMG evaluation than did the attention controls; however, relaxation alone equaled the effects of the self-management preparation. Along these lines, an innovative application of relaxation to hemodialysis was reported by Alarcon, Jenkins, Heestand, Scott, and Cantor (1982). These authors simply presented patients with a relaxation videotape instructing their participation while they were on the dialysis machine. Control subjects viewed a neutral tape. Self-reported anxiety behavior scores obtained after the tape terminated but while the patients were still on the machine showed patients who viewed the relaxation videotape to be more relaxed than controls.

## IV. PREVENTIVE HEALTH CARE

Preventive approaches are usually classified into two groups. Primary prevention (or health promotion) is not directed at any particular disease or disorder; the emphasis is on decreasing the likelihood that risk factors will develop. Secondary prevention refers to changing already developing risk factors or to intervening in the earliest stages of a disease.

### A. Breast Self-Examination

One of the newly evolving areas of secondary prevention is early detection of breast cancer. The evidence strongly indicates that early detection of the lesion is associated with a favorable prognosis (Fisher, Slack, & Bross, 1969; Haagensen, 1971). Two mass screening techniques have been used—mammography and breast self-examination. For reasons of risk, cost, and convenience breast self-examination represents a potentially valuable method for early detection of breast cancer on a large scale. Unfortunately, research has revealed serious limitations with the current self-examination techniques (Celentano & Holtzman, 1983; Holtzman & Celentano, 1983; Sheley, 1983).

Outstanding work addressing the problem of how to train breast self-examination has been reported by Pennypacker, Bloom, Criswell, Neelakantan, Goldstein, and Stein (1982). The Breast Lump Detection Project has developed a model of a human breast into which can be inserted simulated lumps with various characteristics. As the trainee's fingers palpate the model, their locations are automatically transduced so as to monitor the proportion of the model searched, as well as the pattern and duration of the search. A systematic breast examination training procedure using the model has been developed. In applications to date, a trainer demonstrates appropriate search techniques with regard to area of search, palpation topography, palpation pressure, and search duration. The trainer also provides verbal and manual feedback during patient performances.

Pennypacker *et al.* (1982) summarized a randomized-group experiment that compared a 10-minute live training period using the above techniques with a filmed training period, a live demonstration, and neutral reading. When subjects were tested for detecting lumps in live patients, the model-search training procedure was statistically superior to the other three conditions. In another experiment that evaluated model-search training via detecting lumps in breasts of volunteer patients, the trained group detected nearly twice as many lumps as did untrained subjects (Hall, Adams, Stein, Stephenson, Goldstein, & Pennypacker, 1980).

## B. Obesity

Obesity has been of interest to behavior modifiers since the beginning of the behavior therapy movement (e.g., Ferster, Nurnberger, & Levitt, 1962), and it continues to be an area of activity in behavioral medicine. The relatively recent research takes into account that obesity involves energy expenditure as well as eating behavior. Attempts to modify energy expenditure range from prompting and reinforcement designed to increase subjects' activity in their daily routines (Dahlkoetter, Callahan, & Linton, 1979; Stalonas, Johnson, & Christ, 1978) to instruction by professionally qualified trainers in ballet, aerobic dance, and calisthenics (Katahn, Pleas, Thackrey, & Wallston, 1982). Other exercise regimens in the literature include "jogging" (MacKeen, Franklin, Nicholas, & Beskirk, 1983) and use of a bicycle ergometer (Warwick & Garrow, 1981).

Some investigators have examined the role of systematic participation of spouses in weight reduction interventions. Brownell, Heckerman, Westlake, Hayes, and Monti (1978), for example, found that incorporating spouses into a behaviorally based treatment did facilitate initial and follow-up weight loss. Additional support for spouse participation in weight reduction programs has been reported by Fremouw and Zitter (1980) and by Rosenthal, Allen, and Winter (1980). However, the data are not uniformly supportive (e.g., Wilson & Brownell, 1978; Zitter & Fremouw, 1978).

Obviously it is possible to incorporate others than spouses into interventions. A new development along these lines is the controlled evaluation of weight reduction programs conducted at the work place. Brownell, Cohen, Stunkard, Felix, and Cooley (unpublished) obtained mean weight losses ranging from 4.5 to 6.0 kg over 12 to 15 weeks when group competitions for weight loss were arranged. Winning teams received pooled money contributed initially by all participants. Abrams and Follick (1983) obtained a mean weight loss of over 5 kg at 18 weeks by using a multifaceted program that included a "buddy system," along with organizational behavior management techniques such as public posting and recognition for weight loss. A discouraging aspect of worksite programs has been their high attrition rates (Follick, Fowler, & Brown, 1984b). Also worksite programs have not always been impressive as compared with other weight-reduction approaches (cf. Stunkard & Brownell, 1980).

Very low calorie diets (also referred to as protein-sparing modified fasts) offer promise as components in the behavioral treatment of obesity (Wadden, Stunkard, & Brownell, 1983). These diets provide less than 800 calories per day in the form of animal protein (Bistrian, 1978) or egg- or milk-based liquids (Vertes, Genuth, & Hazelton, 1977). Weight losses that follow very low calorie diets alone are rarely maintained at follow-up (Wadden *et al.*, 1983). A potential solution to this problem is the combination of very low calorie diets with behavioral programs targeting modified eating patterns. An innovative integration of a very low calorie diet with a multiple component, self-management program has shown exceptional maintenance of weight loss (Holmes, Ardito, Stevenson, & Lucas, 1984; Stevenson, Lucas, Holmes, & Ardito, 1984). One hundred and twenty-seven massively obese patients lost a mean of 26.3 kg over a treatment period ranging from approximately 10 to 54 weeks. When these patients were later surveyed, reports indicated that 18.9 kg of the original loss remained at a mean follow-up interval of 9.2 months.

A beginning area of behavioral applications to obesity is the delivery of interventions to "special" populations. The most developed of these specialized interventions are for children (Brownell, Kelman, & Stunkard, 1983; Brownell & Stunkard, 1978), adolescents (Coates & Thoresen, 1981; Weiss, 1977), and developmentally retarded persons (Fox, Rotatori, & Burkhart, 1983; Fox, Switzky, Rotatori, & Vitkus, 1982).

## C.  "Type A" Behavior Pattern

A notable development in the history of behavioral medicine was the articulation of relationships between typical modes of behaving and coronary heart disease (see especially Friedman & Rosenman, 1974). There is now considerable agreement that individuals who display "Type A" behavior pattern are differentially likely to suffer coronary heart disease to a degree comparable in magnitude to individuals who smoke and those who have elevated systolic blood pressure and serum cholesterol levels (Review Panel on Coronary-Prone Behavior and Coronary Heart Disease, 1981). Theoretically, the Type A behavior pattern is viewed as a stressful arousal state that has deleterious effects on the individual. The Type A pattern is considered to occur in response to "challenging" environmental conditions and it takes forms such as intense, sustained drive to achieve self-selected goals, reinforcement by recognition, continuous involvement in multiple and diverse activities, extraordinary alertness, hurried speech and gait, clenched fist, and certain facial grimaces (see Bortner & Rosenman, 1967). Paper-and-pencil results and interview-derived ratings of behavior provide empirical referents in behavioral studies of coronary heart disease and Type A behavior.

Several studies have been reported in which measures of Type A behavior taken from nonclinical subjects was used to evaluate anxiety management approaches to the problem (e.g., Roskies, Spevack, Surkis, Cohen, & Gilman, 1978; Suinn & Bloom, 1978). On the whole, results have not been encouraging. Recently, for example, Levenkron, Fisher, Cohen, and Mueller (1983) reported that a comprehensive intervention involving both relaxation and practice at changing "self-statements" was not more effective than was a nonspecific "group support" condition in changing either self-reported Type A behavior or physiological measures among nonclinical subjects.

Preliminary findings from a large-scale, long-term program with acute myocardial infarction patients are considerably more encouraging than are the results from nonclinical subjects. Thoresen, Friedman, Gill, and Ulmer (1982) reported findings from three conditions: a comprehensive and continuing behaviorally based treatment, a condition in which patients were advised by a cardiologist, and a no-treatment control group. At 3 years, recurrence of myocardial infarction among the behaviorally treated patients was significantly lower than recurrence among the cardiologist-led group. The behaviorally treated patients also exhibited significantly less interview-measured "Type A" behavior than did patients in the cardiologist-led treatment and no-treatment conditions.

The Thoresen et al. (1982) experiment differed from previous ones in terms of subjects, measures, and behavioral treatment duration, among other variables. Their relatively more promising results could reflect combinations of these and other factors. Even so, if Type A behavior is an evolving mode of interacting with diverse environmental challenges, it would not be surprising if continuous, long-term intervention into the patient's life is required for meaningful impact.

### D.  Essential Hypertension

Essential hypertension, elevated blood pressure of unknown etiology, is especially a major risk factor for cardiovascular disease (Moyer, 1975). This disorder too has been conceptualized as stress or anxiety related. As a result, a substantial amount of research has involved anxiety-management techniques applied with hypertensive subjects (Seer, 1979; Shapiro, Schwartz, Ferguson, Redmond, & Weiss, 1977).

In what might be referred to as a new use for an old procedure, "stimulus reduction" (also called "Restricted Environmental Stimulation Technique" or REST) has been applied to hypertension, among other disorders (Suedfeld & Kristeller, 1982). The old procedure is sensory deprivation (Zubek, 1969). As currently practiced, stimulus-reduction therapy is accomplished either by having the subject lie in bed for about 24 hours or by having the subject float for 1 hour or so in a tank filled with warm water and Epsom salts. Reductions in blood pressure among hypertensive subjects have been observed from several months to 3 years after 24 hours were spent lying on a bed in a dark and sound-attenuating chamber (Kristeller, Schwartz, & Black, 1982; Suedfeld, Roy, & Landon, 1982). Blood-pressure reductions concurrent with a regimen of frequent 40-minute flotation sessions were reported by Fine and Turner (1982).

## E.   Community Programs

For many years the public health movement has supported large-scale, community-level approaches to primary prevention (e.g., water fluoridation). The basic assumption of contemporary community-wide prevention programs is that success requires regulation of environmental factors and "lifestyle" (Davis & Ng, 1981). The emphasis on environmental regulation and lifestyle is not incompatible with a behavioral view of the problem. Even so, only a handful of community prevention programs have made systematic use of behavioral methods.

The Stanford Heart Disease Prevention Program was a three-community field study that focused on reducing cardiovascular risk by targeting smoking, exercise, and diet (Maccoby, Farquhar, Wood, & Alexander, 1977; Meyer, Nash, McAlister, Maccoby, & Farquhar, 1980). One town received a multimedia campaign during 2 years of intervention. A second town received the media campaign while, in addition, one group of subjects received a regimen of face-to-face training in behavioral self-management along the various risk-factor dimensions. A third town served as an untreated control. Multiple measures of relevant knowledge and of behaviors related to smoking, exercise, and diet were taken at baseline and at three annual surveys. Data for low-risk and high-risk participants were separately analyzed but the results for each were much the same. Both of the media-campaign communities improved on targeted measures relative to the untreated town. The addition of face-to-face behavioral self-management training augmented significantly the effect of the media campaign.

Other community-wide programs have targeted single risk factors. Encouraging results in smoking prevention among adolescents were obtained during 3-year follow-up of one novel curriculum that included peer-taught assertive training, modeling, guided practice, and reinforcement procedures (Perry, Maccoby, & McAlister, 1980). Luepker, Johnson, Murray, and Pechacek (1983) also found durable resistance to smoking among adolescents when peers had conducted a preventive program.

With regard to the problem of obesity, Stunkard (1979, 1981) has argued that nontraditional applications of behavioral principles in large-scale community-wide programs are needed. A recent innovative project along these lines was reported by Wing and Epstein (1982) who obtained encouraging results from a community fund-raising activity (Weight-A-Thon) in which participants solicited sponsors who, in turn, pledged money to the American Cancer Society for weight that participants lost.

Public health methodology shows that simple modifications in environmental conditions can favorably influence the behaviors of many individuals without requiring their participation in any other formal program. An example of creative work in this vein was reported by Brownell, Stunkard, and Albaum (1980). Prompts in the form of inexpensive signs increased reliably the use of stairs adjacent to escalators in three locations.

## F. Worksite Programs

An area of community intervention that recently has received increasing attention is the work place (Parkinson & Associates, 1982). Worksites are recognized as promising settings for health programs because they offer ready access to broad segments of the population (Follick, Abrams, Pinto, & Fowler, 1984a). Worksite interventions thus far have been similar to other community programs in frequently lacking systematic behavioral training or evaluation methods. However, we noted innovative worksite programs for obesity (Abrams & Follick, 1983; Brownell et al., 1984; Stunkard & Brownell, 1980). Innovative worksite programs also have been brought to bear on smoking behavior with promising results (Glasgow, Klesges, Godding, Vasey, & O'Neill, 1984; Scott, Denier, & Prue, 1983; Stachnik & Stoffelmayr, 1983).

Hypertension has been addressed in several worksite interventions. Alderman and Schoenbaum (1975) described a store-wide program for blood-pressure control at a large department store. The program was medication-based, but the authors performed several system manipulations to integrate medication delivery within the organization (e.g., labor union, nurses). Peters, Benson, and Peters (1977a) and Peters, Benson, and Porter (1977b) trained volunteers from large corporate manufacturing offices in simple relaxation and instructed them to take two relaxation breaks each day. Reductions in both systolic and diastolic blood pressure were obtained, as were improvements on self-reported health behavior measures. In a randomized-group experiment targeting blood pressure reductions of individuals in the mild hypertensive range, Drazen, Nevid, Pace, and O'Brien (1982) found limited support for the efficacy of an intervention that entailed changing "self-statements" plus self-managed relaxation.

The worksite model of prevention received encouraging support in a comparative cost analysis of hypertension care provided by physicians at a community clinic versus care provided by nurses under the supervision of physicians at the worksite (Ruchlin, Melcher, & Alderman, 1984). A medication regimen was prescribed in both settings. Blood pressure reductions were greater from the worksite than from the clinic program, and the average cost per unit of blood pressure reduction was significantly less in the worksite condition ($8.25) compared with the clinic program ($28.84).

## V.   METHODOLOGICAL STATUS AND FUTURE DIRECTIONS

Our focus here has been on clinical innovation not on research methodology. Hence, systematic criticism has been omitted. The methodological status of behavioral medicine cannot be ignored entirely, however, and a characterization is offered in the first of three subsections here. There are a great many obvious connections between behavioral medicine and both the behavior therapy and psychosomatic medicine movements. The second subsection here offers an historical perspective on behavioral medicine in light of the histories of these other two traditions. There are some less obvious but potentially important connections between behavioral medicine and a variety of psychological behaviorism known as field behaviorism or interbehaviorism (Kantor, 1959, 1969). The third subsection here proposes that field behaviorism can serve as an organizing conceptual framework for many behavioral medicine activities, and it articulates tentatively a set of interbehavioral "Postulates of Behavioral Medicine."

### A.   Methodological Status

Even though research in behavioral medicine has benefited greatly from the important methodological contributions of behavior therapy, the newer movement inherited a legacy of methodological pluralism as well. One could take advantage of such pluralism and articulate reasonable criticisms of virtually all of the work we have reviewed. For example, it is often possible to characterize actuarially significant results as clinically trivial or to fault intrasubject-replication data as lacking in demonstrable generality. Similarly, by arguing that behavioral medicine is a new movement and by therefore relaxing a few methodological strictures, one could paint a spuriously favorable picture.

The various research areas in behavioral medicine treatment, service delivery, and prevention mirror differing stages in a relatively characteristic subject matter evolution. Reports of successful interventions for individual patients and small patient cohorts appear and are followed by reports of prospective clinical trials with larger groups of patients and, finally, by randomized-group experiments couched in the actuarial tradition. The behavioral medicine literature contains an impressive number of good prospective-group clinical trials. They are particularly meaningful because they have employed clinically relevant measures of intervention effects and because they characteristically have described the effects of intervention on individual patients—not just on composite group averages. Illustrative here is the report of Dworkin *et al.* (unpublished) that, in terms of physicians' prognostic recommendations, 10 of 12 scoliosis patients were significantly aided by postural training based on unobtrusively engineered spinal-curvature biofeedback contingencies.

The literature also contains a fairly large number of reasonably well done randomized-group experiments. By and large, these experiments have compared effects on "symptom" measures of one or more treatments with no treatment at all. While virtually no randomized-group experiment has included a "complete" set of controls (see Kazdin & Wilcoxon, 1976), several experiments represent important pragmatic work within the actuarial tradition. The principle shortcomings that reappear in various places are insufficient sample sizes, inadequate naturalistic assessment, and (often unavoidable) confounds with other ongoing treatments. A few experiments (some just reviewed) have not reflected all of these recurrent problems, but some of the better experiments have yielded the most disappointing evidence of clinical effects from behavioral medicine methods. Since most randomized group experiments do show one or more of these recurrent methodological problems, a degree of skepticism is called for in evaluating strong actuarial claims of clinical efficacy for the treatments embedded in them.

Given the sample-size requirements of true actuarial research, the paradigm tends to restrict scientific access. Furthermore, actuarial results from randomized group experiments often tell us little about individual patients. Hence, the intrasubject replication design logic of the behavior modification movement should serve as one important approach for treatment evaluation in behavioral medicine. There were surprisingly few bona fide intrasubject replication experiments in the material reviewed, i.e., experiments in which intrasubject phase changes were governed by the subject's data (Kazdin, 1982). Notwithstanding the "problem" of limited generality, bona fide intrasubject experimentation, coupled with clinically relevant outcome assessment, is a powerful and insufficiently used approach.

Intervention research in behavioral medicine is already comparable in quality to clinical research in behavior therapy. This should be the case not only because of methodological lessons learned from behavior therapy research but also because, unlike psychiatry, general medicine and dentistry have provided already well-developed measures that behavioral medicine researchers can meaningfully target in intervention studies. (A few examples are measures of the Cobb angle in scoliosis, measures of functional capacity in chronic obstructive airway diseases, measures of blood and urine glucose in diabetes, and measures of gingival inflammation and of cariogenic bacterial action in preventive dentistry.) Given opportunities for sophisticated behaviorists and sophisticated biomedical scientists to pool their efforts, there does exist an impressive potential for significant accomplishment. At the same time, realizing the potential might very well require a general shift toward what might be called "hybrid" methodological thinking.

Between-group experiments and intrasubject experiments are the end points of different intellectual traditions. They stress, differentially, the nomothetic vs idiographic purposes of behavioral researchers. Standing squarely between these two traditions is research that undertakes both intrasubject manipulation of independent variables and between-subject comparisons of dependent variables. Multiple baselines across subjects designs exemplify this hybrid approach and often are ideally suited to behavioral medicine research. This is so because the amount of time and work involved in behavioral medicine interventions and scientifically credible assessment militates strongly against large $N$ actuarial experiments and, at the same time, the problem of truncated generality augurs against excessive use of single, intrasubject replication studies. Hence, multiple baselines across subjects represent a beneficial compromise, and per se they may be ideal for much behavioral medicine research. Multiple baselines across subjects are not without shortcomings, however, e.g., ethical problems in withholding treatment until, say, six other patients have *successively* achieved sufficient baseline stability. Hence identical interventions for successive, not simultaneous, patients might sometimes be preferred as an approach to behavioral medicine research. When coupled with adequate assessment, this can be a persuasive strategy. In general, behavioral medicine research might be well served by a continuing evolution of hybrid methodological thinking. We foresee that rules for adjudicating a general class of "systematically cumulative intrasubject experiments" will, in time, evolve out of the peer review process.

Numerous writers have spelled out substantive directions for valuable research in the future. Among those encountered most frequently are long-term programmatic research on chronic conditions, continued research on the effects of behavioral medicine interventions, research on service delivery as it interfaces with the existing structure of the health care system, and research on the comparative cost effectiveness of behavioral medicine methods.

### B. Behavioral Medicine, Psychosomatic Medicine, and Behavior Therapy

Behavioral medicine is related to psychosomatic medicine in the sense that it has the same generic goal, viz., the application of behavioral science in medicine. In his cogent essay, Agras (1982) explains why psychosomatic medicine failed and why we have a right to expect that behavioral medicine will succeed. In brief, psychosomatic medicine failed because it relied on verbal psychotherapy as a trans-situational treatment modality and because it was without meaningful intervention-oriented research. Its "technology" was both lacking in credibility and weak. In the place of verbal psychotherapy, behavioral medicine has substituted highly specific biofeedback and other training regimens based upon the experimental analysis of behavior (broadly defined). In place of psychometric research on so-called "personality factors," behavioral medicine has substituted experimental research on the clinical effects of various interventions. Hence, behavioral medicine technology is neither incredible nor demonstrably weak. In turn, behavioral medicine need not suffer the fate of the earlier movement.

The failure of psychosomatic medicine might also be related to its postulates, in terms of which mental processes and states (conscious and unconscious) cause biobehavioral "symptoms." This is so because the mentalistic/dualistic postulates of psychosomatic medicine both justified the emphasis on verbal psychotherapy and forestalled the kinds of behavioral thinking on which clinically relevant therapy-outcome research depends. Hence, dividends might accrue to behavioral medicine from paying systematic attention to "postulates," e.g., as we will attempt in the final subsection here.

There are a great many obvious connections between behavioral medicine and behavior therapy, e.g., workers, treatment modalities, research methodologies, and assumptions. Behavior therapy as a movement began in earnest during the latter half of the 1960s. It preceded behavioral medicine by a decade and passed along more than a few of its own features. Among the characteristics of the early behavior therapy movement was more or less uniform allegiance to behaviorism (especially in the form of neobehavioristic learning theory). During the 1970s, however, behavior therapy lost its behaviorism when cognitive and "cognitive–behavioral" methods were included within the field. The cognitive approaches (e.g., Beck, 1970; Mahoney, 1974; Meichenbaum, 1974) *could* have been formulated within the framework of radical behaviorism (Skinner, 1974) or field behaviorism (see below). But they were not. Rather, they took the form of mentalistic dualism in terms of which thoughts regulated actions. Inevitably, behavioral medicine methods also will become mentalistic to some degree.

Another characteristic of the early behavior therapy movement was a systematic difference between American and British definitions of the field. The core of the former was application of learning theory principles, while the core of the latter was application of clinical experimental methods. This difference was never the source of significant difficulty. There might be an evolving difference between American and European approaches to behavioral medicine also—a difference that could be less benign. Yates (1983) reviewed the contents of three behavioral medicine symposia that appeared in 1982 (*British Journal of Clinical Psychology,* Vol. 21, Part 4; *Journal of Consulting and Clinical Psychology,* Vol. 50, No. 6; *Journal of Psychosomatic Research,* Vol. 26, No. 5). On the basis of his review, Yates criticized American behavioral medicine as too intervention oriented and as overemphasizing biofeedback and behavior therapy. Instead, he favored a seemingly emerging European view in which theoretical explanation also is emphasized in research and intervention modes are far less narrowly represented. Differential emphasis on theory vs intervention oriented research is not necessarily important. However, the content of Yates' specific proposals as well as his would-be structure of European behavioral medicine constitute the beginnings of a formal retreat to psychosomatic postualtes with their attendant pitfalls. As noted, there is a sense of inevitability here.

A third characteristic of the early behavior therapy movement was a frequently overstated case for the power of behavioral methods. The protestantism of the early movement as well as methodological naivete fostered incautious claims. Again during the 1970s, there was a shift such that behavior therapists became more critical of their methodologies (cf. Bernstein & Paul, 1971) and of their claims concerning "specifically active" effects from behavioral interventions (cf. Kazdin & Wilcoxon, 1976). Behavioral medicine does not have a protestant tenor, and it is far less naive methodologically than was behavior therapy in the early days. The long-run interests of behavioral medicine as a scientific–professional field are best served by an informed skepticism erected as a safeguard against poor science and against the credibility and technological efficiency problems that result from poor science. The extreme difficulty of doing scientifically acceptable research in the behavioral medicine arena makes the skeptical posture more—not less—important.

Behavior therapy did not revolutionize psychiatry or even clinical psychology. Rather, it became "school," albeit a powerful one, alongside the traditions of psychodynamic and growth approaches. There is no reason to suppose that behavioral medicine will influence the behavior of physicians any more than behavior therapy affected the behavior of mental health professionals. Professional psychology would be well served by recognizing that, inevitably, future physicians will continue to treat organs and diseases (not persons-in-environments) and they will continue to do so within a speciality framework. Professional psychology can become a major service provider in behavioral medicine and should seek to educate physicians toward appropriate referral practices and to develop integrated, multidisciplinary service delivery modes.

## C.  Field Behaviorism and Interbehavioral "Postulates for Behavioral Medicine"

### 1.  FIELD BEHAVIORISM

The practice of behavioral medicine in the middle 1980s is much more technological than scientific. In part, this reflects the technological character of the behavior modification and biofeedback movements out of which behavioral medicine evolved. Demonstrably effective behavior-change technologies are critical to the survival of behavioral medicine and indeed constitute the single most important goal of workers in the field (Agras, 1982). The clinical yields from behavioral technologies to date have been sufficiently impressive to argue for continuation of a fundamentally technological approach to the field. At the same time, some authorities have pointed to the need for one or more unifying conceptual frameworks to guide the growth of behavioral medicine. The best example here is Schwartz (1980, 1981, 1982) who offers Pepper's (1942) root-metaphor theory to justify systems theory (e.g., Miller, 1978) as an integrative framework.

Schwartz's proposals for conceptual integration are related to his notion of BEHAVIORAL medicine as "the application of systems theory and the integration of all scientific disciplines to medicine" (Schwartz, 1982, p. 1046). These disciplines include physics, chemistry, biology, psychology, anthropology, sociology, etc. Other definitions of behavioral medicine exist, however, and the cogency of Schwartz's integration varies as other definitions are applied. Pomerleau has insisted steadfastly on keeping *psychological behaviorism* as a central feature in clinical behavioral medicine. "*Behavioral medicine* can be defined as . . . the clinical use of techniques derived from the experimental analysis of behavior—behavior therapy and behavior modification—for the evaluation, prevention, management, or treatment of physical disease or physiological dysfunction" (Pomerleau & Brady, 1979, p. xii). Pomerleau (1982) has insisted also that modern psychological behaviorism is not restricted to the quasimechanical connectionism of years past and hence that it has much merit as a central feature of the new movement. Heretofore, however, no one has provided an organized scheme for conceptual integration that is consistent with Pomerleau's "narrow" definition of the behavioral medicine field. We attempt to move in that direction in this final section of the chapter by articulating the perspective of field behaviorism and by offering some related (and tentative) Postulates of Behavioral Medicine. Our purpose is to stimulate additional dialogue concerning varieties of psychological behaviorism and the conceptual superstructure of behavioral medicine.

While rallying to the banners of E. C. Tolman, C. L. Hull, and B. F. Skinner for the past 40 or so years, until recently American behaviorists have more or less ignored the systematic writings of J. R. Kantor (Schoenfeld, 1969;

Verplanck, 1983) who promoted an advanced version of behaviorism we refer to here as field behaviorism. Certainly we cannot do justice to the subtleties of Kantor's thinking in this forum. Nonetheless, in educating ourselves about the field of behavioral medicine over the past several years, we have both been struck by the *potential* of field behaviorism as an organizing schema for the area. Accordingly, we provide a brief narrative about field behaviorism here, then introduce a set of "postulates" (e.g., goals, assumptions, interpretations) that can serve to guide the activities of behavioral medicine workers and, simultaneously, can serve as a safeguard against both the mentalistic postulates of psychosomatic medicine and the peripheral/mechanistic posture of classical behavioral modification.

The "field" concept was first formalized in physics. According to Einstein and Infeld (1938), field concepts gained the right to ascendancy when they proved more powerful than mechanical concepts in the domain of electromagnetic phenomena. The essence of field theory in physics is that the behavior of objects does not rest either on properties inherent within the objects (vitalism) or on monolithic causal forces acting between the objects (mechanism). Rather, the behavior of objects reflects the participation of objects in multifaceted event fields that are continually undergoing change. The mechanical theorist, for example, attempted to describe the activity of two electric charges only with reference to the charges or particles themselves; "it needed great scientific imagination to realize that it is not the charges nor the particles but the field in the space between the charges and the particles which is essential for the description of physical phenomena" (Einstein & Infeld, 1938, p. 259).

Kantor's field behaviorism (or "interbehaviorism") is a serious attempt to state a field concept for psychology that preserves and extends the basic natural science (i.e., nonmentalistic, nondualistic) perspective that is the essence of modern behaviorism. To set the stage for the postulates, we offer statements from Kantor on the field concept for psychology, on dualism/mentalism, and on the notion of mechanistic causality.

On the field concept for psychology:

> For a science such as psychology it is advisable to look upon the field as the entire system of things and conditions operating in any event taken in its available totality. It is only the entire system of factors which will provide proper descriptive and explanatory materials for the handling of events. It is not the reacting organism alone which makes up the event but also the stimulating things and conditions, as well as the setting factors (Kantor, 1969, pp. 370–371).

On dualism/mentalism:

> The entire history of psychology up to recent times represented a series of doctrinal changes closely articulated with its spiritual background. The dualistic construction of organisms maintains itself. Thus we have interactions, parallelisms, and, in the experimental period,

psychophysics. Not until the 20th century has there been any serious protest; then the behaviorist with his roots in biological science, threw away the mental half of the constructs of his predecessors. This we might call an *adjustment* to dualism, not a fresh start. The behaviorist objects to the spiritual factor, but he still treats the organism as the same kind of entity dealt with by the dualists. Certainly he does not succeed in making psychology any more scientific by talking about the brain instead of the "mind" (Kantor, 1959, p. 5).

On mechanistic causality:

The alternative to the causal construction is the *interbehavioral field*. All creative agencies, all powers and forces, are rejected. An event is regarded as a field of factors all of which are equally necessary, or, more properly speaking, equal participants in the event. In fact, events are scientifically described by analyzing these participating factors and finding how they are related (Kantor, 1959, p. 90).

### 2.  SIX POSTULATES OF BEHAVIORAL MEDICINE

As noted, the (tentative) Postulates of Behavioral Medicine reflect thinking like that above. Also as noted, they are offered here as prompts for additional systematic dialogue.

*a.   Field Postulate: The Events of Behavioral Medicine Are Composed of Multifactor Fields.* The specific events that are systematically available to the clinician are the interactions of individuals with objects and events, including other individuals. The event field also comprises factors such as the contextual or setting conditions and the media of stimulation (e.g., light, air) that make interactions possible, including the organic state of the individual. Strictly ruled out of the events of behavioral medicine are psychic states or mental processes, conscious or unconscious. The field postulate is an alternative to mentalism/dualism. Subtle interactions such as thinking, perceiving, feeling, imagining, and reflecting are *not* ignored, however, but are conceptualized in the same way as more prominent actions and are approached differently only insofar as they differ in accessibility.

*b.   Holistic Postulate: The Entire Organism, Not Only Specific Components, Participates in Its Performances.* This postulate follows the organismic conception of biology that the individual's activities involve the whole organism and are not composed of parts (e.g., Goldstein, 1939; Kuo, 1967). Bifurcating the individual into mental–physical *or* brain–behavior is not meaningful. Thus, dualisms are ruled out. There are no pure biological causes of behavior. Physiological and other brands of reductionism are rejected. Instead, biological structures and functions are included in behavioral medicine as participating field factors (Delprato, 1979; Kantor, 1947).

*c.   Evolutional Postulate: Behavioral Medicine Works with Multifactor Fields That Have Evolved and Are Evolving.* The event field that provides the basic subject matter always is the outcome of biosocial evolution and evolution is ongoing. An individual's functioning at a particular period is a wholly naturalistic outcome in a continuous stream of developmental processes. Development is a central working concept. In principle, when an individual's developmental history is described, nothing remains to be explained by reference to "causes," either vitalistic or mechanistic.

*d.   Interdisciplinary Postulate: The Practice of Behavioral Medicine Demands Interdisciplinary Cooperation.* This is a corollary to the Field Postulate. The sciences and professions with specialized expertise vis-à-vis participating field factors are called upon to work in concert. In light of the special nature of the field concept, no discipline or science is more basic a priori than is any other, although particular disciplines receive primary emphasis on specific occasions.

*e.   Tactical Postulate: Clinical Procedures Are Seen as Modifications of Field Factors.* Therapy, management, and prevention in behavioral medicine entail the integrated modification of factors in a multifactor field including, as needed, the biological, social, domestic, economic, educational, and vocational factors participating in the patient's life. These modified factors do not produce one-to-one changes in the patient's problem(s). They do modify the fields in which the patient's problem is a participating factor.

*f.   Goal Postulate: The Goals of Behavioral Medicine Are Alterations in Developmental Trajectories.* This is a corollary to the Evolutional Postulate. Development is a central working concept. The individual's developmental history is evolving continuously and can be used to project directions of future development. When field factors are modified, the developmental stream is altered and new trajectories are established. A general goal of treatment, management, and prevention in behavioral medicine practice is to alter patients' developmental trajectories away from disease/dysfunction to health and well-being.

## VI.   SUMMARY

The chapter begins with a brief history of the behavioral medicine movement along with an overview of contemporary activities in the field. Three subsequent sections review technical innovations in major areas of clinical behavioral medicine: (1) treatment, (2) health care delivery, and (3) preventive health care. The final section describes the methodological characteristics of research in behavioral medicine, discusses the field in light of the psychosomatic medicine and behavior modification movements, and calls for a conceptual integration that is authentically behavioristic.

Already the quality of research in behavioral medicine appears comparable to that of research in behavior therapy. Even so, when viewed in terms of contemporary methodological desiderata, most of the work is fairly unimpressive. Possibly needed are "hybrid" experimental approaches in which the inferential power of intrasubject phase manipulations and between-subject outcome comparisons are combined. There is good reason to believe that behavioral medicine will follow the historical course of behavior therapy/modification, not the course of psychosomatic medicine. Behaviorally knowledgeable psychologists can become major service providers in liaison with well-informed medical practitioners. Some potentially deleterious influences on the behavioral medicine movement are (inevitable) mentalistic and dualistic thinking and a retreat toward psychosomatic medicine. Field behaviorism as an organizing schema can, in principle, serve as a safeguard against such untoward influences.

## ACKNOWLEDGMENTS

This review was greatly facilitated by the kind cooperation of many colleagues who supplied reprints, preprints, and various other forms of assistance. We take this opportunity to express our appreciation to them. D.J.D. gratefully acknowledges the support of his participation in the project by a sabbatical leave from Eastern Michigan University and by the Department of Psychology, Rollins College.

## REFERENCES

Abadi, R. V., Carden, D., & Simpson, J. (1979). Controlling abnormal eye movements. *Vision Research,* **19,** 961–963.

Abadi, R. V., Carden, D., & Simpson, J. (1980). A new technique for congenital nystagmus. *British Journal of Ophthalmology,* **64,** 2–6.

Abrams, D. B., & Follick, M. J. (1983). Behavioral weight-loss intervention at the worksite: Feasibility and maintenance. *Journal of Consulting and Clinical Psychology,* **51,** 226–233.

Abramson, D. I. (1974). *Vascular disorders of the extremities* (2nd ed.). New York: Harper.

Abramson, E. E., & Wunderlich, R. A. (1972). Dental hygiene training for retardates: An application of behavioral techniques. *Mental Retardation,* **10,** 6–8.

Agras, W. S. (1982). Behavioral medicine in the 1980s: Nonrandom connections. *Journal of Consulting and Clinical Psychology,* **50,** 797–803.

Alarcon, R. D., Jenkins, C. S., Heestand, D. E., Scott, L. K., & Cantor, L. (1982). The effectiveness of progressive relaxation in chronic hemodialysis patients. *Journal of Chronic Diseases,* **35,** 797–802.

Alderman, M. H., Schoenbaum, E. E. (1975). Detection and treatment of hypertension at the work site. *New England Journal of Medicine,* **293,** 65–68.

Alling, C. C., & Mahan, P. E. (1985). *Facial pain* (3rd ed.). Philadelphia: Lea & Febiger, in press.

Anderson, K. O., & Masur, F. T. (1983). Psychological preparation for invasive medical and dental procedures. *Journal of Behavioral Medicine, 6,* 1–40.

Atkins, C. J., Kaplan, R. M., Timms, R. M., Reinsch, S., & Lofback, K. (1984). Behavioral exercise programs in the management of chronic obstructive pulmonary disease. *Journal of Consulting and Clinical Psychology, 52,* 591–603.

Azrin, N. H., & Nunn, R. G. (1973). Habit-reversal: A method for eliminating nervous habits and tics. *Behaviour Research and Therapy, 11,* 619–628.

Azrin, N. H., Nunn, R. G., & Frantz-Renshaw, S. E. (1982). Habit-reversal *vs.* negative practice treatment of self-destructive oral habits (biting, chewing or licking of the lips, tongue, or palate). *Journal of Behavior Therapy and Experimental Psychiatry, 13,* 49–54.

Bass, H., Whitcomb, J. F., & Forman, R. (1970). Exercise training for patients with chronic obstructive pulmonary disease. *Chest, 57,* 116–121.

Basso, A., Capitani, E., & Vignolo, L. A. (1979). Influence of rehabilitation on language skills in aphasic patients: A controlled study. *Archives of Neurology, 36,* 190–196.

Bates, W. H. (1920). *The cure of imperfect sight by treatment without glasses.* New York: Central Fixation Co.

Beck, A. T. (1970). Cognitive therapy: Nature and relation to behavior therapy. *Behavior Therapy, 1,* 184–200.

Benson, D. F. (1979). Aphasia rehabilitation. *Archives of Neurology, 36,* 187–189.

Bernstein, D. A., & Paul, G. L. (1971). Some comments on therapy analogue research with small animal "phobias." *Journal of Behavior Therapy and Experimental Psychiatry, 2,* 225–237.

Bernstein, I. L. (1978). Learned taste aversions in children receiving chemotherapy. *Science, 200,* 1302–1303.

Bernstein, I. L., & Bernstein, I. D. (1981). Learned food aversions and cancer anorexia. *Cancer Treatment Reports, 65,* 43–47.

Birk, L. (Ed.) (1973). *Biofeedback: Behavioral medicine.* New York: Grune & Stratton.

Bistrian, B. R. (1978). Clinical use of a protein-sparing modified fast. *Journal of the American Medical Association, 240,* 2299–2302.

Blanchard, E. B. (1982). Behavioral medicine: Past, present, and future. *Journal of Consulting and Clinical Psychology, 50,* 795–796.

Boffa, J., & Kugler, J. F. (1970). Development and testing of a junior high school oral hygiene education program. *Journal of School Health, 40,* 557–560.

Bortner, R. W., & Rosenman, R. H. (1967). The measurement of Pattern A behavior. *Journal of Chronic Diseases, 20,* 525–533.

Boshell, B. R., & Gomez-Perez, F. J. (1974). Diabetes mellitus. In H. F. Conn & R. B. Conn (Eds.), *Current diagnosis—4.* Philadelphia: Saunders.

Brownell, K. D., Kelman, J. H., & Stunkard, A. J. (1983). Treatment of obese children with and without their mothers: Changes in weight and blood pressure. *Pediatrics, 71,* 515–523.

Brownell, K. D., Heckerman, C. L., Westlake, R. J., Hayes, S. C., & Monti, P. N. (1978). The effect of couples training and partner cooperativeness in the behavioral treatment of obesity. *Behaviour Research and Therapy, 16,* 323–333.

Brownell, K. D., & Stunkard, A. J. (1978). Behavioral treatment of obesity in children. *American Journal of Diseases of Children, 132,* 403–412.

Brownell, K. D., Stunkard, A. J., & Albaum, J. M. (1980). Evaluation and modification of exercise patterns in the natural environment. *American Journal of Psychiatry, 137,* 1540–1545.

Bryant, P. (1979). Concept and challenge. In B. Ingersall & W. McCutcheon (Eds.), *Clinical research in behavioral dentistry.* Morgantown, WV: West Virginia Univ. Press.

Campbell, D., & Latimer, P. (1980). Biofeedback in the treatment of urinary retention. *Journal of Behavior Therapy and Experimental Psychiatry, 11,* 27–30.

Carney, R. M., Schechter, K., & Davis, T. (1983). Improving adherence to blood glucose testing in insulin-dependent diabetic children. *Behavior Therapy,* **14,** 247–254.

Casas, J. M., Beemsterboer, P., & Clark, G. T. (1982). A comparison of stress reduction behavioral counseling and contingent nocturnal EMG feedback for the treatment of bruxism. *Behaviour Research and Therapy,* **20,** 9–15.

Celentano, D. D., & Holtzman, D. (1983). Breast self-examination competency: An analysis of self-reported practice and associated characteristics. *American Journal of Public Health,* **73,** 1321–1323.

Christie, D. (1968). Physical training in chronic obstructive lung disease. *British Medical Journal,* **2,** 150–151.

Claerhout, S., & Lutzker, J. R. (1981). Increasing children's self-initiated compliance to dental regimens. *Behavior Therapy,* **12,** 165–176.

Clark, G. T., Beemsterboer, P., & Rugh, J. D. (1981). The treatment of nocturnal bruxism using contingent EMG feedback with an arousal task. *Behaviour Research and Therapy,* **19,** 451–455.

Clayden, J. R., Bell, J. W., & Pollard, P. (1974). Menopausal flushing: Double-blind trial of a non-hormonal medication. *British Medical Journal,* **1,** 409–412.

Coates, T. J., & Thoresen, C. E. (1981). Behavior and weight changes in three obese adolescents. *Behavior Therapy,* **12,** 383–399.

Cohen, D. H., & Obrist, P. A. (1975). Interaction between behavior and the cardiovascular system. *Circulation Research,* **37,** 693–706.

Collins, F. L., Epstein, L. H., & Gil, K. M. (1982a). Behavioral factors in the etiology and treatment of myopia. In M. Hersen, R. M. Eisler, & P. M. Miller (Eds.), *Progress in behavior modification* (Vol. 13). New York: Academic Press.

Collins, F. L., Martin, J. E., & Hillenberg, J. B. (1982b). Assessment of compliance with relaxation instructions: A pilot validation study. *Behavioral Assessment,* **4,** 219–223.

Condor, S. W. (1983). The effects of thermal assisted biofeedback training on vasomotor instability in menopausal women. *Biofeedback and Self-Regulation,* **8,** 323 (Abstract).

Corson, J. A., Grant, J. L., Moulton, D. P., Green, R. L., & Dunkel, P. T. (1979). Use of biofeedback in weaning paralyzed patients from respirators. *Chest,* **76,** 543–545.

Costa, G., & Donaldson, S. S. (1979). Effects of cancer and cancer treatment on the nutrition of the host. *New England Journal of Medicine,* **300,** 1471–1474.

Cox, D. J., & Meyer, R. G. (1978). Behavioral treatment parameters with primary dysmenorrhea. *Journal of Behavioral Medicine,* **1,** 297–310.

Craig, T., & Montague, J. L. (1976). Family oral health survey. *Journal of the American Dental Association,* **92,** 326–332.

Creer, T. L. (1982). Asthma. *Journal of Consulting and Clinical Psychology,* **50,** 912–921.

Cummings, K. M., Becker, M. H., Kirscht, J. P., & Levin, N. W. (1981). Intervention strategies to improve compliance with medical regimens by ambulatory hemodialysis patients. *Journal of Behavioral Medicine,* **4,** 111–127.

Dahlkoetter, J., Callahan, D. J., & Linton, J. (1979). Obesity and the unbalanced energy equation: Exercise *vs.* eating habit change. *Journal of Consulting and Clinical Psychology,* **47,** 898–905.

Davis, D. L., & Ng, L. K. Y. (1981). National policy issues for health promotion and disease prevention. In L. K. Y. Ng & D. L. Davis (Eds.), *Strategies for public health: Promoting health and preventing disease.* Princeton, N.J.: Van Nostrand-Reinhold.

Delprato, D. J. (1979). The interbehavioral alternative to brain-dogma. *Psychological Record,* **29,** 409–418.

Delprato, D. J., & McGlynn, F. D. (1984). Behavioral theories of anxiety disorders. In S. M. Turner (Ed.), *Behavioral theories and treatment of anxiety.* New York: Plenum.

Denney, D. R., & Gerrard, M. (1981). Behavioral treatments of primary dysmenorrhea: A review. *Behaviour Research and Therapy,* **19,** 303–312.

Diller, L., & Gordon, W. A. (1981). Interventions for cognitive deficits in brain-injured adults. *Journal of Consulting and Clinical Psychology*, **49**, 822–834.

Dishman, R. K. (1982). Compliance/adherence in health-related exercise. *Health Psychology*, **1**, 237–267.

Downs, J. B., Klein, E. F., Desautels, D., Modell, J. H., & Kirby, R. R. (1973). Intermittent mandatory ventilation: A new approach to weaning patients from mechanical ventilators. *Chest*, **64**, 331–335.

Drazen, M., Nevid, J. S., Pace, N., & O'Brien, R. M. (1982). Worksite-based behavioral treatment of mild hypertension. *Journal of Occupational Medicine*, **24**, 511–514.

Drossman, D. A., Powell, D. W., & Sessions, J. T. (1977). The irritable bowel syndrome. *Gastroenterology*, **73**, 811–822.

Dubner, R., Sessle, B. J., & Storey, A. T. (1978). *The neural basis of oral and facial function*. New York: Plenum.

Dufault, K. S. (1978). Urinary incontinence: United States and British nursing perspectives. *Journal of Gerontological Nursing*, **4**, 28–33.

Dunlap, K. (1932). *Habits: Their making and unmaking*. New York: Liveright.

Dworkin, B. R. (1982). Instrumental learning for the treatment of disease. *Health Psychology*, **1**, 45–59.

Eastman, B. G., Johnson, S. B., Silverstein, J., Spillar, R. P., & McCallum, M. (1983). Understanding of hypo- and hyperglycemia by youngsters with diabetes and their parents. *Journal of Pediatric Psychology*, **8**, 229–243.

Einstein, A., & Infeld, L. (1938). *The evolution of physics*. New York: Simon & Schuster.

Eisenson, J. (1984). *Adult aphasia* (2nd ed.). New York: Prentice-Hall.

Elliott, C. H., & Olson, R. A. (1982). Variations in conditioning procedures for the decannulation of tracheostomy dependent children. *Health Psychology*, **1**, 389–398.

Epstein, L. H., Beck, S., Figueroa, J., Farkas, G., Kazdin, A. E., Daneman, D., & Becker, D. (1981a). The effects of targeting improvements in urine glucose on metabolic control in children with insulin dependent diabetes. *Journal of Applied Behavior Analysis*, **14**, 365–375.

Epstein, L. H., & Cincirpini, P. M. (1977). Behavioral medicine III: Health care delivery. *Association for Advancement of Behavior Therapy Newsletter*, **4**, 7–9, 27.

Epstein, L. H., & Cluss, P. A. (1982). A behavioral medicine perspective on adherence to long-term medical regimens. *Journal of Consulting and Clinical Psychology*, **50**, 950–971.

Epstein, L. H., Figueroa, J., Farkas, G. M., & Beck, S. (1981b). The short-term effects of feedback on accuracy of urine glucose determinations in insulin dependent diabetic children. *Behavior Therapy*, **12**, 560–564.

Epstein, L. H., Katz, R. C., & Zlutnick, S. (1979). Behavioral medicine. In M. Hersen, R. M. Eisler, & P. M. Miller (Eds.), *Progress in behavior modification* (Vol. 7). New York: Academic Press.

Epstein, L. H., & Martin, J. E. (1977). Behavioral medicine. *Association for Advancement of Behavior Therapy Newsletter*, **4**, 5–6.

Epstein, L. H., & Masek, B. J. (1978). Behavioral control of medicine compliance. *Journal of Applied Behavior Analysis*, **11**, 1–10.

Epstein, L. H., & Ossip, D. (1979). Health care delivery. In J. R. McNamara (Ed.), *Behavioral medicine*. New York: Plenum.

Fairburn, C. (1981). A cognitive behavioural approach to the treatment of bulimia. *Psychological Medicine*, **11**, 707–711.

Fernando, C. K., & Basmajian, J. V. (1978). Biofeedback in physical medicine and rehabilitation. *Biofeedback and Self-Regulation*, **3**, 435–455.

Ferster, C. B., Nurnberger, J. I., & Levitt, E. B. (1962). The control of eating. *Journal of Mathetics*, **1**, 87–109.

Figar, S. (1965). Conditional circulatory responses in men and animals. In W. F. Hamilton & P.

Dow (Eds.), *Handbook of physiology: Circulation* (Vol. 3). Washington, D.C.: American Physiological Society.

Fine, T.H., & Turner, J. W. (1982). The effect of brief restricted environmental stimulation therapy in the treatment of essential hypertension. *Behaviour Research and Therapy, 20,* 567–570.

Fisher, B., Slack, N. H., & Bross, I. D. J. (1969). Cancer of the breast: Size of neoplasm and prognosis. *Cancer, 24,* 1071–1080.

Fishman, D. B., & Petty, T. L. (1971). Physical, symptomatic and psychological improvement in patients receiving comprehensive care for chronic airway obstruction. *Journal of Chronic Diseases, 24,* 775–785.

Flom, M. C., Kirschen, D. G., & Bedell, H. E. (1980). Control of unsteady eccentric fixation in amblyopic eyes by auditory feedback of eye position. *Investigative Ophthalmology and Visual Sciences, 19,* 1371–1381.

Follick, M. J., Abrams, D. B., Pinto, R. P., & Fowler, J. L. (1984a). Health promotion in industrial and organizational settings. In G. Stone, S. S. Weiss, J. D. Matarazzo, N. E. Miller, J. Rodin, G. E. Schwartz, C. Belar, M. J. Follick, & J. Singer (Eds.), *Health psychology: A discipline and a profession.* Chicago: Univ. of Chicago Press.

Follick, M. J., Fowler, J. L., & Brown, R. A. (1984b). Attrition in worksite weight-loss interventions: The effects of an incentive procedure. *Journal of Consulting and Clinical Psychology, 52,* 139–140.

Fox, R., Rotatori, A. F., & Burkhart, J. E. (1983). Obesity in mentally retarded and nonretarded populations: Assessment issues. *Advances in Mental Retardation and Developmental Disabilities, 1,* 125–175.

Fox, R., Switzky, H., Rotatori, A. F., & Vitkus, P. (1982). Successful weight loss techniques with mentally retarded children and youth. *Exceptional Children, 49,* 238–244.

Freedman, R. R., Ianni, P., & Wenig, P. (1983). Behavioral treatment of Raynaud's disease. *Journal of Consulting and Clinical Psychology, 51,* 539–549.

Freeman, J. M. (1974). Neural tube defects: Risks of occurrence and recurrence. In J. M. Freeman (Ed.), *Practical management of myelomeningocele.* Baltimore: Univ. Park Press.

Freund, A. M. (1983). *The relationship between blood glucose and symptomatology in insulin-dependent adolescents.* Unpublished masters thesis, University of Florida.

Fremouw, W. J., & Zitter, R. E. (1980). Individual and couple behavioral contracting for weight reduction and maintenance. *Behavior Therapist, 3,* 15–16.

Friedman, M., Rosenman, R. H. (1974). *Type A behavior and your heart.* New York: Knopf.

Garfield, E. (1982). Patient compliance: A multifaceted problem with no easy solution. *Current Contents, 10,* 5–14.

Gianutsos, R. (1980). What is cognitive rehabilitation? *Journal of Rehabilitation, 46,* 37–40.

Gianutsos, R., & Gianutsos, J. (1979). Rehabilitating the verbal recall of brain-injured patients by mnemonic training: An experimental demonstration using single-case methodology. *Journal of Clinical Neuropsychology, 1,* 117–135.

Gianutsos, R., Glosser, D., Elbaum, J., & Vroman, G. M. (1983). Visual imperception in brain-injured adults: Multifaceted measures. *Archives of Physical Medicine and Rehabilitation, 64,* 456–461.

Gilbert, B. O., Johnson, S. B., Spillar, R., McCallum, M., Silverstein, J. H., & Rosenbloom, A. (1982). The effects of a peer-modeling film on children's learning to self-inject insulin. *Behavior Therapy, 13,* 186–193.

Glasgow, R. E., Klesges, R. C., Godding, P. R., Vasey, M. W., & O'Neill, H. K. (1984). Evaluation of a worksite-controlled smoking program. *Journal of Consulting and Clinical Psychology, 52,* 137–138.

Goldfried, M. R. (1971). Systematic desensitization as training in self-control. *Journal of Consulting and Clinical Psychology, 37,* 228–234.

Goldfried, M. R., Decenteceo, E. T., & Weinberg, L. (1974). Systematic rational restructuring as a self-control technique. *Behavior Therapy, 5,* 247–254.

Goldstein, K. (1939). *The organism.* New York: American Book Co.

Haagensen, C. D. (1971). *Diseases of the breast* (2nd ed.). Philadelphia: Saunders.

Hailey, B. J., & White, J. G. (1983). Systematic desensitization for anticipatory nausea associated with chemotherapy. *Psychosomatics, 24,* 287–289.

Hall, D. C., Adams, C. K., Stein, G. H., Stephenson, H. S., Goldstein, M. K., & Pennypacker, H. S. (1980). Improved detection of human breast lesions following experimental training. *Cancer, 46,* 408–414.

Hamberger, L. K. (1982). Reduction of generalized aversive responding in a post-treatment cancer patient: Relaxation as an active coping skill. *Journal of Behavior Therapy and Experimental Psychiatry, 13,* 229–233.

Haynes, R. B., Taylor, D. W., & Sackett, D. L. (Eds.) (1979). *Compliance in health care.* Baltimore: Johns Hopkins Press.

Heller, R. F., & Forgione, A. G. (1975). An evaluation of bruxism control: Massed negative practice and automated relaxation training. *Journal of Dental Research, 54,* 1120–1123.

Helm-Estabrooks, N., Fitzpatrick, P. M., & Barresi, B. (1982). Visual action therapy for global aphasia. *Journal of Speech and Hearing Disorders, 47,* 385–389.

Hilton, L., & Kraetschmer, K. (1983). International trends in aphasia rehabilitation. *Archives of Physical Medicine and Rehabilitation, 64,* 462–467.

Hodgkin, J. E., Balchum, O. J., Kass, I., Glaser, E. M., Miller, W. F., Haas, A., Shaw, D. B., Kimbel, P., & Petty, T. L. (1975). Chronic obstructive airway diseases: Current concepts in diagnosis and comprehensive care. *Journal of the American Medical Association, 232,* 1243–1260.

Hoelscher, T. J., Lichstein, K. L., & Rosenthal, T. L. (1984). Objective vs subjective assessment of relaxation compliance among anxious individuals. *Behaviour Research and Therapy, 22,* 187–193.

Holliday, J. E. (1984). Biofeedback. In J. A. O'Ryan (Ed.), *Pulmonary rehabilitation: From hospital to home.* Chicago: Yearbook Publishers.

Holmes, N., Ardito, E. A., Stevenson, D. W., & Lucas, C. P. (1984). Maintenance of weight loss in a heavily overweight population. In J. Storlie & H. A. Jordon (Eds.), *Behavioral management of obesity.* New York: Spectrum.

Holtzman, D., & Celentano, D. D. (1983). The practice and efficacy of breast self-examination: A critical review. *American Journal of Public Health, 73,* 1324–1326.

Horner, R. D., & Keilitz, I. (1975). Training mentally retarded adolescents to brush their teeth. *Journal of Applied Behavior Analysis, 8,* 301–309.

Horton, A. M. (1979). Behavioral neuropsychology: Rationale and research. *Clinical Neuropsychology, 1,* 20–23.

Horton, A. M. (1982). Behavioral neuropsychology: A brief rationale. *The Behavior Therapist, 5,* 100–102.

Horton, A. M. (1984). Use of the turtle technique with a brain-injured male: A case study. *The Behavior Therapist, 7,* 18, 34.

Jackson, D. D., & Yalom, I. (1966). Family research on the problem of ulcerative colitis. *Archives of General Psychiatry, 15,* 410–418.

Jacobson, E. (1938). *Progressive relaxation.* Chicago: Univ. of Chicago Press.

Jobe, J., Sampson, J., Roberts, D., & Beetham, W. (1982). Induced vasodilation as treatment for Raynaud's disease. *Annals of Internal Medicine, 97,* 706–709.

Johnson, S. B. (1980). Psychosocial factors in juvenile diabetes: A review. *Journal of Behavioral Medicine, 3,* 95–116.

Johnson, S. B., Pollak, T., Silverstein, J. H., Rosenbloom, A. L., Spillar, R., McCallum, M., &

Harkavy, J. (1982). Cognitive and behavioral knowledge about insulin-dependent diabetes among children and parents. *Pediatrics, 69,* 708–713.

Jones, H. G. (1956). The application of conditioning and learning techniques to the treatment of a psychiatric patient. *Journal of Abnormal and Social Psychology, 52,* 414–419.

Kane, W. J. (1977). Scoliosis prevalence: A call for a statement of terms. *Clinical Orthopedics, 126,* 43–46.

Kantor, J. R. (1947). *Problems of physiological psychology.* Granville, OH: Principia Press.

Kantor, J. R. (1959). *Interbehavioral psychology.* Granville, OH: Principia Press.

Kantor, J. R. (1969). *The scientific evolution of psychology* (Vol. 2). Chicago, IL: Principia Press.

Kaplan, R. M., Metzger, G., & Jablecki, C. (1983). Brief cognitive and relaxation training increases tolerance for a painful electromyographic examination. *Psychosomatic Medicine, 45,* 155–162.

Katahn, M., Pleas, J., Thackrey, M., & Wallston, K. A. (1982). Relationship of eating and activity self-reports to follow-up weight maintenance in the massively obese. *Behavior Therapy, 13,* 521–528.

Kazdin, A. E. (1982). Single-case experimental designs. In P. C. Kendall & J. N. Butcher (Eds.), *Handbook of research methods in clinical psychology.* New York: Wiley.

Kazdin, A. E., & Wilcoxon, L. A. (1976). Systematic desensitization and nonspecific treatment effects: A methodological evaluation. *Psychological Bulletin, 83,* 729–758.

Keane, T. M., Prue, D. M., & Collins, F. L. (1981). Behavioral contracting to improve dietary compliance in chronic renal dialysis patients. *Journal of Behavior Therapy and Experimental Psychiatry, 12,* 63–67.

Keefe, F. J., & Surwit, R. S. (1978). Electromyographic biofeedback: Behavioral treatment of neuromuscular disorders. *Journal of Behavioral Medicine, 1,* 13–24.

Keefe, F. J., Surwit, R. S., & Pilon, R. N. (1980). Biofeedback autogenic training and progressive relaxation in the treatment of Raynaud's disease: A comparative study. *Journal of Applied Behavior Analysis, 13,* 3–11.

Kendall, P. C., Williams, L., Pechacek, T. F., Graham, L. E., Shisslak, C., & Herzoff, N. (1979). Cognitive-behavioral and patient education interventions in cardiac catheterization procedures: The Palo Alto medical psychology project. *Journal of Consulting and Clinical Psychology, 47,* 49–58.

King, N. J. (1980). The behavioral management of asthma and asthma-related problems in children: A critical review of the literature. *Journal of Behavioral Medicine, 3,* 169–189.

Kleinknecht, R. A., Klepac, R. K., & Bernstein, D. A. (1976). Psychology and dentistry: Potential benefits from a health-care liason. *Professional Psychology, 7,* 585–592.

Koheil, R., Reg, P. T., & Mandel, A. R. (1980). Joint position biofeedback facilitation of physical therapy in gait training. *American Journal of Physical Medicine, 59,* 288–297.

Kotses, H., & Glaus, K. D. (1981). Applications of biofeedback to the treatment of asthma: A critical review. *Biofeedback and Self-Regulation, 6,* 573–593.

Kristeller, J. L., Schwartz, G. E., & Black, H. (1982). The use of restricted environmental therapy (REST) in the treatment of essential hypertension: Two case studies. *Behaviour Research and Therapy, 20,* 561–566.

Kuo, Z. Y. (1967). *The dynamics of behavior development: An epigenetic view.* New York: Random House.

Labbe, E. L., & Williamson, D. A. (1985). *Treatment of childhood migraine using autogenic feedback training.* Submitted.

Laszlo, J., Lucas, V. S., & Pharm, B. S. (1981). Emesis as a critical problem in chemotherapy. *New England Journal of Medicine, 305,* 948–949.

Lattal, K. A. (1969). Contingency management of toothbrushing behavior in a summer camp for children. *Journal of Applied Behavior Analysis, 2,* 195–198.

Leitenberg, H., Gross, J., Peterson, J., & Rosen, J. C. (1984). Analysis of an anxiety model and the process of change during exposure plus response prevention treatment of bulimia nervosa. *Behavior Therapy*, **15**, 3–20.

Levenkron, J. C., Fisher, E. B., Cohen, J. D., & Mueller, H. S. (1983). Modifying the Type A coronary-prone behavior pattern. *Journal of Consulting and Clinical Psychology*, **51**, 192–204.

Lewinsohn, P. M., Danaher, B. G., & Kikel, S. (1977a). Visual imagery as a mnemonic aid for brain-injured persons. *Journal of Consulting and Clinical Psychology*, **45**, 717–723.

Lewinsohn, P. M., Glasgow, R. E., Barrera, M., Danaher, B. G., Alperson, J., McCarty, D. L., Sullivan, J. M., Zeiss, R. A., Nyland, J., & Rodrigues, M. R. P. (1977b). Assessment and treatment of patients with memory deficits: Initial studies. *JSAS Catalog of Selected Documents in Psychology*, **7**, 79 (Ms. No. 1538).

Libo, L. M., Arnold, G. E., Woodside, J. R., & Borden, T. A. (1983). EMG biofeedback for functional bladder-sphincter dyssynergia: A case study. *Biofeedback and Self-Regulation*, **8**, 243–253.

Luepker, R. V., Johnson, C. A., Murray, D. M., & Pechacek, T. F. (1983). Prevention of cigarette smoking: Three-year follow-up of an education program for youth. *Journal of Behavioral Medicine*, **6**, 53–62.

Lund, A. K., & Kegeles, S. S. (1979). Partial reward schedules and self-management techniques in children's preventive dental programs. In B. Ingersoll & W. McCutcheon (Eds.), *Clinical research in behavioral dentistry*. Morgantown, WV: West Virginia Univ. Press.

Lyles, J. N., Burish, T. G., Krozely, M. G., & Oldham, R. K. (1982). Efficacy of relaxation training and guided imagery in reducing the aversiveness of cancer chemotherapy. *Journal of Consulting and Clinical Psychology*, **50**, 509–524.

Maccoby, N., Farquhar, J. W., Wood, P. D., & Alexander, J. (1977). Reducing the risk of cardiovascular disease: Effects of a community-based campaign on knowledge and behavior. *Journal of Community Health*, **3**, 100–114.

McGlynn, F. D., Cassisi, J. E., & Diamond, E. L. (1985). Diagnosis and treatment of bruxism: A behavioral dentistry perspective. In R. J. Daitzman (Ed.), *Diagnosis and intervention in behavior therapy and behavioral medicine* (Vol. 2). New York: Springer.

MacKeen, P. C., Franklin, B. A., Nicholas, W. C., & Berskirk, E. R. (1983). Body composition, physical work capacity, and physical activity habits at 18 month follow-up of middle-aged women participating in an exercise intervention program. *International Journal of Obesity*, **7**, 61–71.

Mahoney, M. J. (1974). *Cognition and behavior modification*. Cambridge, MA: Ballinger.

Maizels, M., King, L. R., & Firlit, C. F. (1979). Urodynamic biofeedback: A new approach to treat vesical sphincter dyssynergia. *Journal of Urology*, **122**, 205–209.

Malec, J., & Questad, K. (1983). Rehabilitation of memory after craniocerebral trauma: Case report. *Archives of Physical Medicine and Rehabilitation*, **64**, 436–438.

Management of the irritable bowel. (1978). *Lancet*, **2**, 557–558.

Marsden, C. D. (1978). Extrapyramidal disorders. In R. B. Scott (Ed.), *Price's textbook of the practice of medicine* (12th ed.). London and New York: Oxford Univ. Press.

Marshall, H. C., & Gregory, R. T. (1974). Cold hypersensitivity: A simple method for its reduction. *Archives of Physical Medicine and Rehabilitation*, **55**, 119–123.

Martens, L. V., Frazier, P. J., Hirt, U. J., Maskin, L. H., & Prosheck, J. (1973). Developing brushing performance in second graders through behavior modification. *Health Services Report*, **88**, 818–823.

Martin, J. E., Collins, F. L., Hillenberg, J. B., Zabin, M. A., & Katell, A. D. (1981). Assessing compliance to home relaxation: A simple technology for a critical problem. *Journal of Behavioral Assessment*, **3**, 193–197.

Mason, A. S., & Boucher, B. J. (1978). Diabetes mellitus. In R. B. Scott (Ed.), *Price's textbook of the practice of medicine* (12th ed.). London and New York: Oxford Univ. Press.

Meichenbaum, D. H. (1974). *Cognitive behavior modification*. Morristown, NJ: General Learning Press.

Melamed, B. G. (1979). Behavioral approaches to fear in dental settings. In M. Hersen, R. M. Eisler, & P. M. Miller (Eds.), *Progress in behavior modification* (Vol. 7). New York: Academic Press.

Melamed, B. G., & Bennett, C. G. (1985). Behavioral dentistry. In L. J. Siegel & C. Twentyman (Eds.), *Prevention and treatment in behavioral medicine*. New York: Springer, in press.

Melamed, B. G., & Siegel, L. J. (1975). Reduction of anxiety in children facing hospitalization and surgery by use of filmed modeling. *Journal of Consulting and Clinical Psychology, 43,* 511–521.

Meyer, A. J., Nash, J. D., McAlister, A. L., Maccoby, N., & Farquhar, J. W. (1980). Skills training in a cardiovascular health education campaign. *Journal of Consulting and Clinical Psychology, 48,* 129–142.

Milgram, N. W., Krames, L., & Alloway, T. M. (Eds.). (1977). *Food aversion learning*. New York: Plenum.

Miller, E. (1980). Psychological intervention in the management and rehabilitation of neuropsychological impairments. *Behaviour Research and Therapy, 18,* 527–535.

Miller, J. G. (1978). *Living systems*. New York: McGraw-Hill.

Mizes, J. S., & Lohr, J. M. (1983). The treatment of bulimia (binge-eating and self-induced vomiting)—A quasi-experimental investigation of the effects of stimulus narrowing, self-reinforcement and self-control relaxation. *International Journal of Eating Disorders, 2,* 59–65.

Morrow, G. R., & Morrell, C. (1982). Behavioral treatment for the anticipatory nausea and vomiting induced by cancer chemotherapy. *New England Journal of Medicine, 307,* 1476–1480.

Mowrer, O. H., & Mowrer, W. M. (1938). Enuresis—A method for its study and treatment. *American Journal of Orthopsychiatry, 8,* 436–459.

Moyer, J. H. (1975). Hypertension: National significance, general principles of management, and choice of drugs. In H. I. Russek (Ed.), *New horizons in cardiovascular practice*. Baltimore: Univ. Park Press.

Nesse, R. M., Carli, T., Curtis, G. C., & Kleinman, P. D. (1980). Pretreatment nausea in cancer chemotherapy: A conditioned response? *Psychosomatic Medicine, 42,* 33–36.

Page, R. C. (1978). Behavioral research in dentistry: The promise of clinically relevant findings. In P. Weinstein (Ed.), *Advances in behavioral research in dentistry*. Seattle: Univ. of Washington Press.

Parkinson, R. S., & Associates (Eds.) (1982). *Managing health promotion in the work place*. Palo Alto, CA: Mayfield Publishing.

Paul, G. L. (1965). *Insight vs. desensitization in psychotherapy: An experiment in anxiety reduction*. Stanford, CA: Stanford Univ. Press,

Peck, D. F. (1977). The use of EMG feedback in the treatment of a severe case of blepharospasm. *Biofeedback and Self-Regulation, 2,* 273–277.

Peck, C., & King, N. J. (1982). Increasing patient compliance with prescriptions. *Journal of the American Medical Association, 248,* 2874–2877.

Pennebaker, J. W., Cox, D. J., Gonder-Frederick, L., Wunsch, M. G., Evans, W. S., & Pohl, S. (1981). Physical symptoms related to blood glucose in insulin-dependent diabetics. *Psychosomatic Medicine, 43,* 489–500.

Pennypacker, H. S., Bloom, H. S., Criswell, E. L., Neelakantan, P., Goldstein, M. K., & Stein, G. H. (1982). Toward an effective technology of instruction in breast self-examination. *International Journal of Mental Health, 11,* 98–116.

Penta, J. S., Poster, D. S., Bruno, S., & Macdonald, J. S. (1981). Clinical trials with antiemetic agents in cancer patients receiving chemotherapy. *Journal of Clinical Pharmacology, 21,* 11S–22S.

Pepper, S. C. (1942). *World hypotheses*. Berkeley, CA: Univ. of California Press.

Perry, C. L., Maccoby, N., & McAlister, A. L. (1980). Adolescent smoking prevention: A third-year follow-up. *World Smoking and Health*, **5**, 40–45.

Peters, R. K., Benson, H., & Peters, J. M. (1977a). Daily relaxation response breaks in a working population: II. Effects on blood pressure. *American Journal of Public Health*, **67**, 954–959.

Peters, R. K., Benson, H., & Porter, D. (1977b). Daily relaxation response breaks in a working population: I. Effects on self-reported measures of health, performance, and well-being. *American Journal of Public Health*, **67**, 946–953.

Pinkerton, S. S., Hughes, H., & Wenrich, W. W. (1982). *Behavioral medicine: Clinical applications*. New York: Wiley.

Pollack, R. T., & Johnson, S. B. (1979). *Administration and scoring manual for the test of diabetes knowledge*. Gainesville, FL: Johnson.

Pomerleau, O. F. (1982). A discourse on behavioral medicine: Current status and future trends. *Journal of Consulting and Clinical Psychology*, **50**, 1030–1039.

Pomerleau, O. F., & Brady, J. P. (Eds.) (1979). *Behavioral medicine: Theory and practice*. Baltimore: Williams & Wilkins.

Porch, B. E. (1967). *Porch index of communication ability*. Palo Alto, CA: Consulting Psychologists Press.

Quillen, M. A., & Denney, D. R. (1982). Self-control of dysmenorrheic symptoms through pain management training. *Journal of Behavior Therapy and Experimental Psychiatry*, **13**, 123–130.

Ramfjord, S. P., & Ash, M. M. (1983). *Occlusion* (3rd ed.). Philadelphia: Saunders.

Redd, W. H., & Andresen, G. V. (1981). Conditioned aversion in cancer patients. *The Behavior Therapist*, **4**, 3–4.

Reiss, M. L., Piotrowski, W. D., & Bailey, J. S. (1976). Behavioral community psychology: Encouraging low-income parents to seek dental care for their children. *Journal of Applied Behavior Analysis*, **9**, 387–397.

Review Panel on Coronary-Prone Behavior and Coronary Heart Disease. (1981). Coronary-prone behavior and coronary heart disease: A critical review. *Circulation*, **63**, 1199–1215.

Rice, J. M., & Lutzker, J. R. (1984). Reducing noncompliance to follow-up appointment-keeping at a family practice center. *Journal of Applied Behavior Analysis*, **17**, 303–311.

Rose, M. I., & Firestone, P. (1983). Behavioral interventions in juvenile diabetes mellitus. In P. Firestone, P. J. McGrath, & W. Feldman (Eds.), *Advances in behavioral medicine for children and adolescents*. Hillsdale, NJ: Erlbaum.

Rose, M. I., Firestone, P., Heick, H. M. C., & Faught, A. K. (1983). The effects of anxiety management training on the control of juvenile diabetes mellitus. *Journal of Behavioral Medicine*, **6**, 381–395.

Rosen, J. C., & Leitenberg, H. (1982). Bulimia nervosa: Treatment with exposure and response prevention. *Behavior Therapy*, **13**, 117–124.

Rosen, J. C., & Leitenberg, H. (1984). Exposure plus response prevention treatment of bulimia nervosa. In D. M. Garner & P. E. Garfinkel (Eds.), *A handbook of psychotherapy for anorexia nervosa and bulimia*. New York: Guilford Press.

Rosen, R. C., Schiffman, H. R., & Cohen, A. S. (1984). Behavior modification and the treatment of myopia. *Behavior Modification*, **8**, 131–154.

Rosenthal, B., Allen, G. J., & Winter, C. (1980). Husband involvement in the behavioral treatment of overweight women: Initial effects and long-term follow-up. *International Journal of Obesity*, **4**, 165–173.

Roskies, E., Spevack, M., Surkis, A., Cohen, C., & Gilman, S. (1978). Changing the coronary-prone (Type A) behavior pattern in a nonclinical population. *Journal of Behavioral Medicine*, **1**, 201–216.

Rotberg, M. H. (1983). Biofeedback for ophthalmologic disorders. *Survey of Ophthalmology*, **27**, 381–386.

Rotberg, M. H., & Surwit, R. S. (1981). Biofeedback techniques in the treatment of visual and ophthalmologic disorders. *Biofeedback and Self-Regulation*, **6**, 375–388.

Ruchlin, H. S., Melcher, L. A., & Alderman, M. H. (1984). A comparative economic analysis of work-related hypertension care programs. *Journal of Occupational Medicine*, **26**, 45–49.

Sachs, R. H., Eigenbrode, C. R., & Kruper, D. C. (1979). Psychology and dentistry: Potential benefits from a health care liaison. *Professional Psychology*, **10**, 521–528.

Satz, P., & Fletcher, J. M. (1981). Emergent trends in neuropsychology: An overview. *Journal of Consulting and Clinical Psychology*, **49**, 851–865.

Scharer, P. (1974). Bruxism. In Y. Kawamura (Ed.), *Frontiers of oral physiology: Physiology of mastication* (Vol. 1). Basel: Karger.

Schnelle, J. F., Traughber, B., Morgan, D. B., Embry, J. E., Binion, A. F., & Coleman, A. (1983). Management of geriatric incontinence in nursing homes. *Journal of Applied Behavior Analysis*, **16**, 234–241.

Schoenfeld, W. N. (1969). J. R. Kantor's *Objective psychology of grammar* and *Psychology and logic:* A retrospective appreciation. *Journal of the Experimental Analysis of Behavior*, **12**, 329–347.

Schwartz, G. E. (1980). Behavioral medicine and systems theory: A new synthesis. *National Forum*, **4**, 25–30.

Schwartz, G. E. (1981). A systems analysis of psychobiology and behavior therapy: Implications for behavioral medicine. *Psychotherapy and Psychosomatics*, **36**, 159–184.

Schwartz, G. E. (1982). Testing the biopsychosocial model: The ultimate challenge facing behavioral medicine? *Journal of Consulting and Clinical Psychology*, **50**, 1040–1053.

Schwartz, G. E., & Weiss, S. M. (1978). Yale conference on behavioral medicine: A proposed definition and statement of goals. *Journal of Behavioral Medicine*, **1**, 3–12.

Scott, R. R., Denier, C. A., & Prue, D. M. (1983). *Worksite smoking intervention with health professionals.* Paper presented at the meeting of the Association for Advancement of Behavior Therapy, Washington, DC, December.

Seeburg, K. N., & DeBoer, K. F. (1980). Effects of EMG biofeedback on diabetes. *Biofeedback and Self-Regulation*, **5**, 289–293.

Seer, P. (1979). Psychological control of essential hypertension: Review of the literature and methodological critique. *Psychological Bulletin*, **86**, 1015–1043.

Sexton, M. M. (1979). Behavioral epidemiology. In O. F. Pomerleau & J. P. Brady (Eds.), *Behavioral medicine: Theory and practice*. Baltimore: Williams & Wilkins.

Shapiro, A. P., Schwartz, G. E., Ferguson, D. C., Redmond, D. P., & Weiss, S. M. (1977). Behavioral methods in the treatment of hypertension. I. Review of their clinical status. *Annals of Internal Medicine*, **86**, 626–636.

Sheley, J. F. (1983). Inadequate transfer of breast cancer self-detection technology. *American Journal of Public Health*, **73**, 1318–1320.

Shepard, D. S., & Moseley, T. A. E. (1976). Mailed versus telephoned appointment reminders to reduce broken appointments in a hospital outpatient department. *Medical Care*, **14**, 268–273.

Sivak, M., Hill, C. S., Henson, D. L., Butler, B. P., Silber, S. M., & Olson, P. L. (1984). Improved driving performance following perceptual training in persons with brain damage. *Archives of Physical Medicine and Rehabilitation*, **65**, 163–167.

Skinner, B. F. (1974). *About behaviorism*. New York: Knopf.

Solberg, W. K., & Rugh, J. D. (1972). The use of bio-feedback devices in the treatment of bruxism. *Journal, Southern California Dental Association*, **40**, 852–853.

Stachnik, T., & Stoffelmayr, B. (1983). Worksite smoking cessation programs: A potential for national impact. *American Journal of Public Health*, **73**, 1395–1396.

Stalonas, P. M., Johnson, W. G., & Christ, M. (1978). Behavior modification for obesity: The evaluation of exercise, contingency management, and program adherence. *Journal of Consulting and Clinical Psychology*, **46**, 463–469.

Stamler, J. (1979). Research relating to risk factors. *Circulation*, **60**, 1575–1587.

Stevenson, D. W., & Delprato, D. J. (1983). Multiple component self-control program for menopausal hot flashes. *Journal of Behavior Therapy and Experimental Psychiatry*, **14**, 137–140.

Stevenson, D. W., Lucas, C. P., Holmes, N., & Ardito, E. A. (1984). Protein-sparing modified fasting and behavior therapy. In J. Storlie & H. A. Jordan (Eds.), *Nutrition and exercise in obesity management*. New York: Spectrum.

Stunkard, A. J. (1979). Behavioral medicine and beyond: The example of obesity. In O. F. Pomerleau & J. P. Brady (Eds.), *Behavior medicine: Theory and practice*. Baltimore: Williams & Wilkins.

Stunkard, A. J. (1981). The practice of health promotion: The case of obesity. In L. K. Y. Ng & D. L. Davis (Eds.), *Strategies for public health: Promoting health and preventing disease*. Princeton, N.J.: Van Nostrand Reinhold.

Stunkard, A. J., & Brownell, K. D. (1980). Worksite treatment for obesity. *American Journal of Psychiatry*, **137**, 252–253.

Suedfeld, P., & Kristeller, J. L. (1982). Stimulus reduction as a technique in health psychology. *Health Psychology*, **1**, 337–357.

Suedfeld, P., Roy, C., & Landon, P. B. (1982). Restricted environmental stimulation therapy in the treatment of essential hypertension. *Behaviour Research and Therapy*, **20**, 553–559.

Suinn, R. (1975). Anxiety management training for general anxiety. In R. Suinn & R. Weigel (Eds.), *The innovative psychological therapies*. New York: Harper.

Suinn, R., & Bloom, L. J. (1978). Anxiety management training for pattern A behavior. *Journal of Behavioral Medicine*, **1**, 25–35.

Surwit, R. S., & Feinglos, M. N. (1983). The effects of relaxation on glucose tolerance in non-insulin-dependent diabetes. *Diabetes Care*, **6**, 176–179.

Surwit, R. S., Pilon, R. N., & Fenton, C. H. (1978). Behavioral treatment of Raynaud's disease. *Journal of Behavioral Medicine*, **1**, 323–335.

Thoresen, C. E., Friedman, M., Gill, J. K., & Ulmer, D. K. (1982). The recurrent coronary prevention project: Some preliminary findings. *Acta Medica Scandinavica*, **660**, 172–192.

Verplanck, W. S. (1983). Preface. In N. W. Smith, P. T. Mountjoy, & D. H. Ruben (Eds.), *Reassessment in psychology: The interbehavioral alternative*. Washington, DC: Univ. Press of America.

Vertes, V., Genuth, S. M., & Hazelton, I. M. (1977). Supplemented fasting as a large-scale outpatient program. *Journal of the American Medical Association*, **238**, 2151–2153.

Vickers, Z. M., Nielsen, S. S., & Theologides, A. (1981). Odor aversions in cancer patients. *Minnesota Medicine*, **64**, 277–279.

Vignolo, L. A. (1964). Evolution of aphasia and language rehabilitation: A retrospective exploratory study. *Cortex*, **1**, 344–367.

Wadden, T. A., Stunkard, A. J., & Brownell, K. D. (1983). Very low calorie diets: Their efficacy, safety, and future. *Annals of Internal Medicine*, **99**, 675–684.

Warwick, M., & Garrow, J. S. (1981). The effect of addition of exercise to a regime of dietary restriction on weight loss, nitrogen balance, resting metabolic rate and spontaneous physical activity in three obese women in a metabolic ward. *International Journal of Obesity*, **5**, 25–32.

Webster, J. S., Jones, S., Blanton, P., Gross, R., Beissel, G. F., & Wofford, J. D. (1984). Visual scanning training with stroke patients. *Behavior Therapy*, **15**, 129–143.

Webster, J. S., & Scott, R. R. (1983). The effects of self-instructional training on attentional deficits following head injury. *Clinical Neuropsychology*, **5**, 69–74.

Weinberg, J., Diller, L., Gordon, W. A., Gerstman, L. J., Lieberman, A., Lakin, P., Hodges, G., & Ezrachi, O. (1977). Visual scanning training effect on reading-related tasks in acquired right brain damage. *Archives of Physical Medicine and Rehabilitation*, **58**, 479–486.

Weinberg, J., Diller, L., Gordon, W. A., Gerstman, L. J., Lieberman, A., Lakin, P., Hodges, G.,

& Ezrachi, O. (1979). Training sensory awareness and spatial organization in people with right brain damage. *Archives of Physical Medicine and Rehabilitation,* **60,** 491–496.

Weiss, A. R. (1977). A behavioral approach to the treatment of adolescent obesity. *Behavior Therapy,* **8,** 720–726.

Wertz, R. T., Collins, M. J., Weiss, D., Kurtzke, J. F., Friden, T., Brookshire, R. H., Pierce, J., Holtzapple, P., Hubbard, D. J., Porch, B. E., West, J. A., Davis, L., Matovitch, V., Morley, G. K., & Resurreccion, E. (1981). Veterans Administration cooperative study on aphasia: A comparison of individual and group treatment. *Journal of Speech and Hearing Research,* **24,** 580–594.

White, J. J., Suzuki, H., El Shafie, M., Kumar, M., Haller, J. A., & Schnaufer, L. (1972). A physiologic rationale for the management of neurologic rectal incontinence in children. *Pediatrics,* **49,** 888–893.

Whitehead, W. E., Parker, L. H., Masek, B. J., Cataldo, M. F., & Freeman, J. M. (1981). Biofeedback treatment of fecal incontinence in patients with myelomeningocele. *Developmental Medicine and Child Neurology,* **23,** 313–322.

Williamson, D. A. (1981). Behavioral treatment of migraine and muscle-contraction headaches: Outcome and theoretical explanations. In M. Hersen, R. M. Eisler, & P. M. Miller (Eds.), *Progress in behavior modification* (Vol. 11). New York: Academic Press.

Wilson, G. T., & Brownell, K. D. (1978). Behavior therapy for obesity: Including family members in the treatment process. *Behavior Therapy,* **9,** 943–945.

Wineburg, E., Kronenberg, F., Khanukayev, E., & Inz, J. (1983). Hot flashes: Modification of temperature response through biofeedback and hypnotherapy. *Biofeedback and Self-Regulation,* **8,** 324 (Abstract).

Wing, R. R., & Epstein, L. H. (1982). A community approach to weight control: The American Cancer Society Weight-A-Thon. *Preventive Medicine,* **11,** 245–250.

Wolf, S. L. (1983a). An issue of experimental control: EMG feedback applications to stroke patients. *Behavioral Medicine Abstracts,* **4,** 193–197.

Wolf, S. L. (1983b). Electromyographic biofeedback applications to stroke patients: A critical review. *Physical Therapy,* **63,** 1448–1455.

Wolf, S. L., & Binder-Macleod, S. A. (1983a). Electromyographic biofeedback applications to the hemiplegic patient: Changes in lower extremity neuromuscular and functional status. *Physical Therapy,* **63,** 1404–1413.

Wolf, S. L., & Binder-Macleod, S. A. (1983b). Electromyographic biofeedback applications to the hemiplegic patient: Changes in upper extremity neuromuscular and functional status. *Physical Therapy,* **63,** 1393–1403.

Wolf-Wilets, V., Woods, N. F., & Betrus, P. (1981). A pilot study comparing the effectiveness of skin temperature biofeedback and relaxation training for controlling menopausal hot flashes. *Biofeedback and Self-Regulation,* **6,** 413 (Abstract).

Wolpe, J. (1958). *Psychotherapy by reciprocal inhibition.* Stanford, CA: Stanford Univ. Press.

Wright, L., Nunnery, A., Eichel, B., & Scott, R. (1969). Behavioral tactics for reinstating natural breathing in infants with tracheostomy. *Pediatric Research,* **3,** 275–278.

Wright, L., Schaefer, A. B., & Solomons, G. (1979). *Encyclopedia of pediatric psychology.* Baltimore: Univ. Park Press.

Yates, A. J. (1983). Clearing the Augean stables. *Biofeedback and Self-Regulation,* **8,** 619–627.

Zitter, R. E., & Fremouw, W. J. (1978). Individual *vs.* partner consequation for weight loss. *Behavior Therapy,* **9,** 808–813.

Zubek, J. P. (Ed.) (1969). *Sensory deprivation: Fifteen years of research.* New York: Appleton.

# BEHAVIORAL INTERVENTIONS AS ADJUNCTIVE TREATMENTS FOR CHRONIC ASTHMA

PATRICIA A. CLUSS[1]

*University of Pittsburgh School of Medicine*
*Pittsburgh, Pennsylvania*

## I. INTRODUCTION

Bronchial asthma is a disease defined as a "widespread, intermittent narrowing of the bronchial airways which changes in severity over short periods of time either spontaneously or under treatment and is not due to cardiovascular disease; its clinical characteristics are abnormal breathlessness, which may be paroxysmal or persistent, wheezing, and in most cases, relief by bronchodilator drugs" (U.S. Department of Health, Education & Welfare, 1979, p. 3.). Asthma

---

[1] Present address: Staunton Clinic, Sewickley Valley Hospital, Sewickley, Pennsylvania 15143.

PROGRESS IN BEHAVIOR
MODIFICATION, VOLUME 20

is a serious disorder in childhood and leads the list of childhood diseases which are responsible for school absenteeism due to chronic illness (Schiffer & Hunt, 1963). Both children and adults experience paroxysms of dyspnea, cough, and wheezing (McFadden & Austin, 1977) which may be severe and which interrupt normal activities.

## A.  Overview of Chapter

The purpose of this chapter is to provide an up-to-date review of research which has investigated the effectiveness of behavioral methods used as ad- junctive treatments (in addition to pharmacotherapy) for asthma. A description of behavioral studies and their results will be included, as will brief background information about the disease of asthma and a discussion of methodological issues in this area of research.

In preparation for this review, both *Index Medicus* and *Psychological Abstracts* were searched for articles which met the following criteria: the study (1) included a behavorial treatment for bronchial asthma; (2) was published in En- glish in a refereed journal; (3) was not a case report; (4) was not from the "self- management" program genre; and (5) involved either a group or recognized single-case design (Hersen & Barlow, 1976), the latter including a reversal or a return-to-baseline phase. A few words are necessary regarding these inclusion criteria.

*Behavioral treatments.* Studies were selected if they involved a recognized behavioral treatment (progressive muscle relaxation, biofeedback, systematic desensitization, and assertive training) or if the treatment was devised based on classical or operant learning paradigms. Studies assessing the effects of hypnosis and meditation techniques were not included.

*Exclusion of case reports.* One fascinating aspect of the present state of nonpharmacological asthma research is the paucity of well-designed, ran- domized, controlled studies in the area given the long and enthusiastic history of psychology's interest in asthma. Many single-case reports exist which purport to show evidence for the psychosomatic etiology of this disease (e.g., Dekker & Groen, 1956) or for the effectiveness of behavioral techniques in ameliorating asthma symptoms (e.g., Rathus, 1973). Although single-case studies are impor- tant in the initial stages of hypothesis and treatment development, they are essentially clinical observations offered without statistical testing and cannot be weighed heavily as evidence for the general effectiveness of a treatment (Richter & Dahme, 1982).

Walton, for example, published the first report of the application of a behavioral treatment for bronchial asthma in 1960. After 25 years, it is surprising that so few researchers have gone beyond the case report to design studies which might shed a more definitive light on the usefulness of behavioral methods with the disease. Since the author did not wish to reinforce the notion that case reports contribute in a meaningful way to current knowledge in the field, such articles were not included in this review. Investigations which included at least five subjects were arbitrarily designated as "group" studies.

Although it was the intention to include all investigations involving one or a few subjects which met the requirements for good single-case research designs (Hersen & Barlow, 1976), only two such studies were located among the many which "tested" treatments with single or small numbers of subjects.

*Exclusion of self-management programs.* A burgeoning literature in medical journals involves multicomponent self-management programs for patients with bronchial asthma. Although many of these programs include behavior change skills in addition to educational materials, increased attention, and other components, most programs fail to provide more than cursory training in the behavioral methods and do not ensure that even a minimal level of skill is attained by subjects (Thoreson & Kirmil-Gray, 1983). For this reason, such studies are not included here. The interested reader is directed to the work by Fireman and colleagues (Fireman, Friday, Gira, Vierthaler, & Michaels, 1981) for a good example of a self-management program and to the *Journal of Allergy and Clinical Immunology* (1983, Vol. 72, No. 5) for a series of articles describing this particular current field of study.

For readers unfamiliar with asthma research, some background information about the epidemiology, etiology, course, and physiology of bronchial asthma will be presented as a foundation for more accurate interpretation of the studies reviewed.

## B. Epidemiology and Developmental Course

A major methodological problem in epidemiological studies has been the difficulty of differentiating asthma from other respiratory disorders (Gordis, 1973). Nevertheless, it has been estimated that 8.9 million Americans currently have asthma and that approximately 7% have had the disease at some time in the past (U.S. Department of HEW, 1979). Estimates of pediatric incidence of asthma in the United States range from 5 to 15% (American Lung Association, 1975).

Most asthmatics develop the disorder within the first 5 years of life (King, 1980), although onset in adulthood is not unknown and is associated with increased risk of mortality (Ogilvie, 1962). Estimates of childhood asthma which persists to adulthood range from 23 (Rackemann & Edwards, 1952) to 78% (Siegel, Katz, & Rachelefsky, 1978), with severe cases more likely to continue over the years (Aas, 1963). These statistics indicate that from 12 to 77% of children with asthma may become asymptomatic over time, an important base-rate phenomenon to be considered in study design. A slight preponderance of girls with mild asthma gives way to an increasingly high proportion of boys as asthma becomes more severe: boys are four times more likely to develop chronic, intractable asthma by age 14 (McNichol & Williams, 1973).

## C.  Etiology

### 1.  PHYSIOLOGICAL FACTORS

The basic defect in asthma is a predisposition to bronchial hyperreactivity (Crofton & Douglas, 1969) which may be inherited (VanArsdel & Motulsky, 1959). One etiological theory suggests that excessive cholinergic activity in the ariways causes this hyperresponsiveness to stimuli (Richardson, 1977; Richardson & Beland, 1976). Another theory postulates an abnormal functioning of beta-adrenergic receptors which are responsible for maintenance of resting bronchial smooth muscle tone (Szentivanyi, 1968).

The immune system is also implicated in that an overproduction of immunoglobulin E may occur in response to environmental allergens, causing release of chemical mediators such as histamine and prostaglandins from pulmonary mast cells. A list of allergens which may precipitate asthma attacks includes molds, dust, animal dander, pollen, some foods, cigarette smoke, and household sprays. In addition, weather conditions, exercise, and viral infections may trigger bronchoconstriction in asthmatics (Leffert, 1980). Asthma which is *extrinsic,* or allergen induced, has been differentiated from *intrinsic* asthma, for which no specific external allergen can be defined (Rackemann, 1918). Viral infection, as well as various psychological factors, may play a part in the etiology and/or maintenance of intrinsic asthma.

### 2.  PSYCHOLOGICAL FACTORS

Early psychodynamic theorists presumed asthma to be psychogenic in nature (e.g., Dekker & Groen, 1956; French & Alexander, 1941), the latter authors viewing asthma as a "suppressed cry" relating to critical periods of separation conflict. More recent researchers have concluded that psychological factors do not play a causative role in the initial onset of the disease (Creer, 1978), but may be important for some patients in the precipitation of attacks or in the maintenance of the disorder (Levinson, 1979; Luparello, Leist, Lourie, & Swett, 1970; McFadden, Luparello, Lyons, & Bleecker, 1969; McNichol, Williams, Allan, & McAndrew, 1973).

## D.  Measurement of Asthma

Since asthma is, by definition, a variable, intermittent obstruction of the airways, it has been difficult to determine adequate procedures for measuring such an unpredictable process (Chai, Purcell, Brady, & Falliers, 1968). Although physiological measures of lung function are most commonly employed, other measures such as the medication requirements of the child, behavioral measures, including frequency and number of days in the hospital, emergency room visits, and asthma attacks, restrictions on activities and school attendance have been found to be useful indicators of clinical course.

Lung function assessment with spirometric devices is most common in the literature, including forced vital capacity (FVC; the maximum amount of air which can be expired after maximal inspiration), forced expiratory volume in 1 second ($FEV_1$; the volume of air expired in the first second of forced expiration after maximum inspiration), peak expiratory flow rate (PEFR; amount of air expired in the first 0.1 second after maximal inspiration), and maximum midexpiratory flow rate (MMEF).

Use of these convenient methods has been criticized because they are effort dependent, requiring patient cooperation for accuracy of readings, and because the exertion required for valid readings may itself cause bronchoconstriction in some patients (Knapp & Wells, 1978). Non-effort-dependent alternative methods of measurement are available, including whole-body plethysmography or the forced oscillation technique, both of which measure total respiratory resistance (TRR) of the airways.

## E.  Pharmacological Treatment

Treatment with pharmacological agents is the most common procedure, by far, for the management of asthma today. Behavioral interventions are almost always employed in addition to regular-care treatment with one or more of the following drugs: (1) theophylline, the treatment agent of choice in the United States for long-term maintenance therapy, (2) adrenergic compounds, for acute exacerbation of symptoms, (3) cromolyn, an alternative maintenance drug, and (4) corticosteroids, reserved because of unpleasant side effects for patients with severe asthma who do not respond to other drugs (Ellis, 1983).

These drugs may be administered variously as pills, liquids, aerosol sprays, or by injection. The issue of patient compliance to medication regimens is important both for clinical management of the disease and for the appropriate design of studies to test the effects of adjunctive treatments. This issue and its application to research methodology will be addressed in a subsequent section of this chapter.

## II.  BEHAVIORAL INTERVENTIONS

### A.  Introduction

Four behavioral methods, relaxation, biofeedback, systematic desensitization, and assertive training, have been tested to determine their effectiveness in altering asthma symptoms in studies with group designs; results have been reported in a total of 23 published articles. Three studies tested behavioral interventions with alteration of asthma-related behaviors as the goal. A total of 37 treatment groups were studied in these investigations. Table I shows the number of groups studied for each method.

In the review which follows studies are presented by method; investigations which include an asthma regular-care or attention–placebo control group are discussed first in each section since such studies provide the "best test" of treatment effects over time. Designs comparing more than one group, with or without another type of control group, are then presented, followed by uncontrolled one-group studies. Characteristics and results of individual studies are presented in Table II.

### B.  Relaxation Training

Relaxation techniques were among the first behavioral methods used as treatments for asthma. Clinical observations of the role of anxiety and other strong emotions in the precipitation and exacerbation of asthma attacks led to the use of this technique as a counter measure to the physiological arousal which accompanies anxiety. Jacobson's (1938) progressive muscle relaxation (PMR) has been used most frequently and has been shown to decrease pulse rate (Jacobson, 1940), blood pressure (Jacobson, 1939), galvanic skin response, respiration (Wolpe, 1982), and to improve lung function scores in asthmatics (Alexander,

**TABLE I**

Frequency of Behavioral Methods Studied

| Method | Number of groups |
|---|---|
| Relaxation training | 12 |
| Biofeedback training | 16 |
|   EMG feedback | 7 |
|   Feedback of pulmonary function | 8 |
|   Other | 1 |
| Systematic desensitization | 4 |
| Assertive training | 3 |
| Behavior management | 3 (+1 single-subject design) |

## TABLE II

### Investigations of Behavioral Treatments for Asthma

| Authors | Subjects | | Duration | | Experimental conditions | Outcome measures | Results | | | |
|---|---|---|---|---|---|---|---|---|---|---|
| | Type | N | Trt | F.U. | | | Data | p | Direction | Clin. sign?a |
| Alexander (1972) | Inpts Ages 10–15 | 25 | 2 wks | None | Single-group outcome (1) Sitting quietly [5]b; PMRc [5] | A. Δ PEFR B. State/trait anxiety | A. Not reported B. Not reported | NS NS | | No — |
| Alexander et al. (1979) | Inpts Ages 10–15 | 14 | ~5 wks | None | Single-group outcome (1) Sitting quietly [3]; PMR [5]; Use PMR [3] | A. Δ% E. PEFR B. Δ% E. FEV$_1$ C. 10 other pulmonary var. D. Wheezing score | A. −1.2% to +6.7% B. +0.8% to +6.4% C. Not reported D. Not reported | .05 .05 NS NS | | No No — — |
| Alexander et al. (1972) | Inpts Ages 10–15 | 20 16 | 8 days | None | Randomized controlled outcome (1) PMR (2) Sitting quietly | A. Δ PEFR B. Subjective relaxation | A. (1) +21.6 liters/min (2) −6.1 liters/min B. (1) +2.7 (2) +0.4 | .01 .005 | | No — |
| Danker et al. (1975) | Male inpts Ages 8–11 | 6 | ? | None | Single-group outcome (1) Baseline [3–6]; PEFR biofdbk. [?] | A. PEFR | A. Not reported | NS | | No |
| | | 5 | 7 wks | None | Single-group outcome (1) baseline [5–10]; PEFR biofdbck [5–12]; points for achieving criterion | A. Δ PEFR within sessions, pre- vs. posttrt | A. +11.0 liters/min to +23.2 liters/min | NS | | No |
| Davis et al. (1973) | Inpts Ages 6–15 | 8 8 8 | 3 wks | None | Randomized controlled outcome (1) PMR + EMG biofdbk [5] (2) PMR alone [5] (3) Sitting quietly [5] | A. Δ PEFR pre- to posttrt B. Mood adjective checklist | A. (1) +2.3 liters/min (2) −3.3 liters/min (3) −9.5 liters/min B. Not reported | NS NS | | No — |
| Erskine and Schonell (1981) | Outpts Ages 6– | | 13 wks | 6 wks | Randomized-group outcome | A. FEV$_1$ over sessions | A. (1) +2.8 to +2.4 liters/sec | NS | | No |

*(continued)*

## TABLE II (Continued)

| | Subjects | | | Duration | | | Results | | | |
|---|---|---|---|---|---|---|---|---|---|---|
| Authors | Type | N | Experimental conditions | Trt | F.U. | Outcome measures | Data | $p$ | Direction | Clin. sign.?a |
| | 46 | 6 | (1) Muscle relaxation | | | | | | | |
| | | 6 | (2) Mental and muscle relax | | | | (2) +2.0 to +1.8 liters/sec | | | |
| | | | | | | B. Self-report of panic & physical symptoms | B. Not reported | NS | | — |
| Harding and Maher (1982) | Adult volunteers | 8 | Randomized controlled outcome<br>(1) (Asthmatics); biofdbk of cardiac acceleration [2–5] | ? | 2–8 wks | A. Heart rate from baseline to posttrt | A. (1) 75.4 to 89.7 BPM<br>(2) 79.2 to 74.4 BPM<br>(3) Not reported | .001<br>NS | 1 > 2<br>1 & 2<br>=3 | —<br>— |
| | | 8 | (2) (Asthmatics); biofdbk-assisted "cardiac constancy" [1] | | | B. PEFR (baseline to posttrt) | B. (1) 374.1 to 408.1 liters/ min<br>(2) 474.0 to 464.4 liters/ min<br>(3) Not reported | .025<br>NS | 1 > 2<br>1 & 2<br>=3 | No<br>— |
| | | 12 | (3) (Nonasthmatics); biofdbk of cardiac acceleration [1] | | | | | | | |
| Hochstadt et al. (1980) | Inpts Ages 8–13 "over users" of hosp. | 7 | Single-group outcome<br>(1) Time-out from positive reinforcement; contingent positive reinf. for appropriate use of hospital | 1 yr | None | A. Days of hospitalization pre- to posttrt | A. 18.3 to 9.0 days | .01 | | — |
| | | | | | | B. Days to optimal PEFR score pre- to posttrt | B. 9.8 to 4.8 days | .05 | | — |
| | | | | | | C. Interval between hospitalizations | C. 48.9 to 85.3 days | NS | | — |
| Hock et al. (1977) | Outpt male children | ?<br>?<br>? | Randomized controlled outcome<br>(1) PMR [8]<br>(2) Assertive training [8]<br>(3) Regular-care ctl | 8 wks | 1 mo | A. FEV1 at 4 points in time | A. Raw data not rptd. At pre-, mid-, & post-trt<br>At 1 mo F.U. | NS<br>.01 | 1 > 3 | Yes |
| | | | | | | B. Mood scale | B. Raw data not rptd; 10 of 11 factors | NS | | |

130

| Study | N | Design | Tx | F.U. | Outcome | Results | p | Comparison | |
|---|---|---|---|---|---|---|---|---|---|
| Hock et al. (1978) | Output males Ages 10–17<br>9<br>9<br>10<br>7<br>8 | Randomized controlled outcome<br>(1) PMR [8]<br>(2) Assertive training [8]<br>(3) PMR + assertive tng [8]<br>(4) Regular-care control [0]<br>(5) Leaderless peer grp control [8] | 8 wks | 1 mo | A. FEV$_1$ at 4 points in time<br><br>B. Frequency of asthma attacks per week | A. (1) 1.7 to 2.0 liters/sec<br>(2) 1.7 to 1.4 liters/sec<br>(3) 1.8 to 1.9 liters/sec<br>(4) 1.8 to 1.7 liters/sec<br>1.8 to 1.8 liters/sec<br><br>B.   Pre  4  8  F.U.<br>(1) .43 .11 .00 .44<br>(2) .24 .44 .22 1.0<br>(3) .52 .30 .00 .60<br>(4) .39 .29 .29 2.6<br>(5) .26 .38 .75 .13 | .01<br><br><br><br><br><br>.01 | 1 & 3 > 2, 4 & 5<br><br><br><br><br>3 > 1, 3 4 & 5 | Yes<br><br><br><br><br>— |
| Janson-Bjerklie and Clark (1982) | Outputs Ages 18–40<br>8<br>7 | Randomized controlled outcome<br>(1) Feedback of total respiratory resistance (TRR)<br>(2) Random feedback control | 2 wks | None | A. Δ TRR within session over time | A. (1) +.14 to −.38 cm H$_2$O/liters/sec<br>(2) −.23 to −.04 cm H$_2$O/liters sec | .05 | 1 > 2 | ? |
| Khan (1977) | Outpts Ages 8–15<br>20<br><br>20<br>20<br><br>20 | Randomized controlled outcome<br>(1) (Reactors); fdbk of FEV$_1$ [5–8] + "linking training" [10]<br>(2) (Nonreactors); same as group 1<br>(3) (Reactors); regular-care control<br>(4) (Nonreactors); same as group 3 | ? | ~8 mo | A. Frequency of asthma attacks/3 months<br><br>B. Duration of attacks<br><br>C. Asthma severity | A. (1) 27.6 to 11.5<br>(2) 17.0 to 8.0<br>(3) 25.2 to 11.0<br>(4) 20.2 to 26.5<br>B. (1) 43.0 to 22.0<br>(2) 26.5 to 10.7<br>(3) 38.0 to 17.8<br>(4) 33.0 to 31.5<br>C. (1) 52 to 24<br>(2) 32 to 15<br>(3) 50 to 20<br>(4) 51 to 50 | .05?<br><br><br><br>.05?<br><br><br><br>.05? | 2 < 4<br><br><br><br>2 < 4<br><br><br><br>2 < 4 | —<br><br><br><br>—<br><br><br><br>— |
| Khan et al. (1978) | Outputs Ages 8– | Randomized controlled outcome | ? | ~8 mo | A. Δ in No. asthma attacks pre- to posttrt | A. (1) 33.6 to 14.0<br>(2) 49.0 to 25.0 | .05 | 1 + 2 < 3 + 4 | — |

*(continued)*

131

**TABLE II** (*Continued*)

| Authors | Subjects Type | N | Experimental conditions | Duration Trt | F.U. | Outcome measures | Results Data | p | Direction | Clin. sign?[a] |
|---|---|---|---|---|---|---|---|---|---|---|
| | 15 | 5 | (Reactors); fdbk of FEV$_1$ [5] + "linking training" [10] + booster sessions [5] at 1, 2, 3, & 6 mo post-trt | | | B. Δ in amt. of medication | (3) 64.6 to 78.0<br>(4) 30.8 to 39.8<br>B. (1) 10.4 to 4.5<br>(2) 11.2 to 3.4<br>(3) 8.6 to 9.8<br>(4) 8.0 to 6.4 | .05 | 1 + 2 <<br>3 + 4 | — |
| | | 5 | (2) (Nonreactors); same as group 1 | | | C. Δ in No. of emergency rm visits | C. (1) 16.0 to 2.0<br>(2) 1.6 to 0.6<br>(3) 15.6 to 9.5<br>(4) 4.8 to 3.5 | .05 | 1 + 2 <<br>3 + 4 | — |
| | | 5 | (3) (Reactors); regular-care control | | | | | | | |
| | | 5 | (4) (Nonreactors); same as group 3 | | | | | | | |
| Kotses *et al.* (1976) | Campers Ages 8–16 | 18 | Randomized controlled outcome<br>(1) Frontalis EMG biofdbk [9] | 3 wks | None | A. EMG relaxation | A. (1) 15.5 to 11.5 mv<br>(2) 16.2 to 19.3 mv | .025 | 1 < 2 | — |
| | | 18 | (2) Yoked non-contingent feedback control [9] | | | B. Δ PEFR within session over time | B. (1) +26.0 liters/min<br>(2) +1.7 liters/min<br>(3) -3.3 liters/min | .05 | 1 ><br>2 & 3 | ? |
| | | 18 | (3) Regular-care control [0] | | | | | | | |
| Kotses *et al.* (1978) | Campers Ages 8–16 | 10 | Randomized controlled outcome<br>(1) Frontalis EMG biofdbk [9] | 3 wks | None | A. EMG relaxation | A. (1) -3.3 mv<br>(2) -1.1 mv<br>(3) -0.8 mv<br>(4) -0.8 mv | .05<br>NS | 1 > 2<br>3 = 4 | — |
| | | 10 | (2) Yoked non-contingent frontalis control [9] | | | B. PEFR within session | B. (1) +11.1 liters/min<br>(2) +1.7 liters/min<br>(3) -1.8 liters/min<br>(4) -0.2 liters/min | .025<br>NS | 1 > 2<br>3 = 4 | No |
| | | 10 | (3) Brachioradialis EMG biofdbk [9] | | | | | | | |
| | | 10 | (4) Yoked non-contingent brachioradialis control [9] | | | | | | | |

| Study | Subjects (N) | Design / Groups | Duration | Outcome | Results | Statistics | Comparison | |
|---|---|---|---|---|---|---|---|---|
| Miklich et al. (1977) | Inpts Children 19 | Nonrandomized controlled outcome (1) Systematic desensitization; EMG biofdbk for some Ss [?] | ~10 wks | A. Δ %E. PEFR from baseline | A. BL to trt period: (1) −1.9% (2) −4.0% BL to posttrt: (1) +0.1% (2) −9.3% BL to follow-up (1) −5.3% (2) −14.9% | NS .05 NS | 1 > 2 | — No |
| | 7 | (2) Regular-care control [0] | | B. Δ in symptom frequency scores from baseline | B. BL to treatment: (1) −1 (2) −6.3 Other time periods: | .05 NS | 2 > 1 | — |
| Moore (1965) | Output adults and children 12 total | Randomized balanced incomplete block design | 2 mo | A. Δ PEFR pre to post; Δ% efficiency | A. (1) +21.3 liters/min −3.6% (2) +11.4 liters/min −2.5% (3) +75.3 liters/min +19.3% | Both .001 | 3 > 1 & 2 | Yes |
| | 8 | (1) Muscle relaxation [8] | None | | | | | |
| | 8 | (2) Relaxation with suggestion [8] | | B. Δ in no. of asthma attacks | B. (1) −2.5 (2) −3.5 (3) −4.6 | NS | | |
| | 8 | (3) Systematic desensitization [8] | | | | | | |
| Neisworth and Moore (1972) | Output Age 7 1 | Single-case design (ABAB) (1) Baseline (10 days); extinction & DRO (30 days); reversal (10 days); reinstitution of contingencies | 50+ days 11 mo | A. Duration of bedtime episodes of coughing & wheezing | A. BL: x̄ = 68 min Trt: x̄ = 6 min (after day 23) BL: x̄ = 18 min Trt: x̄ = 5 min (after stabilization) | No statistics | | — |
| Philipp et al. (1972) | Output Ages 14–49 half intrinsics, half extrinsics | Randomized controlled outcome (1) Relaxation training [6] | ? | A. Δ $FEV_1$ from initial to posttrt saline suggestion trial | A. Raw data not rptd | NS | | — |
| | 10 | (2) Regular-care control; Both given Mecholyl challenge with information that it was a bronchoconstrictor | None | B. Δ $FEV_1$ from initial to posttrt Mecholyl challenge | B. Raw data not rptd | .01 | 1 > 2 | ? |
| | 10 | | | | | | | |

(continued)

**TABLE II** (*Continued*)

| Authors | Subjects Type | N | Experimental conditions | Duration Trt | F.U. | Outcome measures | Results Data | p | Direction | Clin. sign?[a] |
|---|---|---|---|---|---|---|---|---|---|---|
| Renne and Creer (1976) | Inpts Ages 7–12 | 4 | Multiple baseline Expt 1: Tokens for accuracy of 3 behaviors in use of inhalation therapy apparatus | 1 day | 2 mo | A. Reduction in inaccurate eye fixation, facial posturing, & breathing | A. 98, 98, & 83% reduction, respectively | No statistics | | — |
| | | 2 | Expt 2: Same as above except administered by nurses | | | B. Δ in inhalation treatment effectiveness | B. 4 to 82.3% | No statistics | | — |
| Scherr and Crawford (1978) | Campers Ages 6–15 | | Randomized controlled outcome Expt 1 | 3 wks | None | A. EMG tension over time | A. (1) 16.0 to 11.8 mv (2) 16.2 to 19.7 mv | .05 | 1 > 2 | — |
| | | 12 | (1) EMG biofeedback [9] | | | B. Δ PEFR over time | B. (1) +22 liters/min (2) +2 liters/min (3) −10 liters/min | .01 | 1 > 2 & 3 | No |
| | | 12 | (2) Noncontingent fdbk control | | | | | | | |
| | | 12 | (3) Regular-care control | | | | | | | |
| | | | Expt 2 | 3 wks | None | A. Frontalis EMG tension | A. Raw data not rptd | .05? | 1 > 2 | — |
| | | 10 | (1) Frontalis EMG biofdbk | | | B. Brachioradialis tension | B. Raw data not rptd | NS | | — |
| | | 10 | (2) Noncontingent frontalis feedback | | | C. Δ PEFR | C. Raw data not rptd | .02 | 1 > 2, 3, & 5 | ? |
| | | 10 | (3) Brachioradialis EMG biofeedback | | | | | | | |
| | | 10 | (4) Noncontingent brachioradialis feedback | | | | | | | |
| | | 10 | (5) Regular-care | | | | | | | |

| Study | Subjects | N | Design/Treatment | Duration | Control | Outcome measure | Results | p | Follow-up |
|---|---|---|---|---|---|---|---|---|---|
| Scherr et al. (1975) | Campers Ages 6–15 | 22<br><br>22 | Randomized controlled outcome (1) Relaxation training + EMG biofeedback [18] (2) Regular-care control | 6 wks | None | A. Δ in deviation from E.PEFR<br><br>B. No. asthma attacks<br>C. No. infirmary visits<br>D. Amt steroid usage | A. (1) −1100 to −638 ml (2) −1225 to −850 ml<br>B. (1) 8.4 (2) 31.7<br>C. (1) 6.7 (2) 10.1<br>D. (1) −60% (2) −14% | .05?<br><br>.05?<br>.05?<br>? | Yes<br><br>—<br>—<br>— |
| Steptoe et al. (1981) | Outpt adults Ages 18–58 asthmatics & nonasthmatics | 8<br><br><br>8<br><br>8 | Randomized-group outcome (1) (Asthmatics); instructions to lower airways resistance ($R_t$) + $R_t$ feedback [5] (2) (Nonasthmatics); same as group 1 [5] (3) (Nonasthmatics); attempt to lower $R_t$ with instructions alone [3]; $R_t$ biofdbk added to instructions [2] | ? | None | A. Δ in within-session $R_t$ over time | A. (1) +0.5 to −3.2 mbar/liter (2) −1.2% (3) +8.0% | .001<br>NS  2 = 3 | No |
| Vachon and Rich (1976) | Outpt adults Ages 18–30 | 28 | Expt 1—Single-group outcome (1) Feedback of total respiratory resistance ($R_t$) [1] * A noncontingent fdbk grp was run at a later date, but cannot be considered a control due to time | 1 day | None | A. Δ in $R_t$ over baseline | A. Raw data not rptd | .01 | |

(continued)

135

**TABLE II** (*Continued*)

| Authors | Subjects | | Experimental conditions | Duration | | Outcome measures | Results | | | |
|---|---|---|---|---|---|---|---|---|---|---|
| | Type | N | | Trt | F.U. | | Data | p | Direction | Clin. sign?[a] |
| | | | factor | | | | | | | |
| | | | Expt 2—Nonrandom-group outcome | 1 day | None | A. Δ in $R_t$ over baseline across trials | A. (1) −0.3, −0.6, −0.7, −0.8 | NS, .05, .005, .05 | | Yes |
| | | 7 | (1) Biofeedback of $R_t$ [1] | | | | (2) −0.7, 0.0, −0.5, −0.2 | .05, NS, NS, NS | | No |
| | | 6 | (2) Noncontingent fdbk control [1] | | | | | | | |
| Yorkston et al. (1979) | Outpt adults $\bar{x} = 45$ | | Randomized-group outcome | 5–6 wks | 2 wks | A. Better/worse rating by allergist & psychiatrist | A. Raw data not rptd | NS (for whole grp) (steroid vs nonsteroid pts) | .05? | — |
| | | 9 | (1) PMR [?] | | | | | | | |
| | | 10 | (2) PMR + verbal desensitization [?] | | | B. PEFR pre- to post-trt | B. (1) 216.2 to 231.4 liters/min | NS | | |
| | | 9 | (3) PMR + verbal & practical desensitization | | | | (2) 225.4 to 232.0 liters/min | | | |
| | | | | | | | (3) 236.8 to 259.4 liters/min | | | |
| Yorkston et al. (1974) | Outpt adults $\bar{x} = 42$ | | Randomized-group outcome | 2 wks | 2 yrs | A. % change in E. $FEV_1$ | A. (1) −5% | NS | | No |
| | | 7 | (1) PMR [6] | | | | (2) +20% | .04 | | Yes |
| | | 7 | (2) PMR + systematic desensitization [6] | | | | | | | |

[a] At least a 15% improvement in pulmonary function scores.

[b] Numbers in brackets refer to number of sessions during treatment.

[c] PMR, progressive muscle relaxation.

1972). The interested reader may consult Davidson and Schwartz (1976) for a detailed discussion of the psychobiology of relaxation and related states.

1. GROUP STUDIES WITH REGULAR-CARE OR ATTENTION–
PLACEBO ASTHMA CONTROLS

Five randomized-group studies of this type have been published. In the first of these, Alexander and colleagues (Alexander, Miklich, & Hershkoff, 1972) randomly assigned 20 inpatient chronic asthmatic children to a relaxation treatment group and 16 to a control group receiving regular care including asthma medication. A modified Jacobsonian relaxation procedure was taught to the experimental group during six 15-minute sessions; control subjects were told that the experimenters wanted to "find out if inactivity affects [your] peak flows," and were instructed to sit quietly for 15 minutes. Apparently, treatment subjects received more attention from experimenters than did control subjects. Analysis of within-session PEFR change scores for the last three sessions showed that peak flow scores of the relaxation group increased (improved) $+21.63$ liters/minute, whereas the control group's change scores decreased slightly at $-6.14$ liters/minutes, a significant difference between groups in favor of relaxation subjects.

Phillip, Wilde, and Day (1972) tested their hypotheses that patients taught deep muscle relaxation would show improved respiratory efficiency after a challenge by Mecholyl, a bronchospasm-inducing drug, than would patients untrained in the procedure, and that extrinsic asthmatics would show less reaction to suggestion in the presence of Mecholyl or nebulized saline than would intrinsic asthmatics. Ten patients identified as intrinsics and 10 extrinsics were matched and randomized to a relaxation training group or to a no-treatment control. It is unclear whether all subjects or only a subset were receiving other pharmacological treatment for their asthma symptoms. All subjects underwent an initial Mecholyl trial to determine level of reactivity to bronchoconstricting drug and then were subjected to four suggestion trials during which they received either accurate information about the type of drug or saline solution they were inhaling or inaccurate information. Relaxation subjects then were taught progressive muscle relaxation in five sessions while control subjects received no treatment.

In the final session, experimental subjects were told to practice relaxation for 10 minutes while control subjects waited in the waiting room for the same amount of time. All subjects then inhaled nebulized saline after being told they would receive active drug, then inhaled Mecholyl which was described as a neutral solution. The relaxation-trained group who had a 10 minute pretrial opportunity to practice the technique, showed no significant change in $FEV_1$ scores during inhalation of saline, but demonstrated significantly less deterioration in $FEV_1$ than controls after challenge by Mecholyl. No differences between intrinsics and extrinsics was noted.

In another randomized, controlled study, Davis and colleagues (Davis, Saunders, Creer, & Chai, 1973) tested both a Jacobsonian relaxation treatment procedure and a biofeedback-assisted relaxation group against a regular-care control. Twenty-four inpatient children, ages 6 to 15, were divided into two experimental and one control group. All children were receiving pharmacotherapy in addition to their participation in this research project. When subjects were divided into a "less severe" and "more severe" asthma group, results showed a significant difference among treatment conditions for the less severe group, with both relaxation alone ($+2.5$ liters/minute) and biofeedback ($+5.0$ liters/minute) conditions producing better PEFR results than the control condition ($-10.0$ liters/minute). No significant difference among treatment groups was noted for the more severe asthmatic subjects in this study, nor was there a difference when data from all subjects were analyzed together.

Hock and co-workers (Hock, Bramble, & Kennard, 1977) tested male asthmatic outpatients randomized to a relaxation treatment group, an assertive training group, or a regular-care control. Number of subjects is not specified in the published report. FEV1 was assessed at pre-, mid-, and post-treatment and at a 1 month follow-up session and scores were analyzed by four one-way analyses of variance instead of by repeated measures ANOVA. No differences were found at pretreatment, or at the fourth or eighth week. At follow-up, a significant difference was found between pulmonary function scores of the relaxation group versus the medical control group and versus assertive training subjects; this latter group's scores actually deteriorated from beginning-of-treatment to follow-up assessment.

Hock, Rodgers, Reddi, and Kennard (1978), in a follow-up study, randomly assigned 43 asthmatic children to one of five groups. Relaxation subjects learned progressive muscle relaxation during eight 40-minute sessions; subjects assigned to the assertive training group learned, in the same number of sessions, to "express socially appropriate feelings and rights" (p. 211); the third experimental group was taught a combination of assertive and relaxation training. A regular-care control and a control group of subjects who sat quietly for eight 40-minute leaderless peer group sessions were also included in this design.

Repeated measures analysis of variance of group peak flow data showed a significant difference in treatment outcome for the experimental groups which included relaxation training as compared to those which did not. No difference in lung function scores between the relaxation alone and the assertive training plus relaxation groups was found. Frequency of asthma attacks was also significantly less for the relaxation and the combined treatment groups, whereas subjects taught assertive training alone demonstrated no better outcome than those in the control group.

Overall, of these five randomized group relaxation studies with appropriate controls, all reported statistically significant improvements in pulmonary function scores for relaxation subjects compared to controls. Improvements in lung function which are statistically significant, however, are not necessarily clinically meaningful. If 15% improvement in pulmonary function is set as the minimum clinically significant change (Itkin, 1967; Schonell, 1984), then only the two studies by Hock and co-workers (Hock et al., 1977, 1978) showed results which were clinically as well as statistically meaningful (a 17.7 and 18.8% improvement, respectively). Pulmonary function changes as high as 25% have been found to be undetectable on physician examination (Chai et al., 1968), so it is not clear that even the best results obtained in any of these investigations are at a level which suggests unequivocal effectiveness.

## 2.  STUDIES COMPARING MORE THAN ONE GROUP OR TREATMENT

Moore (1965) reported an early study testing relaxation alone, relaxation plus suggestion, and systematic desensitization in 12 asthmatic adults and children, using a balanced incomplete block design with each patient as his/her own control. Relaxation training was a combination of PMR and autogenic training (Shultz, 1932), taught in eight 30-minute sessions. "Strong reiterated suggestions" (p. 259) that they would show improvement in asthma symptoms between sessions were given to relaxed patients in the relaxation plus suggestion group. Both relaxation groups practiced at home twice daily for 5 minutes. Systematic desensitization (SD) subjects were taught relaxation and were exposed in imagery to three graded hierarchies of asthma-related situations.

Subjects in all three treatments reported fewer asthma attacks during the intervention phase, but the differences in change scores among groups were nonsignificant. The SD intervention, however, resulted in significantly improved PEFR scores over those of the two other groups which did not differ from each other. Analysis of percentage efficiency, a standardized lung function measure, showed that SD subjects improved nearly 20% on this measure, a statistically significant increase compared to the relaxation groups.

Moore implies that subjects in this study were not receiving pharmacotherapy concurrent with behavioral treatment making this research somewhat unusual; few other investigators have expected a relaxation intervention alone to ameliorate bronchoconstriction or other symptoms of asthma. Care should be taken, therefore, in comparing results of this study with others which hypothesize that relaxation has an additive positive effect over that available from drugs alone.

In an investigation devised to test the effects of a systematic desensitization procedure (Yorkston, McHugh, Brady, Serber, & Sergeant, 1974), 14 adult asthmatics were randomized to an SD group or to a relaxation alone group; no control group was included. Subjects were trained in six 30-minute treatment sessions over 2 weeks, were assessed at pretreatment and at each session, and were followed up 2 years later. A statistically significant improvement over time for the desensitization group (20% increase in $FEV_1$) was demonstrated, whereas relaxation subjects showed a decrease in $FEV_1$ over time of 5%. Comparison of a standardized measure (percentage of expected $FEV_1$) gives the same results. After 2 years, desensitization subjects showed a significantly greater reduction in use of drugs including steroids, and were scored by an independent psychiatrist as showing greater clinical improvement than subjects in the relaxation group. Caution must be taken, however, in assuming that improvement at 2-year follow-up was due solely to the effects of a 2-week intervention when no control group was followed and information regarding patient activities during that time was unavailable.

Erskine and Schonell (1981) compared a PMR group and a "mental and muscle relaxation" group which included PMR plus mental imagery of relaxing scenes for 12 moderately to severely asthmatic adult outpatients. Use of asthma medication is not mentioned in the published report of this study. Both groups practiced either PMR alone or with imagery twice daily at home and were assessed weekly during 3 weeks prior to treatment, during treatment, and for 6 weeks post-treatment on $FEV_1$ and self-report of asthma symptoms. Results showed no difference between groups over time on either measure.

Yorkston and colleagues (Yorkston, Eckert, McHugh, Philander, & Blumenthal, 1979) attempted to replicate their earlier (1974) finding that asthmatic adults treated with verbal desensitization improved significantly more than those taught relaxation alone. Twenty-eight subjects were randomized to either a PMR "control" group, a relaxation plus verbal desensitization (RV) group, or a verbal and practical desensitization (RVP) group which attempted to "desensitize patients to expiratory effort by having them gradually accustom themselves to making graduated expiratory efforts without provoking tension" (p. 326). Eighteen subjects were receiving steroids; the medication status of the remaining 10 subjects is not reported.

The authors did not perform analyses of variance on pulmonary function outcome measures, but instead report Fisher's exact test results for patients taking steroids in the relaxation versus both desensitization groups combined, using a better/worse rating as the outcome measure. Richter and Dahme (1982) note the inadequacy of this statistical method and reanalyzed the PEFR data using 3 (Group) $\times$ 2 (Pre–post) ANOVAs for the whole sample and for steroid patients alone. No significant results were found, indicating no evidence for differential change over time for any group or subgroup in this investigation.

## 3.  UNCONTROLLED ONE-GROUP STUDIES

Results of uncontrolled one-group studies, even if significant, allow for little interpretation of beneficial treatment effects due to the lack of information about other factors which might impinge on outcome. Alexander (1972) studied the effect of relaxation on peak flow ratings in 25 inpatient asthmatic children who sat quietly during five 20-minute sessions and who then learned and practiced PMR in five subsequent 20-minute sessions. Mean within-session pre–post PEFR readings for each condition were analyzed; PEFR scores improved significantly more during PMR sessions than during sitting-quietly sessions. Due to an "inconvenient weather change", however, subjects' mean presession pulmonary efficiency level had dropped by over 10% between early (sitting-quietly) and later (PMR) sessions. Reanalysis of these data controlling for this factor resulted in a nonsignificant $F$ value, indicating no evidence for positive effects of relaxation on pulmonary function in asthmatics.

In the final study in this section, Alexander and co-workers (Alexander, Cropp, & Chai, 1979) tested 14 severely asthmatic inpatient children in three phases which included resting quietly, learning and practicing PMR with instructions, and self-initiated PMR while resting quietly. Some subjects were taught PMR individually and some in a group. Pulmonary function was assessed by whole body plethysmography and with a spirometric device immediately postsession and at four subsequent 30-minute intervals, including assessment after two whiffs of a nebulized bronchodilator. These final four assessments were to test for longer term effects and to compare the effects of relaxation with the effects of a commonly used pharmacological treatment.

Results showed no differences for children trained in PMR alone or as part of a group. Of 12 measures of pulmonary function, only peak flow and $FEV_1$ data showed significant differences between resting and relaxation phases. During phase I, these measures declined from presession to 2-hour postsession assessment, consistent with what would be expected 6 to 8 hours after administration of medication; in general, pulmonary function was maintained at presession levels throughout assessment periods in the relaxation phase. The data from this study, therefore, show little evidence for clinically significant improvement in lung function after relaxation training.

## 4. SUMMARY OF RELAXATION STUDIES

Overall, in the 12 relaxation groups studied in the above investigations, the evidence for efficacy of this treatment for asthma is less than substantial. Only five studies demonstrated statistically significant improvement in lung function for relaxation-trained subjects. Of these, only two groups of subjects showed results which were clinically significant. Poor research design, including lack of adequate control groups and small sample sizes, and inadequate statistical analyses are possible contributing factors to the lack of positive results in this area of research.

## C. Biofeedback Interventions

The arrival of biofeedback methodology and experimentation has been of interest to asthma researchers concerned with behavioral models of alterations in physiological functioning. Biofeedback has been seen from several frameworks:

the *operant conditioning* model which emphasizes the learning process resulting from contingent reinforcement for physiological change, the *informational* model in which the biofeedback stimulus is seen to act as a physiological monitor with no direct effect on the physiological activity, and the *skill learning* framework, which proposes the external sensory feedback as a method for the individual to calibrate afferent feedback of visceral responses (Shapiro & Surwit, 1979).

The technique's use as a behavioral treatment for asthma has taken two general forms: feedback of skeletal muscle tension (EMG, or electromyographic biofeedback) and feedback of respiratory function. Muscle tension feedback strategies have been further subdivided into interventions employing EMG feedback to facilitate the effects of relaxation training and those which target directly the interaction between muscle tension and pulmonary function in the absence of relaxation training (Kotses & Glaus, 1981).

The use of EMG biofeedback to facilitate PMR training was motivated by early studies suggesting that progressive muscle relaxation alone was somewhat effective in reducing asthma symptoms. It was theorized that objective information about the level of muscle tension would enhance the general state of relaxation developed during PMR training. Investigators who have employed EMG feedback to examine interactions between muscular and pulmonary variables, however, generally avoid discussion of general relaxation states and focus instead on the effect of relaxation on specific muscle systems. In a related strategy Harding and Maher (1982) investigated the effects of biofeedback-induced voluntary cardiac acceleration on peak expiratory flow rate.

In interventions employing EMG biofeedback, it is necessary not only to demonstrate significant improvement in respiratory outcome variables, but also to show that the ability to reduce muscle tension actually was learned by the subjects. Improvement in asthma symptoms in the absence of evidence for reduced muscle tension disallows the assumption that improvement in pulmonary function was due to the biofeedback intervention (Kotses & Glaus, 1981).

Biofeedback of respiratory function has as its target the asthmatic subject's ability to increase ventilation of the lungs by increasing flow rates or by reducing resistance in the airways. The direct targeting of asthma symptomotology is presumed to be mediated through bronchomotor regulation of airway caliber (Kotses & Glaus, 1981).

A total of 12 published articles have described biofeedback interventions for asthma. Table III shows these studies divided by design characteristics and by the type of biofeedback technique employed.

1. GROUP STUDIES WITH ASTHMA ATTENTION OR REGULAR-
   CARE CONTROLS

Ten studies fall into this category. Since biofeedback involves the utilization of an involved mechanical apparatus, an appropriate attention-placebo con-

## TABLE III

Biofeedback Techniques and Design Characteristics[a]

| Design characteristics[b] | Type of feedback | | |
| --- | --- | --- | --- |
| | EMG | | |
| | To enhance relaxation | Interaction with respiratory variables | Feedback of respiratory variables |
| 1 | Davis et al. (1973) Scherr et al. (1975) | Kotses et al. (1976) Kotses et al (1978) Scherr and Crawford (1978) | Janson-Bjerklie and Clark (1982) Khan (1977) Khan et al. (1978) Vachon and Rich (1976) |
| 2 | — | — | Steptoe et al. (1981) |
| 3 | — | — | Danker et al. (1975) |

[a] Does not include Harding and Maher (1982): Feedback of cardiac acceleration; design characteristics = 1.

[b] 1, Groups studies with asthma regular-care or attention-placebo control; 2, studies comparing more than one group or treatment; 3, uncontrolled one-group studies.

trol group to rule out nonspecific treatment effects is the noncontingent feedback control. With this method, random feedback is given to the subject at approximately the same frequency as that given to treatment subjects, but the feedback signal is not contingent upon production of desired changes in the targeted physiological variable. Many of the interventions described in this section employed this type of attention-placebo control.

Two biofeedback studies with asthma regular-care or attention controls employed EMG biofeedback as a means of facilitating progressive muscle relaxation training. The earliest of these (Davis et al., 1973), was discussed in the section on relaxation investigations and included a relaxation-alone, an EMG biofeedback plus relaxation group, and a regular-care control. Their data showed no significant differences for the sample as a whole, but did indicate that, among less severely asthmatic subjects, both biofeedback and relaxation training resulted in significantly better outcome than did the regular-care control. No muscle tension data are presented in the published report, however, so it is unclear whether muscle relaxation actually occurred in the biofeedback subjects.

Scherr and colleagues (Scherr, Crawford, Sergent, & Scherr, 1975) report an investigation completed at a summer camp for asthmatic children. All children were treated with bronchodilator medication in addition to their participation in the research. The design included 44 subjects assigned to one experimental and one control group. Experimental subjects received 6 weeks of frontalis muscle EMG biofeedback-mediated relaxation training; the control group received regular care which included thrice-daily PEFR assessments.

Results showed that mean PEFR improved significantly (statistically and clinically) for both experimental (+43% increase) and control (+31% increase) subjects during the 2 months of camp. Outcome for biofeedback subjects was significantly better than for controls on peak flow scores, number of infirmary visits, number of asthma attacks, and steroid usage. Since nonspecific treatment effects were not controlled for in this study, it is possible that the differential attention to the biofeedback group was responsible for this outcome.

Four studies (reported in three articles) investigated the effects of EMG biofeedback of specific muscle systems on asthma symptomatology. Kotses, Glaus, Crawford, Edwards, and Scherr (1976) studied the effect of frontalis muscle relaxation on peak expiratory flow in 36 asthmatic children who were assigned to a contingent feedback (CF) group, a noncontingent feedback (NCF) control group, or a regular-care control. All subjects were summer asthma camp residents treated with bronchodilator or steroid medication. Experimental and NCF subjects were trained in nine half-hour sessions over 3 weeks. Each NCF subject was yoked during session to an experimental subject, enabling the investigators to equate the amount of feedback received by experimental and control subjects.

Results showed a strong conditioning of frontalis muscle relaxation for the CF group, whereas NCF subjects' EMG tension values increased over time. In addition, CF subjects showed a marked increase in peak expiratory flow, whereas subjects in both control groups showed essentially no change in lung function during the study. Lack of raw PEFR data in the report precludes determination of clinical significance of these pulmonary changes.

In a subsequent study, Kotses, Glaus, Bricel, Edwards, and Crawford (1978) studied the effects of biofeedback of two separate muscle systems on PEFR using a yoked control design. Subjects were 40 asthmatic children at a summer asthma camp, 23 of whom received some type of asthma pharmacotherapy during the investigation. These researchers wanted to determine if muscle relaxation in any one of a variety of muscles would result in similar changes in peak flow. They provided feedback of electromyographic activity in either the frontalis or brachioradialis muscle, either contingently or noncontingently, to two experimental and two control groups. Children in the frontalis and brachioradialis contingent (FC and BC) groups were paired with noncontingent control children during nine 10-minute sessions. Frontalis contingent subjects showed significantly greater frontalis EMG relaxation than did frontalis noncontingent (FNC) subjects. Brachioradialis contingent and noncontingent subjects did not differ from each other on brachioradialis relaxation during training. Similarly, peak expiratory flow change scores were significantly greater for the FC group than for the FNC group and did not differ for the BC group compared to the BNC group. Therefore, only the group who had received frontalis contingent biofeedback demonstrated statistically, although probably not clinically, significant improvements in pulmonary function after training. Since brachioradialis relaxation was not achieved in the BC group, however, the question of whether successful brachioradialis relaxation might have resulted in improvement in PEFR remains unanswered.

Scherr and Crawford (1978) report two investigations performed in consecutive years at an asthma summer camp for children ages 6 to 15. The first study investigated the effects for 36 subjects of contingent EMG (frontalis) biofeedback (CF), yoked noncontingent EMG feedback (NCF), or regular-care control. A significant conditioning effect for frontalis muscle activity was demonstrated for CF, but not for NCF, subjects. Pulmonary function of all campers improved during the summer, but PEFR for the CF group was significantly improved over that of both control groups.

In an investigation the following summer, 50 campers were assigned to one of five groups: a contingent frontalis (CF) or brachioradialis (CB) group, a yoked noncontingent frontalis (NCF) or brachioradialis (NCB) group, or a regular-care control. Significantly reduced EMG activity was conditioned in FC subjects but was not demonstrated for any other group. As in the Kotses *et al.* (1978) study, pulmonary function scores increased significantly only for the FC group, which was the only group for which significant muscle relaxation occurred.

In an interesting investigation similar in strategy to those targeting the interaction between relaxation in specific muscle systems and respiratory variables, Harding and Maher (1982) provided biofeedback training of cardiac acceleration and measured the effects on airway resistance in asthmatic adults. These investigators postulated that, since narrowing of the bronchial airways appears to be a consequence of vagally mediated increases in smooth muscle tone, voluntary control of output from the vagus nerve should inhibit early asthmatic response. Citing the close anatomical and functional relationship of vagal innervation to the heart as well as to the lungs, the authors suggest that inhibition of vagal efferent activity during biofeedback training for control of heart rate should be general throughout vagal fibers, thus resulting in bronchodilation in the lungs. If so, then voluntary cardiac acceleration could be of potential benefit to asthmatics in the early stages of an attack.

Twenty-four adolescent and adult asthmatics were assigned either to an experimental group that received training in biofeedback-induced voluntary cardiac acceleration or to a control group connected to the biofeedback equipment and told to hold the heart rate meter needle steady during 15 training trials. Following one session for controls or after successful conditioning of heart rate for experimental subjects (two to five sessions), all subjects maintained daily records of asthma symptoms and medication use for at least 2 weeks. Biofeedback subjects were instructed to use the cardiac acceleration technique when they experienced tightness in the chest as a means of aborting attacks.

Eight subjects were dropped from the study due to inability to control heart rate after training or for self-administration of medication during the experiment. Experimental group subjects showed a significant increase in heart rate (16% increase compared to 6% decrease for controls) and PEFR (8% increase compared to controls' 2% decrease) after training. Biofeedback subjects, in addition, showed significant improvement during the post-treatment period on all variables including attack frequency and medication use per week and per attack.

Two flaws in this research make caution necessary in interpreting these otherwise interesting results. First, although an attention control was included in the design, some experimental subjects received five times as many sessions and, thus, significantly more attention, than did controls, making it impossible to rule out nonspecific treatment effects as a causative agent in outcome. Second, data from the 8 subjects dropped from the study, half of whom were unable to achieve voluntary cardiac acceleration, were not included in the analyses. The results suggest, nevertheless, that, for subjects who can learn the technique, biofeedback of cardiac acceleration may improve pulmonary function and may be an effective technique for reducing symptoms of asthma and amount of medication use.

Four studies have tested the effects of biofeedback of respiratory variables and have included an asthma attention control group. The earliest of these (Vachon & Rich, 1976) proceeded in two phases of which the second is the better designed. Subjects for both phases were asthmatic adults between the ages of 18 and 30; none were taking steroids; an unreported number were taking other antiasthma medication. Biofeedback of total respiratory resistance ($R_t$) by the forced oscillation method (see Franetzski, Prestele, & Korn, 1979, for description) was employed in all phases.

In Phase I, 28 subjects received biofeedback training during one 45-minute session. Mean $R_t$ decreased (improved) significantly during the session. An attempt to provide a noncontingent feedback control was conducted at a later time in which 5 subjects received random $R_t$ feedback and showed no tendency to lower total respiratory resistance during sessions.

In the second phase 13 subjects were assigned to concurrent contingent or noncontingent biofeedback groups. Replicating the results found in the earlier phase, contingent feedback subjects showed a 15% reduction in $R_t$ over the session while concontingent feedback subjects showed essentially no change.

Khan (1977) labeled 80 asthmatic outpatients, ages 8 to 15, as "reactors" ($N = 40$) or "nonreactors" ($N = 40$) based on the presence or absence of at least a 15% decrease in $FEV_1$ after inhalation of nebulized saline that had been described as a potent allergen. Half of the reactors and half of the nonreactors were randomized to an experimental or a regular-care control group. Experimental subjects received visual feedback of $FEV_1$ during five to eight training sessions with instructions to decrease airway resistance. In the next 10 sessions, experimental subjects underwent "linking training," designed to help the child use his or her ability to decrease airway resistance in the presence of bronchoconstriction. Subjects in the control group were seen once a week for assessment; all subjects were followed for 1 year.

Unfortunately, no pulmonary function measure was used as an outcome variable in this study. The experimental group as a whole did not differ from controls on number or duration of asthma attacks, medication use, emergency room visits, or hospitalizations. Nonreactors in the experimental group improved significantly more than control nonreactors on number and duration of attacks and on a measure of asthma severity. Results of this study suggest that $FEV_1$ biofeedback training may be useful in ameliorating asthma severity for a subset of asthmatic children who are nonreactive to suggestions of bronchoconstriction, but provide no evidence for effectiveness of the technique for the treatment group as a whole.

In a replication of this previous study, Khan, Staerk, and Bonk (1978) randomly assigned five reactors and five nonreactors, all outpatient children, to an experimental $FEV_1$ biofeedback group and an equal number to a regular-care control. Five sessions of biofeedback training and 10 sessions of "linking training" were provided. All subjects were followed for 1 year, with experimental subjects receiving five booster sessions each at 1, 2, 3, and 6 months posttreatment.

Data on the success of $FEV_1$ conditioning are not presented, nor are posttraining pulmonary function outcome measures. Reported results indicate significant improvement for the biofeedback group on number of attacks and emergency room visits and amount of medication use. It is unclear, however, due to lack of $FEV_1$ conditioning data and an attention control group, whether this result is due to biofeedback training or to some other factor.

In the final investigation in this section, Janson-Bjerklie and Clark (1982) randomly assigned 16 outpatient asthmatic adults to a contingent or noncontingent biofeedback group. None of the subjects was taking steroids, but use of other medications is not reported. Subjects in the contingent feedback experimental group received feedback for lowering total respiratory resistance in five 25-minute sessions. Control subjects received random feedback for the same number of sessions. A differential change over time was evident for the two groups, with mean decrease in $R_t$ significantly greater for experimental than for control subjects. The degree of clinical significance of these results cannot be extrapolated from the data presented.

In the 10 articles discussed in this section, nine reported statistically significant improvements in outcome for subjects trained with a biofeedback intervention compared to asthma regular-care or attention-placebo controls. Of EMG studies, only frontalis muscle feedback was effective in altering pulmonary function. Brachioradialis conditioning was not achieved in any study, however, so effects of relaxation in that muscle on pulmonary variables is not known. Only two of these 10 interventions (Scherr *et al.*, 1975; Vachon & Rich, 1976) achieved results which could be considered clinically significant.

## 2. STUDIES COMPARING MORE THAN ONE GROUP OR TREATMENT

In the only investigation in this category, Steptoe, Phillips, and Harling (1981) studied the ability of 8 asthmatic and 16 nonasthmatic adults to exert voluntary control over respiratory resistance after biofeedback training using the forced oscillation technique. All but one of the asthmatic subjects were taking daily asthma medication. For the asthmatics, a significant improvement in their ability to decrease $R_t$ within session occurred over time; the session 1 change in respiratory resistance averaged $+0.5\%$, whereas by session 4, subjects decreased (improved) $R_t$ an average of $-3.2\%$ over trials. No differences in PEFR or $FEV_1$ across sessions were observed.

## 3. UNCONTROLLED ONE-GROUP STUDIES

The final biofeedback investigations were reported by Danker, Miklich, Pratt, and Creer (1975) in one published report. Subjects in these two studies were inpatients at the National Asthma Center and ranged in age from 8 to 11. In Study 1, six male subjects were provided with visual feedback of peak expiratory flow and were told to maximize "good" PEFRs during an unreported number of sessions. The criterion value for feedback was set initially at a percentage of baseline score and was increased between sessions if all PEFR expirations within session were above the criterion. Results showed no evidence of conditioned increase in PEFR.

In Study 2, five male patients attended 5 to 10 baseline sessions and from 5 to 22 feedback training sessions. New criterion values were set at the beginning of each session at the median of the first three PEFR blows completed. When a subject exceeded or fell below the criterion for three consecutive blows, the criterion was either raised or reduced 5 liters/minute. Although three of five subjects showed significant improvement, no overall group pattern of improvement was demonstrated in this study.

## 4. SUMMARY OF BIOFEEDBACK INTERVENTIONS

Overall, of the 15 studies cited, 11 showed statistically significant differences between the experimental and control groups; only two of these interventions, however, can be said to demonstrate clinically meaningful improvements in pulmonary function after biofeedback training.

This body of research appears to include better attention to design characteristics, including larger groups of subjects and inclusion of appropriate controls, than does the group of studies investigating relaxation interventions. The large proportion of studies with statistically significant results is encouraging,

but lack of clinical significance of the outcome engenders doubt as to the technique's usefulness with clinical populations.

## D.   Systematic Desensitization Interventions

Although the current belief is that factors other than psychological variables are responsible for the initial onset of asthma, few clinicians or researchers would deny that psychological factors including suggestion, anxiety, and/or other strong emotions, may be important for some patients in precipitating attacks and in maintaining the disorder (e.g., Levinson, 1979; Luparello *et al.*, 1969; McNichol *et al.*, 1973). One goal of treating such patients is to increase their ability to think about asthma and its precipitants without creating anxiety or precipitating an attack (Yorkston *et al.*, 1974).

Progressive muscle relaxation training has been employed, as reviewed, by some researchers to assist patients in counteracting the anxiety response. Others, following Wolpe's (1982) contention that the autonomic effects of relaxation are effective in counteracting only relatively weak anxiety responses, have proposed that systematic desensitization of asthma-related anxieties might be more effective. Generally, in these investigations, subjects are trained initially in PMR and then are exposed in a step-by-step manner to weak and then successively stronger asthma-related, anxiety-producing stimuli while maintaining a relaxed state. As exposure is repeated, the stimuli should progressively lose the ability to elicit anxiety and should, therefore, result in a decrease in anxiety-related asthma symptomatology. Four groups of researchers have investigated the effects of systematic desensitization (SD) in published group studies.

### 1.   GROUP STUDIES WITH ASTHMA ATTENTION–PLACEBO OR REGULAR-CARE CONTROLS

Only one study, by Miklich, Renne, Creer, Alexander, Chai, Davis, Hoffman, and Danker-Brown (1977), compared the effects of SD for asthmatics with a regular-care asthma control. The 19 experimental and 7 control subjects were inpatient asthmatic children, all of whom received pharmacotherapy throughout the study. Assignment to groups was "quasirandom" (p. 286) and depended upon whether a therapist was available when a particular subject was ready for treatment. Experimental subjects were significantly older ($\bar{X} = 12.4$ years) than controls ($\bar{X} = 10.1$ years).

A 4-month pretreatment period of assessment was followed by the treatment period, lasting an average of 10 weeks, during which PMR training and SD were completed. Some therapists used EMG biofeedback to enhance relaxation training for an unspecified number of subjects. Ten weeks of posttreatment assessment preceeded 10 weeks of no assessment, followed by resumption of assessment (at approximately 4 months posttreatment) for an average of 6 weeks.

Instead of repeated measures ANOVAs, $t$ tests for differences between group means during each of the four assessment periods were completed. $FEV_1$ scores were much higher for SD subjects than for controls during treatment, posttreatment, and follow-up; control subjects, however, did better than experimental subjects on all measures of symptom frequency during treatment, but not at any other time. Pulmonary function differences were due more to the deterioration of control subjects over time than to improvement by SD subjects who remained less than 2% below their expected $FEV_1$ scores throughout.

The inadequacy of the statistical analyses employed in this study and the fact that experimental subjects were significantly older and, therefore, were more likely to be entering puberty when many children "outgrow" their asthma (Ellis, 1983), make results of this investigation difficult to interpret and preclude clear conclusions regarding the efficacy of this SD intervention.

### 2. STUDIES COMPARING MORE THAN ONE TREATMENT OR GROUP

All three studies in this section have been reviewed previously and are mentioned only briefly here. Moore (1965) compared relaxation, relaxation plus suggestion, and relaxation with "reciprocal inhibition" (systematic desensitization) and found that SD subjects showed significantly improved PEFR scores over those obtained in the other two treatments.

Yorkston et al. (1974), in their investigation of 14 adults randomized to a relaxation or an SD group, demonstrated a 20% increase in $FEV_1$ for SD subjects, whereas relaxation subjects showed no change over time. In an attempt to replicate this finding (Yorkston et al., 1979), 28 subjects were randomized to a relaxation group, an SD group, or a "verbal and practical desensitization" group. There were no significant differences among groups over time.

### 3. SUMMARY

A summary of these four investigations shows that results of three studies were statistically significant in favor of the SD group and that, of these, improvements in two studies were clinically meaningful. These findings are provocative, but further investigation with inclusion of appropriate controls is necessary before an unqualified statement of treatment effectiveness can be made.

## E.  Assertive Training

Hock and his co-workers (Hock et al., 1977, 1978) have investigated the effects of assertive training with male asthmatic children in two studies described previously. Assertive training was chosen as an intervention as a means to "reduce the anxiety and tension of the asthmatic child, and thereby raise the threshold for the manifestation of his physical symptoms" (Hock et al., 1977, p.

593). This approach assumes that asthmatics have a skills deficit in the area of expression of feelings of anger and aggression.

Hock and colleagues (1977) randomized subjects to relaxation, assertive training, or regular-care groups. Group differences in $FEV_1$ were found only at 1 month follow-up when relaxation subjects' pulmonary function was significantly better than that of controls and of subjects who had received assertive training.

In a follow-up study (Hock *et al.*, 1978), 43 children were randomly assigned to PMR, assertive training, or PMR plus assertive training experimental groups, or to a regular-care or a leaderless peer group control. Subjects in the two treatment groups which included relaxation training improved significantly more than subjects in the other three groups.

Results of these two studies suggest that assertive training is not a powerful intervention, at least for male asthmatic children who show no improvement compared to controls after training in this skill. Beneficial effects for the relaxation plus assertive training group probably were due to the PMR component since outcome for the combined group did not differ from that of the relaxation alone group.

## F.  Behavior Management Interventions

The final three studies in this review have a somewhat different focus than those previously described. These investigators targeted management of asthma-related behaviors employing operant techniques instead of attempting to alter directly pulmonary function variables or asthma symptomatology. Two of these three interventions employ single-case research designs.

### 1.  INVESTIGATIONS WITH SINGLE CASE DESIGNS

Neisworth and Moore (1972) successfully treated a 7-year-old asthmatic boy who had developed a continuing pattern of prolonged episodes of coughing and wheezing at bedtime. Parents agreed that they had reinforced their son's "sick" behavior with sympathetic verbal and tactile attention and with administration of medication. Parents participated in a treatment program of ABAB design which included 10 days of baseline recording of duration of bedtime episodes, 30 days of intervention, consisting of extinction (ignoring "sick" behaviors at bedtime) plus differential reinforcement of incompatible behavior, 10 days of a withdrawal condition (return to attention for sick behavior) and, finally, reinstitution of treatment contingencies. A drastic reduction in duration of episodes occurred during treatment phases and was maintained at 11-month follow-up.

Training asthmatic children to use inhalation therapy equipment properly was the goal of two multiple baseline experiments by Renne and Creer (1976). The Intermittent Positive-Pressure Breathing (IPPB) device converts liquid bronchodilator medicine into inhalable form and delivers it under pressure to the patient's airways. Ineffective use of this equipment, which requires that three distinct behaviors be emitted simultaneously in a synchronized manner, results in reduced benefits of treatment and, sometimes, in further hospitalization to bring asthma attacks under control (Renne & Creer, 1976).

In Experiment 1, a reinforcement program was designed to increase accuracy of the three targeted behaviors, eye fixation, proper facial posturing, and diaphragmatic breathing, for four subjects in a multiple baseline design across behaviors, with data pooled across subjects. One 26-trial session was completed for each subject with script, redeemable for a gift, available for each subject upon achievement of criterion. All incorrect behaviors were at zero by end of treatment. Follow-up inspection of records indicated that IPPB treatment effectiveness increased from 4% at pretreatment to 82.3% after completion of training. Generalization of training was maximized by offering additional reinforcement for later appropriate use of the apparatus and occurred for all subjects in postintervention situations when the children actually were suffering from asthma symptoms.

In Experiment 2, a similar procedure was employed with two children, with the difference that eight nurses were trained to implement the intervention. Similar results were obtained, suggesting that knowledge of basic operant learning principles and their use in applied settings by medical personnel may be an appropriate method for increasing effectiveness of this common asthma therapy.

## 2.  UNCONTROLLED ONE-GROUP STUDIES

In the final study Hochstadt, Shepard, and Lulla (1980) implemented an intervention which included time out for inappropriate behavior and contingent positive reinforcement for appropriate behavior for seven asthmatic children who "overused" inpatient hospitalization at a rate in excess of the severity of their asthma. Subjects were assigned a private room on admission and were told that they could be discharged when acceptable PEFR values were obtained. Subjects could not watch television or participate in recreational activities during admission. To reward appropriate use of the hospital, subjects who were symptom-free at regularly scheduled outpatient visits were given access to the hospital recreational facilities for the afternoon. Results showed a significant decrease in days of hospitalization per year from pre- to postintervention and suggest that this type of behavioral intervention for hospital overusers warrants further investigation.

## G.  Summary of Behavioral Interventions

Table IV summarizes the reported effectiveness of behavioral methods used as adjunctive treatments for asthma. Biofeedback, systematic desensitization, and operant interventions were successful in producing statistically meaningful

## TABLE IV

Results of Behavioral Interventions

| Treatment | No. of groups | Studies with significant results (%) | |
|---|---|---|---|
| | | Statistical sign. | Clinical sign.[a] |
| Relaxation | 12 | 55 | 17 |
| Biofeedback | 16 | 67 | 13 |
| Systematic desensitization | 4 | 75 | 50 |
| Assertive training | 3 | 0 | 0 |
| Behavior management | 4[b] | 75 | N/A[c] |

[a] At least a 15% increase in $FEV_1$ or PEFR.

[b] Includes one single-case design.

[c] No pulmonary function outcome data reported.

results for over half the groups studied. Relaxation techniques were somewhat less beneficial overall; training in assertive skills, for those few groups studied, was ineffective in producing amelioration of disease symptoms.

The clinical usefulness of these techniques is less well demonstrated, in that only for systematic desensitization does the outcome meet the common criteria for clinical significance in at least half the studies. Perhaps for adjunctive treatments, however, which are meant to be used *in addition to* asthma medication, interventions can be considered clinically useful even if they result in less than a 15% improvement in pulmonary function. A behavioral treatment which produces a 10% increase in PEFR, for example, when used in addition to a bronchodilator drug which itself effects a clinical improvement, may provide just enough added relief to allow the patient to resume or to maintain daily activities without disruption.

In addition, methodological flaws cause many of these investigations to be less than the "best tests" of behavioral management techniques; such methodological considerations are discussed in the next section.

## III. METHODOLOGICAL ISSUES IN ASTHMA RESEARCH

Overall, attention to methodological issues in this body of research is poor and leaves open to question the validity of results derived from these studies. Three areas of deficiency, including questions of basic research design, the issues of what and how variables should be measured, and general reporting errors, are obvious after a review of the literature.

## A.  Basic Design Issues

The *lack of adequate control groups* in this research has been discussed. Reiteration of the need for attention-placebo or, at least, regular-care asthma controls in group designs and appropriate single case research designs for small *N*'s is worthwhile because of the implications of failure to include such controls. Of the 29 studies cited, 16 (55%) included either a regular-care control, an attention-placebo control, or both, and 2 followed adequate single case design, leaving 11 groups of investigators who compared several treatments without a control or studied one group alone.

Other important design considerations are as follows:

1.  *Failure to follow up.* In only three investigations (10%) were subjects followed beyond 6 months to determine long-term treatment effects. Seventeen studies lacked any follow-up at all, precluding interpretation for long-term effectiveness of these training techniques.

2.  *Small sample sizes.* Small *N*'s bias against finding statistical evidence in support of a particular intervention's usefulness, even if meaningful differences do exist between treatments. Routine use of power analysis (Cohen, 1977; Wing & Jeffery, 1984) during the research design stage would go a long way toward providing investigators with at least the opportunity to discover significant results postintervention.

3.  *Assignment of subjects to groups.* Researchers often fail to add to their designs attention to subject characteristics which may differentiate subpopulations of asthmatics. Since it is not uncommon for children at puberty to outgrow their asthma without therapy (Ellis, 1983), for example, attention to *age* of subjects is necessary; inclusion of both children and adults in a sample, or of a preponderance of young children in one group and a larger number of prepubertal subjects in another is a practice which may confound interpretation of results.

*Sex* of subjects may also be important since four times as many boys as girls have asthma by age 14 (McNichol & Williams, 1973); girls who remain asthmatic by that age may be different in some meaningful way which would cause differential response to treatment.

Attention to *severity of the disorder,* due to differential prognostic implications for mild, moderate, and severe asthmatics, is also important. Fifty percent of the reviewed investigations failed to control for severity. Ellis (1983) suggests objective criteria for grading asthma severity on the basis of history and course of the disease.

In addition, controlling for *intrinsic/extrinsic* or *reactor/nonreactor* characteristics may be important in designing and implementing behavioral interventions (e.g., Richter & Dahme, 1982; Khan, 1977). Asthmatics with a stronger psychological component to the disorder may be differentially amenable to a psychological intervention than subjects whose asthma is clearly allergen based.

## B.   What and How to Measure

### 1.   MEASURES OF ASTHMA OUTCOME

Almost all investigations include some measure of pulmonary function outcome. The pros and cons of various physiological assessment devices have been discussed in the section on measurement.

In addition to physiological pulmonary function measures, behavioral outcome measures, such as frequency of asthma attacks, school absences, hospitalizations, etc., should be employed in order to tap this domain of activity-disrupting sequelae of the disease. Seventy-two percent of studies report both a physiological and behavioral outcome measure.

### 2.   COMPLIANCE TO MEDICATION REGIMENS

A critical issue, both in clinical management of asthma and in the design of studies to test adjunctive treatments for the disease, is that of patient compliance to the medication regimen. Compliance to long-term regimens for chronic disease is poor: approximately 54% of chronically ill patients take their medication as prescribed (Sackett & Snow, 1979). The available data for compliance to theophylline regimens by asthmatic patients indicates an even poorer record: Eney and Goldstein (1976) found that only 11% of their pediatric sample had serum theophylline levels within the therapeutic range; other investigators have found better, although still not encouraging, results (25.5%: Sublett, Pollard, Kadlec, & Karibo, 1979; 50%: Cluss, Epstein, Galvis, Fireman, & Friday, 1984).

In-range serum theophylline levels have shown a clear relationship to adequate pulmonary function (Varni, 1983), so that patients who do not take their medication are at risk for poorer function. Cluss and her colleagues (1984) measured the medication compliance of asthmatic children by adding a riboflavin (vitamin $B_2$) tracer to daily theophylline doses and testing for the presence of riboflavin in the subjects' urine. They found that noncompliant children experienced significantly more wheezing days, showed greater variability in lung function scores, and experienced lower overall lung function during a 2-week period than their more compliant peers.

Unfortunately, although researchers may claim to study specific behavioral methods as adjunctive treatments for asthma in addition to regular-care pharmacological intervention, *no investigator* in the studies reviewed tested for compliance in an outpatient sample. It clearly becomes difficult, then, to determine success or failure of interventions as adjunctive treatments since, for possibly more than half of each sample, the nonpharmacological intervention was the *only* treatment. See Epstein and Cluss (1982) for a review and discussion of compliance techniques and research.

## C.  Errors in Reporting

Poor reporting in published accounts, although not a methodological issue, does cause difficulty for the reader who is interested in such concerns or who simply wishes to determine whether results described are valid. Failure to report sample sizes and raw data, or to describe whether subjects were randomized to groups or were taking concurrent medications is common in this literature. Authors in only 64% of the studies cited, for example, reported clearly whether subjects were taking asthma medications.

## IV.  SUMMARY

Results of this review of the behavioral literature on asthma therapy indicate that systematic desensitization, operant interventions, and biofeedback treatments have been successful in altering pulmonary functioning, asthma symptomatology, and/or asthma-related behaviors, whereas some evidence for the limited effectiveness of relaxation training has been demonstrated. The clinical usefulness of these techniques remains open to interpretation.

It cannot be said, however, that the results reported represent the definitive statement regarding the usefulness of these interventions, due to the lack of methodological sophistication evident in this body of research. Behavioral investigators currently interested in this area have the opportunity to design and implement research strategies which attend to sound methodological considerations and which may present a clearer demonstration of the efficacy of the adjunctive behavioral treatments which have been used with asthma patients for the past several decades.

## REFERENCES

Aas, K. (1963). Prognosis for asthmatic children. *Acta Paediatrica Supplement,* **140,** 87–88.

Alexander, A. B. (1972). Systematic relaxation and flow rates in asthmatic children: Relationship to emotional precipitants and anxiety. *Journal of Psychosomatic Research,* **16,** 405–410.

Alexander, A. B., Cropp, G., & Chai, H. (1979). Effects of relaxation training on pulmonary mechanics in children with asthma. *Journal of Applied Behavior Analysis,* **12,** 27–35.

Alexander, A. B., Miklich, D., & Hershkoff, H. (1972). The immediate effects of systematic relaxation training on peak expiratory flow rates in asthmatic children. *Psychosomatic Medicine,* **34,** 388–394.

American Lung Association (1975). *Introduction to lung diseases* (6th edition).

Chai, H., Purcell, K., Brady, K., & Falliers, C. (1968). Therapeutic and investigational evaluation of asthmatic children. *Journal of Allergy,* **41,** 23–36.

Cluss, P., Epstein, L., Galvis, S., Fireman, P., & Friday, G. (1984). Effect of compliance for chronic asthmatic children. *Journal of Consulting and Clinical Psychology,* **52,** 909–910.

Cohen, J. (1977). *Statistical power analysis for the behavioral sciences,* New York: Academic Press.

Creer, T. (1978). Asthma: Psychologic aspects and management. In E. Middleton, Jr., C. Reed, & E. Ellis (Eds.), *Allergy: Principles and practice* (pp. 796–797). St. Louis: Mosby.

Crofton, J., & Douglas, A. (1969). *Respiratory diseases.* Oxford: Blackwell.

Danker, P., Miklich, D., Pratt, C., & Creer, T. (1975). An unsuccessful attempt to instrumentally condition peak expiratory flow rates in asthmatic children. *Journal of Psychosomatic Research,* **19,** 209–213.

Davidson, R., & Schwartz, G. (1976). The psychobiology of relaxation and related states: A multiprocess theory. In D. Mostotsky (Ed.), *Behavior control and modification of physiological activity.* New York: Prentice-Hall.

Davis, M., Saunders, D., Creer, T., & Chai, H. (1973). Relaxation training facilitated by biofeedback apparatus as a supplemental treatment in bronchial asthma. *Journal of Psychosomatic Research,* **17,** 121–128.

Dekker, E., & Groen, J. (1956). Reproducible psychogenic attacks of asthma: A laboratory study. *Journal of Psychosomatic Research,* **1,** 58–67.

Ellis, E. (1983). Asthma in childhood. *Journal of Allergy and Clinical Immunology,* **72,** 526–539.

Eney, R., & Goldstein, E. (1976). Compliance of chronic asthmatics with oral administration of theophylline as measured by serum and salivary measures. *Pediatrics,* **57,** 513–517.

Epstein, L., & Cluss, P. (1982). A behavioral medicine perspective on adherence to long-term medical regimens. *Journal of Consulting and Clinical Psychology,* **50,** 950–971.

Erskine, J., & Schonell, M. (1981). Relaxation therapy in asthma: A critical review. *Psychosomatic Medicine,* **43,** 365–372.

Fireman, P., Friday, G., Gira, C., Vierthaler, W., & Michaels, L. (1981). Teaching self-management skills to asthmatic children and their parents in an ambulatory care setting. *Pediatrics,* **68,** 341–348.

Franetzski, M., Prestele, K., & Korn, V. (1979). A direct-display oscillation method for measurement of respiratory impedance. *Journal of Applied Physiology,* **46,** 956.

French, T., & Alexander, F. (1941). *Psychosomatic medicine: Monograph series* (vol. 4). Washington, D.C.: National Research Council.

Gordis, L. (1973). *Epidemiology of chronic lung diseases in children.* Baltimore: Johns Hopkins Univ. Press.

Harding, A., & Maher, K. (1982). Biofeedback training of cardiac acceleration: Effects on airway resistance in bronchial asthma. *Journal of Psychosomatic Research,* **26,** 447–454.

Hersen, M., & Barlow, D. (1976). *Single-case experimental designs: Strategies for studying behavior change.* Oxford: Pergamon.

Hochstadt, N., Shepard, J., & Lulla, S. (1980). Reducing hospitalizations of children with asthma. *Journal of Pediatrics,* **97,** 1012–1015.

Hock, R., Bramble, J., & Kennard, D. (1977). A comparison between relaxation and assertive training with asthmatic male children. *Biological Psychiatry,* **12,** 593–596.

Hock, R., Rodgers, C., Reddi, C., & Kennard, D. (1978). Medico-psychological interventions in male asthmatic children: An evaluation of physiological change. *Psychosomatic Medicine,* **40,** 210–215.

Itkin, I. (1967). Bronchial hypersensitivity to mecholyl and histamine in asthma subjects. *Journal of Allergy,* **40,** 245–256.

Jacobson, E. (1938). *Progressive relaxation.* Chicago: Univ. of Chicago Press.

Jacobson, E. (1939). Variation of blood pressure with skeletal muscle tension and relaxation. *Annals of Internal Medicine*, **12**, 1194–1212.

Jacobson, E. (1940). Variation of pulse rate with skeletal muscle tension and relaxation. *Annals of Internal Medicine*, **13**, 1619–1625.

Janson-Bjerklie, S., & Clark, E. (1982). The effects of biofeedback training on bronchial diameter in asthma. *Heart and Lung*, **11**, 200–207.

Khan, A. (1977). Effectiveness of biodfeedback and counter-conditioning in the treatment of bronchial asthma. *Journal of Psychosomatic Research*, **21**, 97–104.

Khan, A., Staerk, M., & Bonk, C. (1978). Role of counter-conditioning in the treatment of asthma. *Journal of Psychosomatic Research*, **17**, 389–392.

King, N. (1980). The behavioral management of asthma and asthma-related problems in children: A critical review of the literature. *Journal of Behavioral Medicine*, **3**, 169–189.

Knapp, T., & Wells, L. (1978). Behavior therapy for asthma: A review. *Behavior Research and Therapy*, **16**, 103–115.

Kotses, H., & Glaus, K. (1981). Applications of biofeedback to the treatment of asthma: A critical review. *Biofeedback and Self-Regulation*, **6**, 573–593.

Kotses, H., Glaus, K., Bricel, S., Edwards, J., & Crawford, P. (1978). Operant muscular relaxation and peak expiratory flow rate in asthmatic children. *Journal of Psychosomatic Research*, **22**, 17–23.

Kotses, H., Glaus, K., Crawford, P., Edwards, J., & Scherr, M. (1976). Operant reduction of frontalis EMG activity in the treatment of asthma in children. *Journal of Psychosomatic Research*, **20**, 453–459.

Leffert, F. (1980). The management of chronic asthma. *Journal of Pediatrics*, **97**, 875–885.

Levinson, R. (1979). Effects of thematically relevant and general stressors on specificity of responding in asthmatic and nonasthmatic subjects. *Psychosomatic Medicine*, **41**, 28–39.

Luparello, T., Leist, N., Lourie, C., & Swett, P. (1970). The interaction of psychologic agents on airway reactivity in asthmatic subjects. *Psychosomatic Medicine*, **32**, 509–513.

McFadden, E., & Austin, K. (1977). Asthma. In G. Thorn, R. Adams, E. Braunwald, K. Isselbacher, & R. Petersdorf (Eds.), *Harrison's principles of internal medicine* (8th edition). New York: McGraw-Hill.

McFadden, E., Luparello, T., Lyons, H., & Bleecker, E. (1969). The mechanism of suggestion in the induction of acute asthma. *Psychosomatic Medicine*, **31**, 134–143.

McNichol, K., & Williams, K. (1973). Spectrum of asthma in children. *British Journal of Medicine*, **4**, 7–11.

McNichol, K., Williams, H., Allan, J., & McAndrew, I. (1973). Spectrum of asthma in children—III. Psychological and social components. *British Journal of Medicine*, **4**, 16–20.

Miklich, D., Renne, C., Creer, T., Alexander, A., Chai, H., Davis, M., Hoffman, A., & Danker-Brown, P. (1977). The clinical utility of behavior therapy as an adjunctive treatment for asthma. *Journal of Allergy and Clinical Immunology*, **60**, 285–294.

Moore, N. (1965). Behaviour therapy in bronchial asthma: A controlled study. *Journal of Psychosomatic Research*, **9**, 257–276.

Neisworth, J., & Moore, F. (1972). Operant treatment of asthmatic responding with the parent as therapist. *Behavior Therapy*, **3**, 95–99.

Ogilvie, A. (1962). Asthma: A study in prognosis of 1000 patients. *Thorax*, **17**, 183–189.

Philipp, R., Wilde, G., & Day, J. (1972). Suggestion and relaxation in asthmatics. *Journal of Psychosomatic Research*, **16**, 193–204.

Rackemann, F. (1918). A clinical study of one hundred and fifty cases of bronchial asthma. *Archives of Internal Medicine*, **22**, 522.

Rackemann, F., & Edwards, M. (1952). Asthma in children: A follow-up study of 688 patients after an interval of 20 years. *New England Journal of Medicine*, **246**, 815–823.

Rathus, S. (1973). Motoric, autonomic, and cognitive reciprocal inhibition of a case of hysterical bronchial asthma. *Adolescence, 8,* 29–32.

Renne, C., & Creer, T. (1976). Training children with asthma to use inhalation therapy equipment. *Journal of Applied Behavior Analysis, 9,* 1–11.

Richardson, J. (1977). The neural control of human tracheobronchial smooth muscle. In K. Austin & L. Lichtenstein (Eds.), *Asthma II: Physiology, immunopharmacology, and small muscle.* New York: Academic Press.

Richardson, J., & Beland, J. (1976). Noradrenergic inhibitory nervous system in human airways. *Journal of Applied Physiology, 41,* 764–771.

Richter, R., & Dahme, B. (1982). Bronchial asthma in adults: There is little evidence for the effectiveness of behavior therapy and relaxation. *Journal of Psychosomatic Research, 26,* 533–540.

Sackett, E., & Snow, J. (1979). The magnitude of compliance and noncompliance. In R. Haynes, D. Taylor, & D. Sackett (Eds.), *Compliance in health care.* Baltimore: Johns Hopkins Press.

Scherr, M., & Crawford, P. (1978). Three-year evaluation of biofeedback techniques in the treatment of children with chronic asthma in a summer camp environment. *Annals of Allergy, 38,* 288–292.

Scherr, M., Crawford, P., Sergent, C., & Scherr, C. (1975). Effect of biofeedback techniques on chronic asthma in a summer camp environment. *Annals of Allergy, 35,* 289–295.

Schiffer, C., & Hunt, E. (1963). Illness among Children. Children's Bureau Publ. No. 405, U.S. Department of Health, Education, and Welfare. Washington, D.C.: U.S. Govt. Printing Office.

Schonell, M. (1984). *Respiratory medicine* (2nd edition, revised by I. Campbell). Edinburgh: Churchill Livingstone.

Shapiro, D., & Surwit, R. (1979). Biofeedback. In O. Pomerleau & J. Brady (Eds.), *Behavioral medicine: Theory and practice.* Baltimore: Williams & Wilkins.

Shultz, J. (1932). *Autogenic training.* Stuttgart: Thieme.

Siegel, S., Katz, R., & Rachelefsky, G. (1978). Asthma in infancy and childhood. In E. Middleton, C. Reed, & E. Ellis (Eds.), *Allergy: Principles and practice* (vol. 2). St. Louis: Mosby.

Steptoe, A., Phillips, J., & Harling, J. (1981). Biofeedback and instructions in the modification of total respiratory resistance: An experimental study of asthmatic and non-asthmatic volunteers. *Journal of Psychosomatic Research, 25,* 541–551.

Sublett, J., Pollard, S., Kadlec, G., & Karibo, J. (1979). Noncompliance in asthmatic children: A study of theophylline levels in a pediatric emergency room population. *Annals of Allergy, 43,* 95–97.

Szentivanyi, A. (1968). The beta-adrenergic theory of atopic abnormality in bronchial asthma. *Journal of Allergy, 42,* 203–232.

Thoreson, L., & Kirmil-Gray, K. (1983). Self-management and the treatment of childhood asthma. *Journal of Allergy and Clinical Immunology, 72,* 596–606.

United States Department of Health, Education, & Welfare, Public Health Service (1979). NIH Publ. No. 79-387. Asthma and the other allergic diseases: NIAID Task Force Report.

Vachon, L., & Rich, E. (1976). Visceral learning in asthma. *Psychosomatic Medicine, 38,* 122–130.

VanArsdel, P., Jr., & Motulsky, A. (1959). Frequency and heritability of asthma and allergic rhinitis in college students. *Acta Genetica, 9,* 101–114.

Varni, T. (1983). *Clinical behavioral pediatrics: An interdisciplinary biobehavioral approach.* Oxford: Pergamon.

Walton, D. (1960). The application of learning theory to the treatment of a case of bronchial asthma. In H. Eysenck (Ed.), *Behaviour therapy and the neuroses,* Oxford: Pergamon.

Wing, R., & Jeffery, R. (1984). Sample size in clinical outcome research: The case of behavioral weight control. *Behavior Therapy, 15,* 550–556.

Wolpe, J. (1982). *The practice of behavior therapy* (2nd edition). Oxford: Pergamon.

Yorkston, N., Eckert, E., McHugh, R., Philander, D., & Blumenthal, M. (1979). Bronchial asthma: Improved lung function after behavior modification. *Psychosomatics, 20,* 325–331.

Yorkston, N., McHugh, R., Brady, R., Serber, M., & Sergeant, H. (1974). Verbal desensitisation in bronchial asthma. *Journal of Psychosomatic Research, 18,* 371–376.

# HEALTH BEHAVIOR CHANGE AT THE WORKSITE: CARDIOVASCULAR RISK REDUCTION

JAMES F. SALLIS

*Division of General Pediatrics*
*University of California, San Diego*
*La Jolla, California*

ROBERT D. HILL
STEPHEN P. FORTMANN
JUNE A. FLORA

*Stanford Center for Research in Disease Prevention*
*Stanford University Medical Center*
*Stanford, California*

## I.  INTRODUCTION

In 1978, cardiovascular diseases (CVD) killed 966,000 people in the United States, making it the largest cause of death of both men and women. Many of these deaths were in the prime working age group of 45–64, and there were an

PROGRESS IN BEHAVIOR
MODIFICATION, VOLUME 20

estimated 20.7 million persons whose activities were limited by heart conditions (U.S. Department of Health and Human Services, 1982). CVD may account for $230 billion per year in medical costs, lost productivity, and income (*Sourcebook of Health Insurance Data, 1981–1982,* 1983). The massive human and economic toll of CVD has led to national and international efforts to discover methods of reducing CVD morbidity and mortality.

Behavioral techniques have shown promise in their ability to promote heart healthy behavior changes in the areas of cigarette smoking (Lichtenstein & Brown, 1982) blood pressure (Jacob, Kraemer, & Agras, 1977), overweight (Brownell, 1982) hyperlipidemia (Carmody, Fay, Pierce, Connor, & Matarazzo, 1982), sedentary lifestyle (Martin & Dubbert, 1982), and Type A behavior (Suinn, 1982), though the need for improved intervention in all areas is apparent (Agras, 1982). The recognition of the utility of behavioral approaches for heart disease prevention has been accompanied by efforts to devise systems whereby behavior change technology can be disseminated to populations at high risk, as well as to the general public. Community health education programs have produced important decreases in CVD risk factors in several trials, and efforts to refine community-based interventions are under way (Farquhar, Fortmann, Wood, & Haskell, 1983). One of the basic tenets of community interventions is that existing organizations should be utilized for educational purposes whenever possible (Rothman, 1979). One category of existing organizations which has the potential to play a major role in community-based CVD prevention programs is the workplace. The unique attributes of worksites which can aid health promotion and the ways in which health promotion may benefit employees and employers are outlined below.

## A.  Potential of Worksite Interventions

The reasons for the increasing interest in the workplace as a setting for health promotion activities are both varied and compelling. Nearly 75,000,000 Americans are employed outside the home (U.S. Department of Commerce, 1980), so a very large portion of the population may be reached with educational messages at the worksite. The reach extends even more if one considers the impact on the family. The physical convenience of worksite health programs, the perception that programs are benefits, and the ease of information diffusion throughout the population on site make the worksite a nearly ideal setting for health promotion (Chadwick, 1982). The complex and long-lasting social networks that exist in work situations also provide a vehicle whereby knowledge and behavior can be disseminated and supported among work groups (Rogers & Kincaid, 1978; Colletti & Brownell, 1982).

Chesney and Feuerstein (1979) listed several advantages of worksite programs. The working population is large and varied in age, ethnic composition, and socioeconomic level. As more women enter the workforce the mix of genders becomes more balanced. Though layoffs and turnover are salient events, a general stability facilitates the continuity of interventions, but it is especially valuable in allowing for the collection of long-term follow-up data.

Since worksite interventions take place in the "natural environment," as opposed to a clinic, generalization of intervention effects should be greater. A worksite program can provide cues for health behaviors in the work environment which could favorably affect adherence to regimens and maintenance of gains. Company policies could be altered to restrict hazardous actions (e.g., ban smoking in public areas) or provide incentives for salutary actions (e.g., give bonuses to those who quit smoking). Formalized communication channels, which could be used in part for health purposes, include newsletters, bulletin boards, memorandum distribution, posters, and learning centers with audio and video resources.

Management, employee, and union organizations may be able to foster the acceptance of worksite health promotion activities, as each has an investment in the improvement of health. The employer could consider the potential value of a health promotion program in recruiting competent personnel, reducing turnover, improving the perception of the company's social responsibility, and improving worker morale. For management, however, a clear demonstration that programs could affect economic variables such as absenteeism, health care costs, or productivity, may be most convincing. Unfortunately, clear evidence that health promotion programs produce such benefits is currently lacking (Blair, Blair, Howe, Pale, Rosenberg, & Parker, 1980; Donoghue, 1977; Verbrugge, 1982), though the possibility remains that improved studies will document these relationships.

In summary, worksites are small communities with formal and informal communication systems, large and small groups of people who interact over long periods of time, and representatives from many social groups. The workplace is in existence for purposes which are not usually health related, but the resources, policies, and incentives which are mobilized for profit making could also be partially utilized for health promotion. Personnel, medical, in-service, and health and safety departments all have functions which are consistent with cardiovascular health enhancement and have resources that could be utilized to that end. Given the large percentage of the population which could be reached by heart health promotion programs at the worksite, successful intervention efforts could have a significant impact on the public health problem of cardiovascular diseases. Thus, for many reasons, there is a great deal of interest in cardiovascular risk reduction programs at the worksite (Cohen, 1985).

## B.  Basis for Evaluation

The purpose of this chapter is to critically review studies of heart health behavior change at the workplace and to provide guidelines for further research and practice. This review differs from previous ones (Fielding, 1982, 1984) in its emphasis on methodological evaluation and consideration of the organizational context of the intervention programs.

Studies relating to cardiovascular risk reduction which were available in early 1985, are reviewed under the following headings: (1) hypertension control, (2) smoking cessation, (3) physical activity and exercise promotion, (4) weight control, (5) stress reduction, and (6) multiple risk factor interventions.

Many of the studies reviewed are single-group designs, utilizing measurements before and after an intervention (see Tables I–VI). This program evaluation model does not allow for casual attributions, but it can suggest whether an intervention is feasible and shows promise.

Other studies are classified as quasi-experimental (Cook & Campbell, 1979), because nonrandomized groups were compared. A common study of this type includes evaluation of one worksite which received an intervention and a second worksite which received no intervention. Another common variation was to compare individuals who self-selected various levels of exposure to a single intervention program. This type of design cannot demonstrate that an intervention is causally related to outcome, but it is a design that is well suited to evaluation of organizational interventions.

A design less frequently found in the worksite literature is the randomized, controlled outcome study. Usually, individuals within a worksite were randomly assigned to treatment or control conditions or to comparative treatment conditions. This true experimental design will allow causal interpretations, but does not control for the effects of variation between worksites and may be compromised by diffusion of the education program to control individuals. Only one study randomly assigned entire worksites to experimental conditions.

## II.  REVIEW OF STUDIES

### A.  Worksite Behavioral Hypertension Treatment Programs

Blood pressure is directly and consistently related to CVD incidence (Pooling Project Research Group, 1978), and it has been estimated that there are 24 million hypertensives in the United States (Marx & Kolata, 1978). While medical treatment has been found to be effective in reducing blood pressure and mortality (Hypertension Detection and Follow-up Cooperative Group, 1979), specific behavioral methods such as relaxation procedures (Jacob *et al.,* 1977), weight reduction (Hovell, 1982), and sodium restriction (MacGregor, 1983) are also effective in reducing blood pressure.

Worksite programs of screening and medical treatment can be effective (Alderman, Green, & Flynn, 1980; Alderman, Madhavan, & Davis, 1983; and

Foote & Erfurt, 1983), but their efficacy is limited by lack of volunteers for screening, lack of follow through on physician referrals, and high rate of non-adherence to medications. These are all problems which could be addressed by behavioral researchers. One experimental study found that an incentive program for adherence yielded more regular medication taking and lower blood pressures (Haynes, Gibson, Hackett, Sackett, Taylor, Fogle, & Verdesca, 1976) than a control condition.

Several nonpharmacologic interventions have been found to be successful in reducing blood pressure (see Table I). Low-intensity programs such as a 10-minute education program and self-monitoring of blood pressure have shown some promise (Zimmerman, Bauman, Safer, & Leventhal, 1983; Bertera & Cuthie, 1984). Brief psychotherapy treatments were superior to a health education control condition at a 2-month follow-up (Drazen, Nevid, Pace, & O'Brien, 1982).

The most promising nonpharmacological intervention for hypertension to date is relaxation training. In a randomized study of hypertensives, who were uncontrolled by medication, relaxation was found to produce blood pressure reductions in the clinic and during the working day (Southam, Agras, Taylor, Kraemer, 1982) which persisted for 15 months (Agras, Southam, & Taylor, 1983b). In a small, randomized study of relaxation training and stress management, blood pressure reductions were maintained at a 3-year follow-up, and there was a suggestion of reduced medical costs (Charlesworth, Williams, & Baer, 1984). An ongoing study of 400 hypertensives at Lockheed Corporation is demonstrating high adherence rates (90% attendance at sessions) and greater blood pressure declines in the relaxation group than in the control group (Agras, Chesney, Taylor, & Sevelius, 1983a).

All of the reviewed studies of behavioral treatment of hypertension at the worksite have been experimental except one, and all have shown treatment effects. Relaxation training appears to produce meaningful decreases in blood pressure, which are generalized and maintained. It is important to study the cost-effectiveness of relaxation training in comparison to other available treatments because it is a very time-consuming intervention on the part of the staff and employees. There are other behaviorally based blood pressure reduction techniques, such as dietary sodium reduction and weight loss, which should be tesed with hypertensives at worksites. There is also a potential to explore implementing behavioral programs for the entire worksite population for the prevention of hypertension.

## B. Worksite Smoking Cessation Programs

In recent years cigarette smoking in the United States has steadily declined. Although this decline is promising, more than 53 million adults are currently

**TABLE I**

Hypertension Control

| Source | Company and population | Design[a] | Sample size | Program intervention | Program duration | Follow-up[b] | Results |
|---|---|---|---|---|---|---|---|
| Agras et al. (1983); Southam et al. (1982) | Syntex Corporation | 3 | 37 hypertensive employees | 24-hour blood pressure readings at 20-minute intervals<br>1. Relaxation training group<br>2. Control group | 40 minutes per week for 10 weeks | 15 months | Pretest to follow-up changes in clinic and worksite blood pressure (SBP/DBP[c] mm Hg)<br>Worksite group:<br>−5.7/−6.5<br>($p < .01$)<br>Clinic group:<br>−6.3/8.3<br>($p < .01$) |
| Charlesworth et al. (1984) | Not reported | 1 | 54 hypertensive employees | Group programs<br>1. Relaxation training and stress management<br>2. Delayed intervention | 1 hour per week for 10 weeks | 10 weeks and 3 years | 40 Subjects completed study (74%)<br>Blood pressure decline from pretreatment to posttreatment (SBP/DBP) (mm Hg)<br>1. −6.1/−2.9<br>2. −3.8/−2.6<br>Change in delayed intervention group during extended |

| Study | Type[a] | Setting | Sample | Intervention | Duration | Follow-up[b] | Results |
|---|---|---|---|---|---|---|---|
| | | | | | | | baseline: +.5/+.2 3-year follow-up of 32 subjects. Mean BP change from baseline: −7.4/−5.3 |
| Drazen et al. (1982) | 3 | Not reported | 22 mildly hypertensive volunteers | Behavioral treatment 1. Anxiety management 2. Rational emotive therapy/ assertiveness training 3. Health education counseling | 10-week sessions | 2 months | Blood pressure decline from pre- to post-test (SPB/DBP) mm Hg 1. −12.9/−11.6 2. −16.3/−8.3 3. −7.1/−10.9 |
| Haynes et al. (1976) | 2 | Steel Co. (5000 employees) | 38 uncontrolled hypertensive men | Group 1: behavioral treatment (incentives for adherence) Group 2: No treatment control | 6 months | 1 year | Changes at follow-up treatment group ($p$) 21.3% improved compliance .001 5.4 mm Hg change in DBP .001 Control group 1.5% compliance decline NS 1.9 mm Hg change in DBP NS |

[a] 1, case study; 2, quasi-experimental evaluation; 3, randomized, controlled trial.
[b] Follow-up specifies time elapsed since program inception.
[c] SBP/DBP, systolic blood pressure/diastolic blood pressure.

classified as cigarette smokers, and smoking is still the primary preventable cause of death and disability in the nation (Department of Health and Human Services, 1982).

Smoking prevalence is related to occupation. More smokers are found among blue collar workers, and employed women are more likely to smoke than women who do not work outside the home (Sterling & Weinkam, 1976). Smoking-related costs to business are high. For example, Kristein (1983) estimated that each smoking employee costs the employer $336 to $601 per year. It has been estimated that 3% of American and 6% of Canadian companies have antismoking programs (Companies put up the ''no smoking'' sign, 1980), but very few of these efforts have been evaluated (Danaher, 1980; Orleans & Shipley, 1982). In a survey conducted by the National Interagency Council on Smoking and Health (1983) involving 3000 companies, almost half of the companies had policies related to smoking in the workplace, and smoking cessation programs were the third most frequent type of health program.

Several case studies of worksite smoking cessation programs have been reported (see Table II). One multicomponent program yielded a high cessation rate which was verified (Miller & Rodway, 1980), but another did not (Mossman, 1978). Two incentive programs produced high recruitment rates and promising cessation rates (Rosen & Lichtenstein, 1977; Stachnick & Stoffelmayr, 1983), and two small group treatment programs produced significant but unremarkable reductions in cigarette smoking (Flow, 1980; Glasgow, Klesges, Godding, Vasey, & O'Neil, 1984).

The lack of research in this area is surprising given the extent of the smoking problem and the opportunity for high-frequency, long-term contact with smokers at the worksite. Future research could consider variations on the incentive program such as lotteries, varying the use of social support, evaluating the effects of antismoking policies and media campaigns, and comparing the costs and effects of incentive systems and skills training.

## C.  Worksite Physical Activity Programs

Epidemiologic studies have shown that physically active people are less likely to die of CVD (Salonen, Puska, and Tuomihehto, 1982; Paffenbarger & Hyde, 1984). Despite numerous benefits of physical activity, such as weight loss (Thompson, Jarvie, Lahey, & Cureton, 1982) and increases in high-density lipoproteins (Haskell, 1984), it has been estimated that half of American adults are extremely sedentary (Department of Health and Human Services, 1980). Even this estimate probably understates the degree of inactivity that characterizes modern society.

Commitment of large companies to promoting employee fitness appeared to be virtually nonexistent in 1961 (Duggar & Swengros, 1969), but Hitchings

**TABLE II**

Smoking Cessation

| Source | Company and population | Design[a] | Sample size | Program intervention | Program duration | Follow-up[b] | Results |
|---|---|---|---|---|---|---|---|
| Flow (1980) | Not reported | 3 | 218 | Group versus self-help techniques | Not specified | 4 months | Group treatment was superior to self-help |
| Glasgow et al. (1984) | Telephone company | 3 | 36 | 1. Abrupt reduction 2. Gradual reduction 3. Gradual reduction and feedback | 5 to 7 weeks | 6 months | Group 1: 8% attrition 0% abstinence Group 2: 28% reduction in cigarette consumption 0% abstinence Group 3: No information |
| Miller & Rodway (1980) | Cummins Engine Co. | 1 | 33 | Smoking education program/peer support | 15 sessions over 1 year | 4.5 months | 77% abstinent at follow-up; validated by carbon monoxide report |
| Mossman (1978) | Sandia Laboratories | 1 | 118 responded to follow-up | 5-day plan for employees and spouses | 5 daily sessions then 6 weekly follow-ups | 1 year | 25% reported abstinence at follow-up |
| Rosen & Lichtenstein (1977) | Ambulance rental service | 1 | 31 | Nonsmokers at work given monthly bonus | 1 year | 1 year | 4 of 12 smokers reported abstinence at work |

*(continued)*

**TABLE II** (*Continued*)

| Source | Company and population | Design[a] | Sample size | Program intervention | Program duration | Follow-up[b] | Results |
|---|---|---|---|---|---|---|---|
| Dawley *et al.* (1984) | Hospital employees | 1 | 15 | Group intervention | 1 hour per week for 10 weeks | 8.5 months | 53% (7 of 13) reported cessation |
| Nepps (1984) | Johnson & Johnson | 1 | 36 | 9 modules of materials for self-help quitting | Approx. 9 weeks | 9 months | 22% (8 of 36) quit by end of treatment 14% (5 of 31) were confirmed abstinent at last follow-up 33% picked up three or more modules |
| Stachnik & Staffelmayr (1983) | Bank, professional organization, manufacturing company | 2 (three replications) | Not reported | 20 one-hour meetings over 7-month period. No smoking contests, lotteries, and contracts. | 7 months | 6 months | 57% of smokers enrolled in program 85% reported abstinence after 6 months 49% reduction in smokers at worksite |

(1979) recently reported that over 400 major corporations have elaborate gymnasium facilities to promote exercise at the worksite. In a survey of California employers, Fielding and Breslow (1983) found that 14.2% of employers offered some type of fitness program for employees. Thus, despite projections that worksite fitness programs will not be cost-effective (Everett, 1979; Chadwick, 1982), employers are apparently proceeding with the development of such programs. Several authors (Haskell and Blair 1980; Pate & Blair, 1983) have considered the benefits of exercise and the promise and problems of physical activity programs in work settings.

A number of case studies and quasi-experiments found that participants in worksite physical activity programs reduce cardiovascular risk factors, improve fitness, improve psychological functioning, and improve job satsifaction (Durbeck, Heinzelmann, Schacter, Haskell, Payne, Moxley, Nemiroff, Limoncelli, Arnoldi, & Fox, 1972; Koerner, 1973; Fogle & Verdesca, 1975; Pauly, Palmer, Wright, & Pfeiffer, 1982; Horne, 1975; Yarvote, McDonagh, Goldman, & Zuckerman, 1974) more than nonparticipants (see Table III). These studies had methodological problems, and programs requiring expensive gymnasia may not be cost-effective.

Two studies of mandatory fitness programs for firefighters (Barnard & Anthony, 1980; Puterbaugh & Lawyer, 1983) suggest that exercise can decrease serum cholesterol and blood pressure, as well as decrease the heart rate response to work-related stress. One study suggested that brief physical activity can reduce fatigue in office workers (Laporte, 1966).

A controlled trial of an on-site fitness program attempted to document effects on fitness and productivity (Cox, Shephard, & Corey, 1981). Approximately 25% of employees in the experimental and control companies completed initial and 6-month follow-up assessments. Short-term improvements in fitness, psychological functioning, absenteeism, and turnover were documented in the experimental company. At the 18-month follow-up (Song, Shephard, & Cox, 1982), there was substantial attrition from the exercise program, but favorable effects on abscnteeism, turnover, and medical costs for the experimental company were still evident (Shepherd, Corey, Renzland, & Cox, 1982). Estimates of total savings from the exercise program were $744 per employee per year (Shephard, 1983). It was concluded that the exercise program had beneficial effects, which diffused to some extent throughout the test company. Other large studies suggest that fitness programs can reduce medical and disability costs (Bowne, Russell, Morgan et al., 1984) and that adherence to worksite exercise programs is associated with superior job performance (Bernacki & Baun, 1984).

Evaluations of worksite fitness programs suggest that programs were associated with improved fitness, reduced CVD risk factors, improved job satisfaction, and decreased turnover among participants. In these studies low recruitment rates and high attrition rates for general employees were common, with time conflicts being the most common reason for inattendance (Durbeck et al., 1972).

**TABLE III**

Weight Loss

| Source | Company and population | Design | Sample size | Program intervention | Program duration | Follow-up | Results |
|---|---|---|---|---|---|---|---|
| Abrams and Follick (1983) | 1 hospital | 3 | 133 96% female | Behavior modification program structured versus unstructured maintenance groups | 10 weekly sessions/4 biweekly follow-ups | 6 months | Weight loss at follow-up Structured maintenance group: 4.4 kg Unstructured maintenance group: 1.5 kg 48% attrition in first 10 weeks |
| Brownell et al. (1984) | 1. 3 banks 2. Manufacturing firm 3. Factory | 2 | 1. $n=176$ of 570 workers 2. $n=53$ of 226 workers 3. $n=48$ of 1200 workers | 1. Weight loss competition among 3 banks 2. Weight loss competition among random teams 3. Weight loss competition among divisions | 1. 12 weeks 2. 13 weeks 3. 15 weeks | 6 months | Mean weight loss at 6 months 1. 6.0 kg (9.7% reduction in overweight) 2. 5.4 kg (9% reduction in overweight) 3. 4.5 kg (7.8% reduction in overweight) Overall attrition: .05% |
| Brownell et al. (1983) | Members of United Store-workers Union | 3 | 179 women from 15,000 workers | Compared combinations of lay versus professional led weight loss groups in worksite versus clinic setting in weekly versus frequent meetings | 16 meetings | 6 months | Overall attrition: 42.4 Overall weight loss at 6 month follow-up: 2.8 kg |
| Colvin et al. (1983) | Medical students | 3 | 23 | Public posting of weights | 11 weekly | 6 months | Weight loss at follow-up |

| Study | Setting | | N | Intervention | Sessions | Follow-up | Results |
|---|---|---|---|---|---|---|---|
| | and staff | | | and monetary vs social incentives | weigh-ins | | Social group: 3.1 lb below baseline<br>Money group: 6.0 lb below baseline<br>46% reported attrition |
| Follick *et al.* (1984) | 1 hospital | 3 | Not reported | Behavior modification incentives for attendance versus standard protocol | As in Abrams & Follick, 1983 | 6 months | Attrition at follow-up; Incentive group: 29%; Nonincentive group: 92%<br>Mean weight loss in both groups: 3.5 kg (regained at follow-up) |
| Fowler *et al.* (1983) | 1 hospital | 3 | 57 | 1. Professionally led group<br>2. Self-help group | 1. 14 weekly sessions<br>2. 16 sessions | 8 months | Attrition at follow-up; Professional group: 80%; Self-help group: 54% ($p < .001$)<br>Mean weight loss at follow-up; Professional group: 2.2 kg; Self-help group: 0.0 kg ($p = $ NS) |
| Kelly (1979) | Boston Police Officers greater than 20% overweight | 1 | 53 | 12-week diet, activity, and education group | 12 weeks | 1 year | Postintervention weight loss of 10.9 lb; 50% follow-up (mean weight loss of 11.4 lb) |
| Sanger and Bichanich (1977) | 1 hospital | 1 | 176 | Dietary instruction | Weekly sessions | Ongoing | Average weight loss of 1.17 lb per week; 6% met their goals; 68% attrition rate |

*(continued)*

173

**TABLE III** (*Continued*)

| Source | Company and population | Design | Sample size | Program intervention | Program duration | Follow-up | Results |
|---|---|---|---|---|---|---|---|
| Schumacher et al. (1979) | 1 hospital | 1 | 70 | Dietary instruction, physical activity, behavior modification, intergroup competition | 8 weekly sessions plus follow-up | None | Average weight loss 1.3 lb/wk Attrition: 21% |
| Stunkard and Brownell (1982) | 15,000 member union | 3 | 40 obese female employees | Behavioral treatment a. Professionally led group 1. Worksite setting 2. Medical setting b. Lay group at worksite 1. Weekly meetings 2. Frequent meetings | 16 weeks | 6 months | Mean weight loss at 6 months: 1.2 kg Attrition: 60% No differences among groups |
| Peterson et al. (1985) | Texas Instruments in Attleboro, MA | 3 | 63 | Behavioral modification program 1. Professional leaders 2. Trained lay leaders | 12 one-hour meetings over 16 weeks | 8 months | Attendance did not differ by group 38% (24 of 63) completed follow-up mean weight loss at 6 months 1. 10.8 kg 2. 7.6 kg |
| Seidman et al. (1984) | Lockheed Missiles | 1 | 2499 at six sites | Team competition with cash and social rewards. Also, film, seminar, books, newspaper articles, and nutrition fair. | 3 months | 3 months | 40% of target population was recruited 70% of subjects completed final weigh-in Mean weight loss was 3.3 kg |

The general belief that worksite exercise programs produce psychological and productivity improvements in employees has yet to be empirically validated. Studies are needed which randomly assign subjects to exercise or control conditions, controlling for expectancy effects. Exercise programs which do not require expensive facilities should be developed because they are more likely to be adopted by large numbers of companies. For example, aerobics classes after work or incentive programs to engage in exercise at home may be more cost-effective.

## D. Worksite Weight Loss Programs

It is estimated that between 15 and 50% of American adults are overweight (Brownell, 1982). Obesity is related to hypertension, myocardial infarction, sudden death, and cerebrovascular accidents (Dawber, 1980). Montegriffo (1968) examined 10,269 employees of a manufacturing firm and found 60% of the 40- to 49-year-old men had higher than "desirable" weight. Foreyt, Scott, and Gotto (1980) reviewed a number of promising worksite weight reduction programs, and between 10 (Fielding & Breslow, 1983) and 16% of large firms (National Interagency Council on Smoking and Health, 1983) may offer weight loss programs.

Early case studies on weight reduction programs produced conflicting results (see Table IV). In a program offered to hospital employees (Sanger & Bichanich, 1977), the drop-out rate was 68% and only 6% of participants met their weight loss goals. Other programs for hospital employees (Schumacher, Groth, Kleinsek, & Seay, 1979) and police officers (Kelly, 1979) were more encouraging.

In the first of a series of studies, an attempt was made to improve maintenance of weight loss in hospital employees (Abrams & Follick, 1983). After a 10-week behavioral treatment, which also included social/organizational influence procedures, subjects were assigned to maintenance groups consisting of either a structured program or a group discussion. While the overall weight loss for the sample was small at the 6-month follow-up, the structured maintenance program was found to significantly aid maintenance. Drop-out rate was high. In the second study (Follick, Fowler, & Brown, 1984), a monetary incentive system was highly effective in improving attendance, but there were no differences between groups in weight loss, and maintenance was poor. In the third study, attendance was higher in professionally led groups than in self-help groups, but weight loss was minimal and did not differ between groups at post-treatment or at an 8-month follow-up. (Fowler, Abrams, Peterson, & Follick, 1983). A fourth study showed significant but essentially equal weight loss in professionally led and self-help groups. Change was maintained at the 6-month follow-up, and the self-help intervention was more cost-effective (Peterson, Abrams, Elder, & Beaudin, 1985).

Another series of studies (Stunkard & Brownell, 1980; Brownell, Stunkard, & McKeon, 1983) explored the relative benefits of lay versus professional leaders and weekly versus intensive scheduling. Attrition exceeded 40% overall, but it was reduced by phone call reminders. Lay and professional leaders produced similar results. Frequent, as compared to weekly, meetings led to better attendance but not more weight loss. Lay leaders were more cost-effective, but overall weight loss was minimal.

The most promising worksite programs utilize incentives and group competition. Monetary and social contingencies produced weight loss without behavioral skills training in one study (Colvin, Zopf, & Myers, 1983). A group competition program at Lockheed was associated with high participation rate and moderate weight loss at low cost (Seidman, Sevelius, & Ewald, 1984). In a series of evaluations (Brownell, Cohen, Stunkard, Felix, & Cooley, 1984), competing teams of employees tried to win a pool of money by losing the most weight. Behavioral manuals were provided and public feedback of group weight loss was prominently displayed. These low-cost programs had relatively high recruitment and very low attrition rates, produced moderate weight loss, and were well received by employees and managers.

The question of efficacy must continue to be addressed in the weight loss area. Group-based approaches have continually yielded disappointing results, so the transferability of this clinical approach to worksite settings must be questioned. However, even the relatively successful incentive programs have produced only modest weight loss and maintenance. Though procedures have been found to decrease attrition in group programs, use of incentive programs may circumvent this problem. Based on the discrepant results between group training and competition approaches, there is reason to believe that successful worksite programs are very different from successful clinic-based programs. Incentive-based programs have been found to be more effective, more cost-efficient, and to stimulate more participation than group programs.

## E.  Worksite Stress Reduction Programs

The area of stress reduction is one of the most challenging areas of worksite health promotion (Schwartz, 1980). Though estimates are very difficult to make, the effects of work-related stress may cost industry nearly 75 billion dollars per year in employee absenteeism, lost worker productivity, and rising medical cost (Wallis, 1983). The stressful effects of many objective and subjective characteristics of the work environment have been studied (Holt, 1982), but the relationship between heart disease and job satisfaction, job pressures, and occupational mobility seem to be most widely documented (House, 1975). Fielding and Breslow (1983) found that 16.6% of California employers had offered a worksite stress management program.

**TABLE IV**

Stress Reduction

| Source | Company and population | Design | Sample size | Program intervention | Program duration | Follow-up | Results |
|---|---|---|---|---|---|---|---|
| Carrington et al. (1980) | New York Telephone Co. | 3 | 154 men | Taught via audiotape<br>a. Muscle relaxation<br>b. Meditation (a)<br>c. Meditation (b)<br>d. Meditation (b)<br>e. Waiting list | 2 weeks | 5.5 months | Groups b and c practiced more than group a<br>Groups b and c reported fewer symptoms than group d |
| Murphy (1984) | Highway workers (normotensive) | 1 | 38 | 1. EMG biofeedback<br>2. Muscle relaxation<br>3. Wait-list control | 2 weeks (10 sessions) | 3 months | 12% attrition<br>50% nonadherence<br>No group differences on anxiety or job satisfaction |
| Patel et al. (1981) | Manufact. firm (N = 1268) | 3 | 192 high risk employees<br>37% >50<br>61% male | Treatment group (93)<br>Health education lecture<br>Relaxation training<br>Biofeedback training<br>Control group (99)<br>One health education lecture | 8 weeks | 8 months | Mean changes at follow-up<br>a. Blood pressure (SBP/DBP mm Hg)<br>Treatment group: −15.3/−6.8<br>Control group: −6.1/−.6 ($p$ <.001)<br>b. Log plasma renin<br>Treatment group: −.40<br>Control group: −.09 ($p$ = NS)<br>c. Plasma aldosterone (pmol/liter)<br>Treatment group: +12.2 |

*(continued)*

**TABLE IV** (*Continued*)

| Source | Company and population | Design | Sample size | Program intervention | Program duration | Follow-up | Results |
|---|---|---|---|---|---|---|---|
| Peters *et al.* (1977a) | Rubber co. | 3 | 140 volunteers 54 nonvolunteers | Group A: (58) relaxation training<br>Group B: (39) asked to sit quietly<br>Group C: (39) volunteer control<br>Group D: (54) nonvolunteer control | 12 weeks | None | Control group: +4.2 ($p$ = NS)<br>Group A improvement over Group B ($p$)<br>a. Symptoms .05<br>b. Illness days .05<br>c. Performance .05<br>d. Satisfaction .05 |
| Peters *et al.* (1977b) | | | Same as Peter *et al.* (1977a) | | 12 weeks | None | Blood pressure change from baseline (SBP/DBP mm Hg)<br>Group A: −11.6/−7.9<br>Group B: −6.5/−3.1<br>Group C: +.4/−.6<br>Group D: −.1/0 |
| Seamonds (1982) | Large financial company | 1 | 5000 | Referral to appropriate resources (quasi-control group) | Not applicable | 6 months | Changes in treatment group at follow-up<br>1. Decreased Absenteeism for 61% of treated employees<br>2. Some reduction in reported |

Type A behavior may be a mediator of stress and its health effects (Glass, 1977). The type A behavior pattern seems to be prevalent in working groups (Roskies, Kearney, Spevak, Surkis, Cohen, & Gilman, 1979; Chesney, Sevelius, Black, Ward, Swan, and Rosenman, 1981), and while no type A modification programs at the worksite have been adequately evaluated (Manuso, 1983), this may be an important area for future research (Suinn, 1982).

been reported. Meditation and "sitting quietly" were more effective in reducing symptom reports and blood pressure than a control condition (Peters, Benson, Porter, 1977a; Peters, Benson, & Peters, 1977b). In a 6-month follow-up of a randomized study, meditation groups were adhering better than a relaxation group, and meditators reported fewer stress symptoms than controls (Carrington, Collings, Benson, Robinson, Wood, Lehrer, Woolfolk, & Cola, 1980). A relaxation-based intervention with high-risk men reduced blood pressure more than a control condition in a large study with an 8-month follow-up (Patel, Marmot, & Terry, 1980). However, a small study found that a brief stress reduction course reduced workday anxiety but decreased job satsifaction (Riley, Frederiksen, Winett, & Love, 1983). A variety of other approaches have been studied (see Table V).

An interesting study, comparing relaxation training to an organizational development approach to stress reduction is in progress. Preliminary results show a significantly lower attrition rate in the organizational stress group (Dexter, 1984).

While several experimental studies suggest that a variety of stress reduction interventions can have beneficial psychological and physiological effects, confidence in these studies is diminished because of the inadequacy of the measures used. There is a need for reliable and valid measures of work stress (e.g., Steinmetz, Kaplan, & Miller, 1982) as well as better conceptualizations of the effects of stress on work-related variables. All studies should monitor for undesirable side effects of stress interventions (Riley et al., 1983).

The different approaches taken by investigators in this area are of some interest. Benson and colleagues (Peters et al., 1977a,b; Carrington et al., 1980) utilized low-risk employee volunteers, while Patel et al. (1981) identified employees at high risk for CVD and demonstrated large blood pressure reductions. Dexter (1984) assigned entire work groups to interventions and is attempting to make organization-wide changes. The latter approach may be particularly appropriate in the stress management area because of the strong links between the work environment, including relations with co-workers, and CVD (House, 1975).

## F.  Worksite Multiple Risk Factor Programs

All of the previously reviewed programs have targeted one risk factor, but it can be argued that multiple risk factor interventions are more desirable. No

**TABLE V**

Physical Activity Promotion

| Source | Company and population | Design | Sample size | Program intervention | Program duration | Follow-up | Results |
|---|---|---|---|---|---|---|---|
| Barnard and Anthony (1980) | LA City Fire Dept. | 2 | 300 firemen (program involved 2856 firemen) | 1. Strenuous exercise 45 minutes daily 2. Police department as quasi-control | Ongoing | 7 years | 1. Mean changes (1971–78) Resting HR[a]: −15.5 bpm Reduction in cholesterol ($p < 05$) Reduction in DBP ($p < 05$) 2. Slight weight gain |
| Durbeck et al. (1972) | NASA managers | 2 | 259 men volunteered of 998 eligible | Group 1: stress lab (circuit training in gym) Group 2: group jogging Group 3: individual program | 6 months | 1 year | Exercise frequency (weekly) 1. Stress lab/jogging group: −1.3 per week 2. Individual program: 1.2 per week Reductions in SBP/DBP, and weight related to attendance in stress lab |
| Fogle and Verdesca (1975) | Western Electric Company managers | 2 | 103 employees between 35 and 47 years | Exercise onsite 3 times/week Group 1 (37): attended more than twice per week | 7 months | None | Mean pre post changes ($p$) HR WT SBP DBP 1. NS >.05 NS <.05 2. NS NS >.05 NS |

| | | | | | | | |
|---|---|---|---|---|---|---|---|
| Horne (1975) | Mobile Oil executives | 1 | 154 middle-aged men | Group 2 (42): attended one or two sessions per week; Group 3 (24): attended less than once per week | Ongoing | 1 year | Mean diff. active vs control ($p$) Resting HR: $-9$ bpm .05; SBP/DBP $-5/-2$ mm Hg NS; CHOL: $-$ %/mg .05; Weight: $-2$ lb NS |
| Koerner (1973) | Xerox Corp. executives | 1 | 40 men $x = 41$ years | 1. Program group: exercising employees (21 months) 2. Preprogram group: nonexercising employees | Ongoing | 21 months | Improved fitness and lower resting HR in program participants |
| Pauly et al. (1982) | Xerox Corp. | 1 | 73 employees $x = 36$ years | Daily exercise for 20-min sessions in gym | 14 weeks | None | Change pre vs post test ($p$) Resting HR: $-4.4$ bpm .05; Systolic BP: $-3.95$ mm Hg .05; CHOL: $-14.4$ mg/dl .05; TRIG: $-19.2$ mg/dl .05 |
| Puterbaugh | Portland Fire | 3 | 27 male firemen | 1. Supervised running | 12 weeks | None | Postalarm HR correlated |

3. NS NS NS <.05

*(continued)*

181

**TABLE V** (*Continued*)

| Source | Company and population | Design | Sample size | Program intervention | Program duration | Follow-up | Results |
|--------|------------------------|--------|-------------|----------------------|------------------|-----------|---------|
| and Lawyer (1983) | Dept. | | | 1. 40 minutes 3 times per week<br>2. Unsupervised running<br>3. No extra activity | | | inversely with VO2 maximum:<br>1. +20% in VO2 maximum: −5.6 lb<br>2. +19% in VO2 maximum: +0.5 lb<br>3. −2% in VO2 maximum: +1.3 lb |
| Shephard *et al.* (1982) | 2 insurance companies | 2 | 1858 employees | 1. 3 thirty-minute weekly exercise sessions ($N = 1281$ employees)<br>2. No exercise requirement ($N = 577$ employees) | 6 months | None | 1. 34% enrolled 34% of enrollees high attenders<br>47% reported greater job satisfaction<br>63% reported less fatigue<br>Significant reduction in % body fat<br>Decreased absenteeism and turnover of enrollees |

| Reference | Company/Population | | Sample | Intervention | | | Results |
|---|---|---|---|---|---|---|---|
| Song et al (1982) | Same as Shepard et al. (1981) | 2 | | | 6 months | 18 months | Participation rate: 17.2% Mean absences per month was less for high adherers (.08) than for others (.40). Less turnover in high adherer group. |
| Yarvote et al. (1974) | Exxon Corp. executives | 1 | 232 men | Exercise requested 2 to 3 times per week in gym | 6 months | 1 year | Mean change at 1 year ($p$) Weight −4.0 lb .001 BP: −7.3/−4.3 mm Hg .001 pulse: −13.6 bpm .001 CHOL: −2.5 %/mg NS |
| Bowne et al. (1984) | Prudential Insurance Co. 1389 employees | 1 | 669 | Availability of gym, exercise programs, and health seminars | 1 year | 1 year (records were checked for 5 years prior to program) | 20% reduction in disability days in participants (direct savings of $91 per subject per year) major medical costs decreased 38% for women and increased for men cholesterol, weight, and BP did not change significantly |

[a] Abbreviations: SBP/DBP, systolic blood pressure/diastolic blood pressure; HR, heart rate; CHOL, cholesterol; TRIG, triglycerides.

single factor intervention would be appropriate for all employees, so the benefits of such a program would only be available to a portion of the workforce. Multiple risk factor interventions should maximize the probability of health behavior change for each employee. Since all risk factor reduction programs have common elements (e.g., staff, measurement, publicity), combining programs could capitalize on such shared overhead and enhance cost efficiency (Collings, 1982).

Multiple risk programs often utilize employee health screenings, and this feedback component, termed health hazard appraisal (Goetz, Duff, & Bernstein, 1980) has been studied. A program consisting of extensive physical examinations was associated with an increase in medical usage (Wood, 1975). A California company provided screening, feedback, and educational materials, and found improvements in physical activity, cholesterol, blood pressure, and smoking, among participants after 1 year (Rodnick, 1982). Users of automated blood pressure monitoring devices at work also improved reported health habits (Bertera & Cuthie, 1984). While experimental trials are needed to verify benefits of health hazard appraisal, Wynder and Arnold (1978) caution against the diversion of resources from intervention to screening.

The U.S. Air Force (Arnold & Jacobsen, 1981), Campbell Soup Company (Wear, 1983), Kimberly-Clark Corporation (1977), and others (reviewed in Parkinson & associates, 1982) have developed comprehensive health promotion programs for their employees. While many of these are innovative, no evaluations of their effectiveness have been reported.

Most evaluations of multiple risk factor programs have had positive results (see Table VI). Meyer and Henderson (1974) found that men at high risk for CVD who participated in behavioral group sessions with their spouses had more weight loss, exercise, and dietary changes at follow-up than subjects assigned to health education or physician consultation groups. A long-term project at a New York State Agency had relatively high recruitment rates and was associated with risk factor improvements, reduced sick leave, and less stress (Bjurstrom & Alexiou, 1978). Costs of the program were modest. An experimental study found that a behavioral group program for teachers produced significant changes in fitness, weight, blood pressure, and job satisfaction (Blair, Collingwood, Reynolds, Smith, Hagan, & Sterling, 1984). Results of other small group studies have been generally positive (Grove, Reed, & Miller, 1979; Bruno, Arnold, Jacobson, Winick, & Wynder, 1983).

The Johnson and Johnson Live for Life Program is an ambitious health promotion program in industry (Wilbur, 1983). In addition to physical examinations, behavior change programs, and referral services, employees at each site are trained to make environmental changes at the worksite. Early reports of a quasi-experimental evaluation indicate that subjects at treatment sites made more changes in exercise, weight control, smoking cessation, and well-being. Changes were also seen in self-reported sick days, satsifaction with job and co-workers, and ability to handle job strain. A similarly comprehensive program at Control Data Corporation is currently being evaluated (Naditch, 1980).

In the largest worksite study conducted (World Health Organization European Collaborative Group [WHO], 1983) 66 worksites in four countries were randomly assigned to treatment or control conditions in a 6-year study. The behavioral targets were (1) reduction of dietary fat and cholesterol, (2) smoking cessation, (3) weight reduction, (4) increase in exercise, and (5) adherence to medication regimens for hypertensives. Middle-aged men were screened, and those with highest risk received three or four brief appointments each year with the company physician and nurse. There was also a general information campaign consisting of booklets, posters, films, and personal letters. While there were differences in results among countries, overall changes in risk factors (11% reduction in risk) were significant. Death due to coronary heart disease was lower in the intervention condition, but not significantly so. A 12-year follow-up of ten British factories showed continuing benefits for the intervention group on dietary and smoking behaviors, but not on exercise (Bauer, Heller, & Challah, 1985). This large European study demonstrated that multiple risk reduction at the worksite can be carried out on a large scale and can have a significant impact on risk of cardiovascular diseases.

The interest in and success of multiple risk programs (e.g., WHO, 1983) suggests that they will be used with increased frequency for large companies. The consistently positive results of both large and small experiments suggest that multiple risk programs are a high priority for continued development.

## III. DISCUSSION

The different areas of worksite heart health behavior change interventions vary dramatically in their states of development. From a scientific point of view, multiple risk factor reduction programs have been most thoroughly researched while smoking cessation programs for workers have received the least attention. The finding that the pattern of program implementation differs from the pattern of activity within the scientific community (Fielding & Breslow, 1983) is cause for some concern. In many instances the reach and efficacy of interventions which were reviewed were found to be rather disappointing, yet it is reasonable to expect that the more successful programs would tend to be published. Thus, effectiveness of purely service-oriented programs must be questioned at this point, and evaluation of all worksite risk reduction efforts must be considered a requirement.

While keeping in mind that the worksite risk reduction literature is at an

## TABLE VI

### Multiple Risk Reduction

| Source | Company and population | Design | Sample size | Program intervention | Program duration | Follow-up | Results |
|---|---|---|---|---|---|---|---|
| Bertera & Cuthie (1984) | Hospital employee volunteers | 2 | 193 | 1. Blood pressure screening, brief counseling, access to blood pressure cuff 2. Blood pressure screening, brief counseling | 1 year | 1.1 years | Frequent self-monitors reported more lifestyle changes Both groups decreased blood pressure at follow-up |
| Bjurstrom and Alexiou (1978) | New York State Dept of Education ($N$=approx. 2400) | 2 | 800 | 1. Exercise program 2. Seminars on risk factors | 15 weeks | 1 year | Mean changes at follow-up ($p$) a. Weight: 13.8 lb .01 b. CHOL: −9.6 mg/% .01 c. SBP/DBP: −1.5/−1.3 mm Hg NS d. Hours/employee/year absences: −4.7 e. Attrition: 39% |
| Blair et al. (1984) | Teachers in four schools | 2 | 119 | 1. Group sessions on exercise, stress, and nutrition 2. Control | 10 weeks | 10 weeks | Significant differences in treatment group on exercise, fitness, and job satisfaction |
| Bruno et al. (1983) | New York Telephone employees | 3 | 145 employees with serum cholesterol (240–350 mg%) | Eight 1-hour group sessions led by health educator on lunch hours | 8 weeks | 1 month | 55% attended 4 sessions mean changes at follow-up |

Bruno et al. continued results:

| | Treatment | Control |
|---|---|---|
| a. Serum cholesterol (mg%) | −24 | −7 |
| b. % ideal wt (kg) | −2.4 | +1.1 |

| Source | Company and population | Design | Sample size | Program intervention | Program duration | Follow-up | Results |
|---|---|---|---|---|---|---|---|
| Grove et al. (1979) | Blue Cross/ Blue Shield ($N$ = 2200) | 1 | 1108 women | Medical exam. Health education | 3 weeks | 6 months | Follow-up results Smoking: 7% quit rate Weight: −7.45 lb DBP: −2.72 mm Hg CHOL: −19.0 mg/100 ml |
| Meyer and Henderson (1974) | Varian Corp. | 3 | 36 "high risk" employees (aged 35–55) | Group 1 (12): behavior modification Group 2 (10): individual counseling Group 3 (14): physician visit | 11 weeks | 3 months | Mean changes at follow-up ($p$) a. Weight: Group 1: −12.18 lb .01 Group 2: −10.64 lb .01 Group 3: −6.21 lb .025 |

| Author (year) | Setting | No. | Sample | Intervention | Duration | Follow-up | Results |
|---|---|---|---|---|---|---|---|
| Rodnick (1982) | Manufacturing firm | 2 | 292 59% male | Comprehensive medical exam and interpretation with educational material | 1 year | None | b. Cigarettes reduced<br>  Group 1: 13 — NS<br>  Group 2: 12 — NS<br>  Group 3: 9 — NS<br>c. CHOL/TRIG (mg/100 ml)<br>  Group 1: 44/68 — .01<br>  Group 2: 27/37 — .05<br>  Group 3: 17/70 — .05 |
| WHO (1983) | Large worksites in United Kingdom, Belgium, Italy, and Poland | 3 | 66 factories 49,781 men | Health screening information. 3 to 4 physician visits per year for high risk group | 6 years | Not applicable | Risk factor changes<br>1. Blood pressure 13% increase 24% decrease<br>2. Significant chol decrease in men<br>3. 9% smoking cessation reported<br>4. No change in weight<br>Mean differences between treatment and control groups<br>Cholesterol (mg%) −1.2<br>Smokers (%) −1.9<br>Weight (kg) −.04<br>SBP (mmHg) −2.0<br>Fatal CHD (%) −7.4<br>Total risk −11.1 |
| Wilbur (1983) | Johnson and Johnson Co. | 2 | 3046 "at risk" employees | Comprehensive health ed. intervention<br>1. physical activity<br>2. hypertension<br>3. weight and diet<br>4. smoking<br>5. stress reduction | 2 years | Ongoing | % change from baseline at 1 year<br>           Treatment   Control<br>Above ideal wt   −1%   +6%<br>Smokers   −15%   −4%<br>Well being   +5%   +2%<br>BP>140/90 mmHg   mi32%   −9%<br>Sick days   −9%   +14% |
| Wood (1975) | New York phone co. | 1 | 3984 | Free medical check-up and referral | 1 year | None | Health Care Maintenance Group<br>37% increase in hospitalization<br>No changes in absenteeism<br>Blood pressure −71% controlled in 195 hypertensives |

early stage and in large part comprises studies of low methodological rigor, some conclusions can be summarized.

1. Programs are feasible. About 50 programs of various size have been evaluated and reported in the past decade and 10–15% of companies may be already offering some form of risk reduction program for employees. Both public and private organizations have offered them and workers at all levels have participated in risk reduction programs.

2. Generalizations about the effectiveness of programs are difficult, in part because outcomes can be measured at several levels. Effects on health behaviors, physiological risk, and work-related variables can be assessed. However, multiple risk factor programs appear to be effective in reducing CVD risk, especially in high risk employees. Several large studies which are underway will provide additional information on participation, effects, and costs of programs.

One published study has documented that relaxation training can produce generalized, long-term blood pressure reductions in uncontrolled hypertensives. Relaxation-based stress reduction programs have produced a vareity of physiological and psychological effects, but measurement problems and small sample sizes limit confidence in the results of most studies. Physical activity programs have been associated with many benefits, but no experimental study has verified any benefits to the organization. Worksite weight control programs produce weight reductions that are probably not clinically meaningful, but which could be important if applied to large populations. There are insufficient data with which to judge the efficacy of worksite smoking control programs. The available findings suggest that the worksite has untapped potential as a setting for heart health behavior change programs and that further research and development is worthwhile.

3. Significant problems have been identified in each intervention area which must be overcome before progress in the field can continue. Low rates of recruitment and retention are serious problems which need to be addressed across all programs. Research is needed on the determinants of initial and continued participation in health programs and methods to improve the reach of interventions.

4. Savings to the employer are cited as inducements to conduct health promotion programs, but the cost studies to date have been inconclusive. Inadequate methodology and incomplete measurement of cost and benefit variables have been found in all studies. While there are promising indications that some weight reduction programs are cost-effective (Brownell *et al.*, 1984) and fitness programs may reduce absenteeism (Song *et al.*, 1982), these studies are not definitive.

5. Most intervention programs merely transplanted a clinical model of treatment to the workplace setting. Very few of the characteristics of worksites

listed at the beginning of this paper have been systematically utilized to improve the efficacy of worksite interventions. When organizational characteristics, such as opportunities for social support and intergroup competition were utilized, as in several weight loss programs, results were encouraging.

6.  The effective components of programs in all areas have not been identified.

It must be concluded that the scientific basis for believing that worksite heart health programs are effective is generally weak with the exception of multiple risk factor programs for high-risk individuals. However, the cost-effectiveness of worksite programs has not been convincingly demonstrated in any area. The research to date has demonstrated the feasibility of programs and has identified barriers to effectiveness. The challenge is for behavioral researchers to develop broadly applicable and effective interventions, well suited to the workplace. Some recommendations for future work in this area are presented below.


## IV.   RESEARCH DIRECTIONS

Viewing this literature from a public health perspective allows for the formulation of research priorities for the field of worksite health behavior promotion in general.

1.   Probably the greatest need is for development of programs which are effective and feasible for use in small worksites, because health programs are concentrated in large companies (Fielding & Breslow, 1983). This is a tremendous challenge, which will likely require interventions that do not rely on expensive or time-consuming techniques. Another strategy to be tested is developing regional consortia of small companies so that resources can be pooled for health promotion (Basch, Zelasko, & Burkholder, 1985). However, it is vital that appropriate programs are offered to some of the 40% of the workforce which are employed in smaller establishments (U.S. Department of Commerce, 1980).

2.   It is time to assess the efficacy of utilizing the unique characteristics and resources of work organizations. Programs designed to capitalize on social support among employees, to place cues in the work environment which stimulate healthier behavior, to use formal communication systems such as newsletters or computer mail for health education, and to alter policies in a health promoting direction can be implemented and evaluated. These types of interventions could be used by themselves or in combination with skills training or interpersonal approaches. We should not continue merely to treat individuals at worksites, but should also treat the worksite itself. To accomplish this, investigators are encouraged to familiarize themselves with aspects of organizational psychology (Dun-

nette, 1976), organizational development (Kotter, 1978), and organizational diagnosis (Weisbord, 1978).

3.   Investigators are encouraged to use comprehensive measurement systems. Measurement of the appropriate behavioral and physiological outcomes could be complemented with assessment of emotional and cognitive effects. Economic and noneconomic outcomes that are of interest to organizations should be measured in all studies, including job satisfaction, absenteeism, health care utilization, and possibly turnover and organizational climate. A recent paper by Hunter and Schmidt (1983) describes a model for calculating the economic utility of organizational interventions, which may be useful for the evaluation of health promotion programs, but investigators should also report such variables as total program cost, cost per employee, and cost per unit of risk reduction. Long-term, large-scale programs should monitor the populations for morbidity and mortality from CVD and other chronic disease that may be affected, such as cancer and lung diseases (e.g., WHO, 1983).

4.   Different strategies of intervention need to be compared in cost-effectiveness. Comparisons between single risk versus multiple risk programs and the targeting of high-risk individuals versus the entire workforce are recommended.

5.   Multidisciplinary teams should be formed to conduct this research, not only because the team approach will enhance the effectiveness of programs, but also because the worksite is a suitable laboratory for many purposes. It seems that epidemiologists, cardiologists, communication scientists, health educators, economists, exercise physiologists, nutritionists, and social, organizational, and health psychologists, could all contribute to the benefit from this enterprise.

6.   Future research must be experimental or quasi-experimental in design. Evaluations of single programs will not advance the field. However, true experiments in which sufficient numbers of work units are randomized into conditions will continue to be rare. Therefore, quasi-experiments in which one or two experimental worksites or departments are compared to similar control sites will be the best design possible in many cases and should be considered acceptable in this context. Single-case experimental design principles (Hersen & Barlow, 1976) can be applied to worksites and their use would greatly improve the methodological rigor of the worksite risk reduction literature. Multiple baselines across worksites or across different risk factors would allow for demonstration of causation of change while eliminating some practical problems of conducting randomized experiments in a field setting.

Finally, there has been a large proliferation of proprietary health promotion firms and consultants who develop and implement services at worksites for a fee. To the extent that they offer scientifically based, effective interventions, they may be useful. However, the danger in these service-oriented programs is that they make unrealistic claims, do not evaluate their projects, and are unqualified to deal with all of the implementation and evaluation issues. Aggressive marketing of ineffective programs could arouse resistance in the business community and thus impede the development of worksite interventions which could benefit the public health.

## ACKNOWLEDGMENTS

Work on this project was supported by NIH Grant HL21906 and Dr. Sallis was partially supported by NIH Training Grant HL 07034. The authors thank Margaret A. Chesney for her direction and valuable comments on an earlier draft of this manuscript.

## REFERENCES

Abrams, D. B., & Follick, M. J. (1983). Behavioral weight loss intervention at the worksite: Feasibility and maintenance. *Journal of Consulting and Clinical Psychology, 51,* 226–233.

Agras, W. S. (1982). Behavioral medicine in the 1980s: Nonrandom connections. *Journal of Consulting and Clinical Psychology, 50,* 797–803.

Agras, W. S., Chesney, M. A., Taylor, C. B., & Sevelius, G. (1983a). *The Lockheed hypertension project*. Presented at Society of Behavioral Medicine, Baltimore, March.

Agras, W. S., Southam, M. A., & Taylor, C. B. (1983b). Long-term persistence of relaxation-induced blood pressure lowering during the working day. *Journal of Consulting and Clinical Psychology, 51,* 792–794.

Alderman, M., Green, L. W., & Flynn, B. S. (1980). Hypertension control programs in occupational settings. *Public Health Reports, 95,* 158–163.

Alderman, M. H., Madhaven, S., & Davis, T. (1983). Reduction of cardiovascular disease events by worksite hypertension treatment. *Hypertension, 5* (supplement V), V138–V143.

Arnold, C. B., & Jacobson, C. (1981). Risk reduction in the U.S. Air Force primary prevention HEART program. *Preventive Medicine, 10,* 270–276.

Barnard, R. J., & Anthony, D. F. (1980). Effect of health maintenance programs on Los Angeles City Firefighters. *Journal of Occupational Medicine, 22,* 667–669.

Basch, C. E., Zelasko, S., & Burkholder, B. (1985). An alternative approach for worksite health promotion: The consortium model. *Health Education, 15,* 22–24.

Bauer, R. L., Heller, R. F., & Challah, S. (1985). United Kingdom heart disease prevention project: 12-year follow-up of risk factors. *American Journal of Epidemiology, 121,* 563–569.

Bernacki, E. J., & Baun, W. B. (1984). The relationship of job performance to exercise adherence in a corporate fitness program. *Journal of Occupational Medicine, 26,* 529–531.

Bertera, R. L., & Cuthie, J. C. (1984). Blood pressure self-monitoring in the workplace. *Journal of Occupational Medicine, 26,* 183–188.

Bjurstrom, L. A., & Alexiou, N. G. (1978). A program of heart disease intervention for public employees. *Journal of Occupational Medicine, 8,* 521–531.

Blair, S. N., Blair, A., Howe, H. G., Pate, R., Rosenberg, M., & Parker, G. M. (1980). Leisure time physical activity and job performance. *Research Quarterly for Exercise and Sport, 51,* 718–723.

Blair, S. N., Collingwood, T. R., Reynolds, R., Smith, M., Hagan, D., & Sterling, C. L. (1984). Health promotion for educators: Impact on health behaviors, satisfaction, and general well-being. *American Journal of Public Health, 74,* 147–149.

Bowne, D. W., Russell, M. L., Morgan, J. L., Optenberg, S. A., & Clarke, A. E. (1984). Reduced disability and health care costs in an industrial fitness program. *Journal of Occupational Medicine,* **26,** 809–816.

Brownell, K. D. (1982). Obesity: Understanding and treating a serious, prevalent, and refractory disorder. *Journal of Consulting and Clinical Psychology,* **50,** 820–840.

Brownell, K. D., Cohen, R. Y., Stunkard, A. J., Felix, M. R. J., & Cooley, N. B. (1984). Weight loss competitions at the work site: Impact on weight, morale, and cost-effectiveness. *American Journal of Public Health,* **74,** 1283–1285.

Brownell, K. D., Stunkard, A. J., & McKeon, P. E. (1983). Weight reduction at the work site: A promise partially fulfilled. *American Journal of Psychiatry,* **142,** 47–52.

Bruno, R., Arnold, D., Jacobson, L., Winick, & Wynder, E. (1983). Randomized controlled trial of a nonpharmacologic cholesterol reduction program at the worksite. *Preventive Medicine,* **12,** 523–532.

Carmody, T. P., Fey, S. L., Pierce, D. K., Connor, W. E., & Matarazzo, J. D. (1982). Behavioral treatment of hyperlipidemia: Techniques, results, and future directions. *Journal of Behavioral Medicine,* **5,** 91–116.

Carrington, P., Collings, G. H., Benson, H., Robinson, H., Wood, L. W., Lehrer, P. M., Woolfolk, R. L., & Cole, J. W. (1980). The use of meditation-relaxation techniques for the management of stress in a working population. *Journal of Occupational Medicine,* **22,** 221–231.

Chadwick, J. H. (1982). Health behavior change at the worksite: A problem-oriented analysis. In R. S. Parkinson & Associates. *Managing health promotion in the workplace: Guidelines for implementation and evaluation* (pp. 144–161). Palo Alto: Mayfield.

Charlesworth, E. A., Williams, B. J., & Baer, P. E. (1984). Stress management at the worksite for hypertension: Compliance, cost-benefit, health care and hypertension-related variables. *Psychosomatic Medicine,* **46,** 387–397.

Chesney, M. A., & Feuerstein, M. (1979). Behavioral medicine in the occupational setting. In J. R. McNamara (Ed.), *Behavioral approaches to medicine: Application and analysis* (pp. 267–290). New York: Plenum.

Chesney, M. A., Sevelius, G., Black, G. W., Ward, M. M., Swan, G. E., & Rosenman, R. H. (1981). Work environment, Type A behavior, and coronary heart disease risk factors. *Journal of Occupational Medicine,* **23,** 551–555.

Cohen, W. S. (1985). Health promotion in the workplace: A prescription for good health. *American Psychologist,* **40,** 213–216.

Colletti, G., & Brownell, K. D. (1982). The physical and emotional benefits of social support: Application to obesity, smoking, and alcoholism. In M. Hersen, R. M. Eisler, & P. M. Mill (Eds.), *Progress in behavior modification* (Vol. 13). New York: Academic Press.

Collings, G. H. (1982). Managing the health of the employee. *Journal of Occupational Medicine,* **24,** 15–17.

Colvin, R. H. Zopf, K. J., & Myers, J. H. (1983). Weight control among coworkers: Effects of monetary contingencies and social milieu. *Behavior Modification,* **7,** 64–75.

Companies put up the "no-smoking" sign. (1978). *Business Week* **68** (May 29).

Cook, T. D., & Campbell, D. T. (1979). *Quasi-experimentation: Design and analysis for field settings.* Chicago: Rand-McNally.

Cox, M., Shephard, R. J., & Corey, P. (1981). Influence of an employee fitness programme upon fitness, productivity and absenteeism. *Ergonomics,* **24,** 795–806.

Danaher, B. G. (1980). Smoking cessation programs in occupation settings. *Public Health Reports,* **95,** 149–157.

Dawber, T. R. (1980). *The Framingham study: The epidemiology of atherosclerotic disease.* Cambridge, MA: Harvard Univ. Press.

Dawley, H. H., Fleischer, B. J., & Dawley, L. T. (1984). Smoking cessation with hospital employees: An example of worksite smoking cessation. *The International Journal of the Addictions,* **19,** 327–334.

Department of Health and Human Services. (1980). *Health, United States 1977–1978.* Washington, D.C.: U.S. Govt. Printing Office.

Department of Health and Human Services. (1982). *Health consequences of smoking: A report of the Surgeon General.* Washington, D.C.: U.S. Govt. Printing Office.

Dexter, G. A. (1984). Comparing relaxation training and organization development as work site stress management treatments. Unpublished manuscript (Stanford University).

Donoghue, S. (1977). The correlation between physical fitness, absenteeism, and work performance. *Canadian Journal of Public Health,* **68,** 201–203.

Drazen, M., Nevid, J. S., Pace, N., & O'Brien, R. M. (1982). Worksite-based behavioral treatment of mild hypertension. *Journal of Occupational Medicine,* **24,** 511–514.

Duggar, B., & Swengros, G. (1969). The design of physical activity programs for industry. *Journal of Occupational Medicine,* **2,** 322–329.

Dunnette, M. R. (Ed.) (1976). *Handbook of industrial and organizational psychology.* Chicago: Rand-McNally.

Durbeck, D. C., Heinzelmann, F., Schacter, J., Haskell, W. E., Payne, G. H., Moxley, R. T., Nemiroff, M., Limoncelli, D. D., Arnoldi, L. B., and Fox, S. M. (1972). The National Aeronautics and Space Administration-U.S. Public Health Service health evaluation and enhancement program. *American Journal of Cardiology,* **30,** 784–790.

Everett, M. D. (1979). Strategies for increasing employees' level of exercise and physical fitness. *Journal of Occupational Medicine,* **7,** 463–467.

Farquhar, J. W., Fortmann, S. P., Wood, P. D., & Haskell, W. L. (1983). Community studies of cardiovascular disease prevention. In N. M. Kaplan & J. Stamler (Eds.), *Preventive cardiology.* Philadelphia: Saunders.

Fielding, J. E. (1982). Effectiveness of employee health improvement programs. *Journal of Occupational Medicine,* **24,** 907–916.

Fielding, J. E. (1984). Health promotion and disease prevention at the worksite. *Annual Review of Public Health,* **5,** 237–266.

Fielding, J. E., & Breslow, L. (1983). Health promotion programs sponsored by California employers. *American Journal of Public Health,* **73,** 538–542.

Flow, D. L. (1980). *A comparison of two smoking cessation techniques conducted in an occupational setting.* Doctoral dissertation, Oregon State Univ. University Microfilms International. 80--21937.

Fogle, R. K., Verdesca, A. S. (1975). The cardiovascular conditioning effects of a supervised exercise program. *Journal of Occupational Medicine,* **17,** 240–246.

Follick, M. J., Fowler, J. L., & Brown, R. A. (1984). Attrition in worksite weight-loss interventions: The effects of an incentive procedure. *Journal of Consulting and Clinical Psychology,* **52,** 139–140.

Foote, A., & Erfurt, J. C. (1983). Hypertension control at the worksite: Comparison of screening and referral alone, referral and follow-up, and on-site treatment. *New England Journal of Medicine,* **308,** 809–813.

Foreyt, J. P., Scott, L. W., & Gotto, A. M. (1980). Weight control and nutrition education programs in occupational settings. *Public Health Reports,* **95,** 127–136.

Fowler, J. L., Abrams, D. B., Peterson, G. S., & Follick, M. J. (1983). *Worksite weight loss: Professionally led vs. self-help.* Presented at Society of Behavioral Medicine, Baltimore, March.

Glasgow, R. E., Klesges, R. C., Godding, P. R., Vasey, M. W., and O'Neill, H. K. (1984). Evaluation of a worksite-controlled smoking program. *Journal of Consulting and Clinical, Psychology,* **52,** 137–138.

Glass, D. C. (1977). *Behavior patterns, stress, and coronary disease.* Hillsdale, N.J.: Erlbaum.

Goetz, A. A., Duff, J. F., & Bernstein, J. E. (1980). Health risk appraisal. *Public Health Reports,* **95,** 119–126.

Grove, D. A., Reed, R. W., & Miller, L. C. (1979). A health promotion program in a corporate setting. *Journal of Family Practice,* **9,** 83–88.

Haskell, W. L. (1984). Exercise-induced changes in plasma lipids and lipoproteins. *Preventive Medicine* **13,** 23–26.

Haskell, W. L., and Blair, S. N. (1980). The physical activity component of health promotion in occupational settings. *Public Health Reports,* **95,** 109–110.

Haynes, R. B., Gibson, E. S., Hackett, B. C., Sackett, D. L., Taylor, D. W., Roberts, R. S., & Johnson, A. L. (1976). Improvement of medication compliance in uncontrolled hypertension. *Lancet,* **1,** 1265–1268.

Hersen, M., & Barlow, D. H. (1976). *Single-case experimental designs: Strategies for studying behavior change.* Oxford: Pergamon.

Hitchings, B. (1979). Healthy trend toward corporate exercise programs. *Business Week,* **91–92,** April 3.

Holt, R. R. (1982). Occupational stress. In L. Goldberger & S. Breznitz (Eds.), *Handbook of stress: Theoretical and clinical aspects.* New York: Free Press.

Horne, W. M. (1975). Effects of a physical activity program on middle-aged sedentary corporation executives. *American Industrial Hygiene Association Journal,* **35,** 241–245.

House, J. S. (1975). Occupational stress as a precursor to coronary disease. In W. D. Gentry & R. B. Williams (Eds.), *Psychological aspects of myocardial infarction and coronary care.* St. Louis: Mosby.

Hovel, M. F. (1982). The experimental evidence for weight loss treatment of essential hypertension: A critical review. *American Journal of Public Health,* **72,** 359–368.

Hunter, J. E., and Schmidt, F. L. (1983). Quantifying the effects of psychological interventions on employee job performance and work-force productivity. *American Psychologist,* **38,** 473–478.

Hypertension Detection and Follow-up Cooperative Group. (1979). Five year findings of the hypertension detection and follow-up program. *Journal of the American Medical Association,* **242,** 2562–2571.

Jacob, R. G., Kraemer, H. C., & Agras, W. S. (1977). Relaxation therapy in the treatment of hypertension. *Archives of General Psychiatry,* **34,** 1417–1427.

Kelly, K. L. (1979). Evaluation of a group nutrition education approach to effective weight loss and control. *American Journal of Public Health,* **69,** 813–814.

"Kimberly-Clark health management program aimed at prevention." (1977). *Occupational Health and Safety,* 25–27.

Koerner, D. R. (1973). Cardiovascular benefits from an industrial physical fitness program. *Journal of Occupational Medicine,* **15,** 700–707.

Kotter, J. P. (1978). *Organizational dynamics: Diagnosis and intervention.* Reading, MA: Addison-Wesley.

Kristein, M. M. (1983). How much can business expect to profit from smoking cessation? *Preventive Medicine,* **12,** 358–381.

Laporte, W. (1966). The influence of a gymnastic pause upon recovery following post office work. *Ergonomics,* **9,** 501–506.

Lichtenstein, E., & Brown, R. A. (1982). Current trends in the modification of cigarette dependence. In A. S. Bellack, M. Hersen, & A. E. Kazdin (Eds.), *International handbook of behavior modification and therapy.* New York: Plenum.

MacGregor, G. A. (1983). Dietary sodium and potassium intake and blood pressure. *Lancet,* **1,** 750–753.

Manuso, J. S. (1983). The Equitable Life Assurance program. *Preventive Medicine,* **12,** 658–662.

Martin, J. W., and Dubbert, P. M. (1982). Exercise applications and promotion in behavioral medicine: Current status and future directions. *Journal of Consulting and Clinical Psychology,* **50,** 1004–1017.

Marx, J. L., & Kolata, G. B. (1978). *Combating the #1 killer: Epidemiology of heart disease.* Washington, D.C.: American Association for the Advancement of Science.

Meyer, A. J., & Henderson, J. B. (1974). Multiple risk factor reduction in the prevention of cardiovascular disease. *Preventive Medicine,* **3,** 225–236.

Miller, G. H., & Rodway, J. S. (1980). The Cummins Engine Company stop smoking program. *Journal of the Indiana State Medical Association,* **73,** 233.

Montegriffo, V. M. E. (1968). Height and weight of a United Kingdom adult population with a review of anthropometric literature. *Annals of Human Genetics,* **31,** 309–399.

Mossman, P. B. (1978). Changing habits: An experience in industry. *Journal of Occupational Medicine,* **20,** 213.

Murphy, L. R. (1984). Stress management in highway maintenance workers. *Journal of Occupational Medicine,* **26,** 436–442.

Naditch, M. P. (1980). The Control Data Corporation StayWell Program. *Behavioral Medicine Updates,* **2,** 9–10.

National Interagency Council on Smoking and Health (1983). *Smoking and the workplace: Business Survey.* New York: Unpublished report.

Nepps, M. M. (1984). A minimal contact smoking cessation program at the worksite. *Addictive Behaviors* **9,** 291–294.

Orleans, C. S., & Shipley, R. H. (1982). Worksite smoking cessation initiatives: Review and recommendations. *Addictive Behaviors,* **7,** 1–16.

Paffenbarger, R. S., & Hyde, R. T. (1984). Exercise in the prevention of coronary heart disease. *Preventive Medicine,* **13,** 3–22.

Parkinson, R. S., & associates (Eds.) (1982). *Managing health promotion at the worksite: Guidelines for implementation and evaluation.* Palo Alto: Mayfield.

Pate, R. R., & Blair, S. N. (1983). Physical fitness programming for health promotion at the worksite. *Preventive Medicine,* **12,** 632–643.

Patel, C., Marmot, M. G., & Terry, D. J. (1981). Controlled trial of biofeedback-aided behavioural methods in reducing mild hypertension. *British Medical Journal,* **28,** 2005–2008.

Pauly, J. T., Palmer, J. A., Wright, C. C., & Pfeiffer, G. J. (1982). The effect of a 14-week employee fitness program on selected physiological and psychological parameters. *Journal of Occupational Medicine,* **24,** 457–463.

Peters, R. K., Benson, H., & Porter, D. (1977a). Daily relaxation response breaks in a working population: I. Effects on self-reported measures of health, performance, and well-being. *American Journal of Public Health,* **67,** 946–953.

Peters, R. K., Benson, H., & Peters, J. M. (1977b). Daily relaxation response breaks in a working population: II. Effects on blood pressure. *American Journal of Public Health,* **67,** 954–959.

Peterson, G., Abrams, D. B., Elder, J. P., & Beaudin, P. A. (1985). Professional versus self-help weight loss at the worksite: The challenge of making a public health impact. *Behavior Therapy,* **16,** 213–222.

Pooling Project Research Group. (1978). Relationship of blood pressure, serum cholesterol, smoking habit, relative weight, and ECG abnormalities to incidence of major coronary events: Final report of the pooling project. *Journal of Chronic Disease,* **31,** 201–306.

Puterbaugh, J. S., & Lawyer, C. H. (1983). Cardiovascular effects of an exercise program: A controlled study among firemen. *Journal of Occupational Medicine,* **25,** 581–586.

Riley, A. W., Frederiksen, L. W., Winett, R. A., & Love, S. Q. (1983). *A comprehensive evaluation of a stress management program: A time for caution in organizational health promotion.* Presented at Society of Behavioral Medicine, Baltimore, March.

Rodnick, J. E. (1982). Health behavior changes associated with health hazard appraisal counseling in an occupational setting. *Preventive Medicine,* **11,** 583–594.

Rogers, E. M., & Kincaid, D. L. (1978). *Communication networks: Toward a new paradigm for research.* New York: Free Press.

Rosen, G. M., & Lichtenstein, E. (1977). An employee incentive program to reduce cigarette smoking. *Journal of Consulting and Clinical Psychology,* **45,** 957.

Roskies, E., Kearney, H., Spevak, M., Surkis, A., Cohen, C., & Gilman, S. (1979). Generalizability and durability of treatment effects in an intervention program for coronary-prone (Type A) managers. *Journal of Behavioral Medicine,* **2,** 195–208.

Rothman, J. (1979). Three models of community organization practice, their mixing and phasing. In F. M. Cox, J. L. Erlich, J. Rothman, & J. E. Tropman (Eds.), *Strategies of community organization* (3rd ed.). Chicago: Peacock Publ.

Salonen, J. T., Puska, P., & Tuomihehto, J. (1982). Physical activity and risk of myocardial infarction, cerebral stroke, and death: A longitudinal study in Eastern Finland. *American Journal of Epidemiology,* **115,** 526–537.

Sanger, M. R., & Bichanich, P. (1977). Weight-reducing program for hospital employees. *Journal of the American Dietetics Association,* **71,** 535–536.

Schumacher, N., Groth, B., Kleinsek, J., & Seay, N. (1979). Successful weight control program for employees. *Journal of the American Dietetics Association,* **74,** 466–467.

Schwartz, G. E. (1980). Stress management in occupational settings. *Public Health Reports,* **95,** 99–108.

Seamonds, B. C. (1982). Stress factors and their effect on absenteeism in a corporate employee group. *Journal of Occupational Medicine,* **24,** 393–397.

Seidman, L. S., Sevelius, G. G., & Ewald, P. (1984). A cost-effective weight loss program at the worksite. *Journal of Occupational Medicine,* **26,** 725–730.

Shephard, R. J. (1983). Employee health and fitness: The state of the art. *Preventive Medicine,* **12,** 644–653.

Shephard, R. J., Corey, P., Renzland, R., & Cox, M. (1982). The influence of an employee fitness and lifestyle modification program upon medical care costs. *Canadian Journal of Public Health,* **73,** 259–263.

Song, T. K., Shephard, R. J., & Cox, M. (1982). Absenteeism, employee turnover, and sustained exercise participation. *Journal of Sports Medicine,* **22,** 392–399.

*Sourcebook of Health Insurance Data, 1981–1982.* (1983). Washington, D.C.: Health Insurance Association of America.

Southam, M. A., Agras, W. S., Taylor, C. B., & Kraemer, H. C. (1982). Relaxation training: Blood pressure lowering during the working day. *Archives of General Psychiatry,* **39,** 715–717.

Stachnik, T., & Stoffelmayr, B. (1983). Worksite smoking cessation programs: A potential for national impact. *American Journal of Public Health,* **73,** 1395–1396.

Steinmetz, J. I., Kaplan, R. M., & Miller, G. L. (1982). Stress management: An assessment questionnaire for evaluating interventions and comparing groups. *Journal of Occupational Medicine,* **24,** 923–931.

Sterling, T. D., & Weinkam, J. J. (1976). Smoking characteristics by type of employment. *Journal of Occupational Medicine,* **18,** 743–754.

Stunkard, A. J., & Brownell, K. D. (1982). Work-site treatment for obesity. *American Journal of Psychiatry,* **137,** 252–253.

Suinn, R. M. (1982). Intervention with type A behaviors. *Journal of Consulting and Clinical Psychology,* **50,** 797–803.

Thompson, J. K., Jarvie, G. J., Lahey, B. B., & Cureton, K. J. (1982). Exercise and obesity: Etiology, physiology, and intervention. *Psychological Bulletin,* **91,** 55–79.

U.S. Department of Commerce (1980). *County Business Patterns* Washington, D.C.: Department of Commerce (CBP 80-2).

U.S. Department of Health and Human Services. (1982). *Vital Statistics of the United States, 1978* (Vol. II. Mortality). Washington, D.C.: Department of Health and Human Services (Publ. No. 83-1101).

Verbrugge, L. M. (1982). Work satisfaction and physical health. *Journal of Community Health, 7,* 262–283.

Wallis, C. (1983). Stress: Can we cope? *Time,* **June 6,** 48–54.

Wear, R. F. (1983). The Campbell Soup Company program. *Preventive Medicine, 12,* 667–671.

Weisbord, M. R. (1978). *Organizational diagnosis: A workbook of theory and practice.* Reading, MA: Addison-Wesley.

Wilbur, C. S. (1983). The Johnson and Johnson program. *Preventive Medicine, 12,* 672–681.

Wood, L. W. (1975). The Bronx study—A trial of health care management. *Journal of Occupational Medicine, 17,* 648–651.

World Health Organization European Collaborative Group (WHO) (1983). Multifactorial trial in the prevention of coronary heart disease: 3. Incidence and mortality results. *European Heart Journal, 4,* 141–147.

Wynder, E. L., & Arnold, C. B. (1978). Mini-screening and maxi-intervention. *International Journal of Epidemiology, 7,* 199–200.

Yarvote, P. M., McDonagh, T. J., Goldman, M. E., & Zuckerman, J. (1974). Organization and evaluation of a physical fitness program in industry. *Journal of Occupational Medicine, 16,* 589–598.

Zimmerman, R. S., Baumann, L. J., Safer, M., & Leventhal, H. (1983). *Providing a service in the pursuit of science: Hypertension education at the worksite.* Presented at Society of Behavioral Medicine, Baltimore, March.

# THE ROLE OF BEHAVIORAL CHANGE PROCEDURES IN MULTIFACTORIAL CORONARY HEART DISEASE PREVENTION PROGRAMS

PAULINE M. LANGELUDDECKE

*Professorial Psychiatric Unit*
*The University of Sydney*
*Royal North Shore Hospital of Sydney*
*Sydney, Australia*

## I.  INTRODUCTION

Cognizant of the major role of lifestyle factors in increasing the risk of coronary heart disease (CHD), a number of large scale behavioral change programes aimed at preventing CHD have been undertaken throughout the last 15 years. The better known programes include the Stanford Heart Disease Prevention Project (1), the North Karelia Study (2), the Multiple Risk Factor Intervention Trial (3), and the WHO International Collaborative Study (4). The importance of such programes cannot be overstated. Coronary heart disease constitutes by far the major single cause of death in industrialized nations (5). It should also be borne in mind that the risk factors for CHD, (i.e., cigarette smoking, hypertension, hyperlipidemia, overweight, and insufficient exercise) play a role in the etiology of other prevalent chronic degenerative diseases (e.g., chronic obstructive pulmonary disease, cerebrovascular accidents) and that the living patterns which are promoted to minimize CHD risk are widely recognized as sound health practices (6). Thus, the development of intervention programs which are effective in correcting coronary risk-inducing behaviors has important implications for reducing morbidity in, and improving the general health of, populations in the developed nations.

Behavioral changes which have been demonstrated, or are presumed, to reduce CHD risk are cessation of cigarette smoking; adjustment of dietary intake to reduce serum cholesterol and triglyceride levels; control of total caloric intake to attain and maintain desirable body weight; reduced sodium intake aimed at blood pressure reduction; improved stress management skills to reduce blood pressure levels and modify the Type A (coronary prone) behavior pattern; and the adoption of a regimen of frequent aerobic exercise to improve cardiovascular functioning and to facilitate weight control (1–4). Experimental clinical psychologists have paid considerable attention to the development and modification of these health-related behaviors. Research over the last 15 to 20 years has demonstrated the importance of behavioral procedures in increasing the effectiveness (at least in the short term) of treatment programs aimed at weight reduction (7,8), cessation/reduction of cigarette smoking (9), serum lipid level reduction (10), improved physical fitness (11–13), blood pressure reduction (14), and modification of Type A behavior (14). Accordingly, it is widely held that behavioral approaches may provide the theoretical and empirical basis for effective behavioral change programs aimed at preventing chronic diseases such as CHD (15–20). For example, Pomerleau, Bass, and Crown (17) predicted that ''the successful application of behavioural principles to problems in preventive medicine may prove to be as important . . . as the development of effective antibacterial agents was in the first half of the century'' (p. 1277). In the light of such optimism, the present article assesses the role of behavioral change procedures in multifactorial preventive programs for CHD. First of all, general guidelines for intervention in such programs, based on research and theory in experimental clinical psychology, will be outlined. Thereafter, the large-scale, multifactorial CHD prevention programs which have been conducted over the last 15 years will be reviewed in terms of their emphasis on behavioral procedures, and their effectiveness in achieving lasting improvements in target behaviors and the coronary risk factors.

CHD intervention studies will be considered under two major headings, namely ''community'' and ''clinic-based'' trials. Community studies are defined as those in which intervention and evaluation (i.e., changes in coronary risk-related behavior patterns and coronary risk factor status) involves entire populations, regardless of their initial CHD risk. Clinic-based trials include those in which treatment is confined to persons initially identified as having a high CHD risk. Community trials typically have a lower mean baseline value on the behavioral and physiological coronary risk indices than is the case for clinic studies. More importantly, in studies involving high risk samples, reductions in various coronary risk indices (particularly serum lipid and blood pressure levels) subsequent to the first assessment can be expected due to regression toward the population mean as a consequence of error in the initial assessments. Practical and methodological advantages and disadvantages of clinic-based as opposed to community-based trials are discussed by Syme (21) and Farquhar (22), and will not be considered here.

Omitted from the present article are the following. First, preventive trials for CHD conducted in the 1960s, which were typically directed toward single coronary risk factors (particularly the reduction of serum lipid levels) have been excluded because of their methodological shortcomings and the fact that little information is available on the nature of the intervention procedures adopted. Second, studies designed to assess the impact on CHD incidence of hypertension control (e.g., 23–25) or serum lipid reduction (e.g., 26,27) which involve pharmacological (rather than lifestyle) intervention are outside of the scope of the present article. Finally, the important issue of the impact which changes in coronary risk factor status (as a result of behavior change) can be expected to have on CHD morbidity and mortality is peripheral to the present discussion. This topic is discussed in a number of other articles (e.g., 3, 28,29).

## II.  GUIDELINES FOR INTERVENTION AIMED AT CHANGING CORONARY RISK-RELATED BEHAVIORS

A behavioral analysis of the problem of modifying coronary risk-inducing living patterns points first to a number of social, economic, and political factors at a societal or cultural level in westernized nations which foster and reinforce unhealthy living patterns. These are discussed by Henderson and Enelow (30), and include the social acceptability (i.e., social reinforcement) of unhealthy living patterns, the powerful advertising campaigns waged by the manufacturers of risk-related products (particularly cigarettes), minimal emphasis on facilities aimed at health promotion in the health care system, and the fact that health insurance schemes generally fail either to provide incentives for maintaining a health-promoting lifestyle or to reimburse subscribers for the use of preventive health care services. Interventions aimed at altering these unfavorable environmental contingencies are dependent upon the actions of legislators and community agents (i.e., are beyond the control of the individual), and are referred to as "managerial" (as opposed to personal) prevention measures (31). Such measures include legislation aimed at removing or heavily restricting the availability of unhealthy substances, widespread propaganda on the relation of lifestyle to health and disease, economic incentives for maintaining health-promoting living patterns (*e.g.*, reduced health insurance premiums), and greater emphasis on health-promotion facilities in the allocation of health resources. One would expect managerial measures to play an important and effective role in preventive health programs which are conducted on a community basis.

In most preventive health programmes, the onus for behavioral change is on the individual rather than on community agencies. Research in experimental clinical psychology would suggest the following principles to be pertinent to the development of effective behavioral change programs at an individual level. First, it is necessary to modify the subject's attitudes, beliefs, and perceptions such that he/she is aware of the urgent need to modify unhealthy living patterns and has an expectation of the possibility of doing so (32). Coronary risk factor screening and health education can be expected to play an important role in establishing a cognitive framework which is conducive to long-term behavioral change in CHD prevention programs. Since CHD is asymptomatic in its preclinical stages, it is primarily through assessment and feedback of the individual's status on each of the coroi.ary risk indices and provision of information on the implications of this for immediate and future CHD risk that individuals may be alerted to the immediate need to favorably change their unhealthy living patterns. Similarly, through well designed health education programs individuals may be informed of (1) the implications of the advancement of CHD to a clinical stage in terms of quality and quantity of life, (2) the significant role of unhealthy living patterns in increasing CHD risk, and (3) the extent to which they are able to improve their coronary risk profile through appropriate changes in their living patterns. Such information can be expected not only to motivate people (particularly those whose CHD risk is high) to change their unhealthy lifestyles, but also to favorably influence the individual's perception of his/her ability to do so.

While health education and screening procedures are generally regarded as an important component of preventive health programs, when used alone they have generally proved ineffectual in achieving lasting improvements in target behaviors (33–37). For example, in his assessment of health education programs, Haggerty (34) concluded that

> "A careful review of the literature leaves one with only a few studies meeting two criteria: that alterations in behaviour rather than knowledge or attitudes should be the end result of intervention; and that rigorous research methods with controls or at least good comparisons should be used. When such rigorous criteria are used, few health education programmes have shown much effect on behaviour" (p.279)

The disappointing findings of health education programs are hardly surprising given the wealth of psychological research demonstrating that favorable cognitive change is a necessary, but rarely a sufficient condition for achieving lasting improvements in well established, unhealthy living patterns (e.g., 30,38,39).

A functional analysis of the behaviors which are targets for change in preventive health programs assists in explaining why screening/health education alone generally fail to result in lasting improvements in target behaviors. First, the behaviors which are to be extinguished (e.g., cigarette smoking, overeating) are habits which are maintained by immedite positive reinforcers (e.g., pleasant taste) and negative reinforcers (e.g., termination of aversive states). Second, attempts to establish new behaviors (e.g., daily aerobic exercise) or to modify well established eating or drug usage patterns often initially have adverse effects on the subject's physical and/or mental well being (e.g., muscle soreness due to exercise, irritability and weight gain when stopping smoking). These act as punishers for the desired behaviors. Third, since the onset of disease symptomatology is temporally divorced from, and intangibly linked with, unhealthy living patterns, the threat of disease is a fairly weak deterrent and is less salient than the immediate enjoyment derived from these behaviors. Moreover, since CHD prevention programs are directed toward reduction of risk rather than the treatment of actual symptoms of disease, the individual can expect little (if any) positive feedback in the form of improvements in symptomatology through changing his/her lifestyle. In addition to the unfavorable response contingencies which foster and reinforce coronary risk-inducing behaviors, a number of the behaviors which are targets for change (particularly cigarette smoking and undesirable eating patterns) are under the control of a wide array of discriminative stimuli. In short, a functional analysis of unhealthy living patterns suggests them to be highly resistant to change.

Behavioral change principles and procedures which are relevant to the modification of undesirable patterns of eating and exercise and cigarette smoking are well documented, and will be merely summarized for present purposes. Behavioral intervention at the individual level is based on a functional analysis of the nature and magnitude of target behaviors and the environmental conditions relevant to their occurrence (see above), and involves an individually tailored behavioral change regimen. The objectives for behavioral change which are established are clearly defined to provide both a clear understanding of the subject's goals and an objective yardstick against which progress can be measured. To create the opportunity for immediate reinforcement, the emphasis is on attaining short-term goals which are realistic (i.e., which the individual is highly likely to attain) given his/her present behavioral skills rather than on less influential long-term behavioral objectives. A detailed account of the behavioral means of attaining his/her objectives for coronary risk factor change can be expected to facilitate adherence to the necessary behavioral regimen. The individual's chances of successfully affecting and maintaining the desired behavioral changes are likely to be greatly increased through the careful self-monitoring of target behaviors and the systematic use of self-management procedures such as stimulus control and contingency management techniques. Furthermore, to positively reinforce favorable behavioral change and in turn maintain a high level of commitment to furthering/maintaining healthy living patterns, it is necessary to objectively measure and provide feedback of changes in the individual's coronary risk factor status at frequent intervals.

Given that the goal of intervention is lasting improvement in target behaviors, social support from the home and (if possible) work environment for new, desirable living patterns may facilitate long-term behavioral change. In view of the highly complex and recalcitrant nature of behaviors such as cigarette smoking, overeating and sedentary living patterns, booster sessions (i.e., continued therapeutic contact on a less frequent basis) after the initial formal treatment program has ended are likely to be an important component of intervention. Booster sessions enable continued supervision over the implementation of behavioral change techniques and create the opportunity for continued assessment and feedback of progress toward long-term behavioral goals.

There is no sound empirical basis at this stage for deciding whether CHD prevention programs should attempt to simultaneously correct the array of unhealthy living patterns rather than attending to only one of these behaviors at any one time. However, the following considerations suggest that the former, more global approach to behavioral change is likely to prove more effective. First of all, in attending to the entire array of behaviors, greater opportunity is afforded for the individual to commit himself/herself to the establishment and maintenance of a healthy lifestyle. Second, greater opportunity is afforded for reinforcement of favourable behavioral change. Third, the simultaneously correction of a wide range of health-related behaviors is likely to have a greater beneficial impact on the subject's perception of self-efficacy than could be expected through increased control over only one aspect of his/her repertoire. Fourth, behaviors which adversely effect CHD risk are often interrelated, both physiologically and psychologically. Therefore, favorable changes in one behavior may act to facilitate favorable changes in another. Finally, since target behaviors often share a number of cue stimuli and/or act as cue stimuli for each other, attending to only one aspect of the coronary prone individual's repertoire of health-related living patterns may result in a number of discriminative stimuli for other unhealthy behaviors remaining intact.

## III.   COMMUNITY-BASED STUDIES

In the majority of community-based trials, intervention has focused on (1) the delivery of general health information on living patterns which increase coronary risk (either through the mass media or occupational health education programs); (2) screening and feedback of coronary risk factor status; and/or (3) medical counseling aimed at reducing CHD risk. Very little attention has been devoted to the role of behavioral procedures in such programs.

## A. Screening–Health Education Programs

In one of the earliest community studies, conducted in California, the effectiveness of a screening–health education approach to coronary risk factor change was evaluated in a sample of over 2500 asymptomatic adults who volunteered for assessment of their coronary risk profile (40). Results of the individual tests were sent to the persons screened and to the physician of their choice. In addition, the first 1280 subjects screened received an educational program involving four lectures plus standard American Heart Association literature on smoking cessation, hypertension control, and dietary change aimed at weight loss and serum lipid reduction. Approximately three-quarters ($N = 1817$) of the sample attended for reassessment of their coronary risk 10 to 11 months later, the level of attendance at follow-up being significantly lower for persons allocated to the educational program than for the remainder of the sample. Findings were presented in terms of change in the prevalence of abnormal scores on the coronary risk factors for the entire cohort and the health education subgroup (see Table I). Results were the same for both groups; the prevalence of cigarette smoking, overweight, and hypercholesterolaemia at follow-up was not significantly reduced, and the proportion of subjects with hypertension (i.e., > 140/90 mm Hg) or hypertriglyceridemia (>2 mmol/liter) rose significantly.

Despite the disappointing findings reported by Aronow et al. (40), four large, controlled studies evaluating the effectiveness of coronary risk factor intervention programs which center on screening and health education techniques have subsequently been conducted. The first of these, the Stanford Three Community Study (1), evaluated the long-term effectiveness of a community health education program in improving the coronary risk factors. In the second study, known as CHAD (Community Syndrome of Hypertension, Atherosclerosis and Diabetes) (41), screening and health education procedures were incorporated into the local medical care system. The remaining two trials are still in progress, one being an international study evaluating an occupational screening–health education program (3), and the other being a community study involving all adult males in a Swedish community within a particular age range (42). The design and findings of these studies will be briefly outlined.

In the Stanford study (1), two towns (Gilroy and Watsonville) received an extensive mass media health education campaign (involving television, radio, billboards, newspapers) of 2 years duration aimed at smoking cessation, dietary change (to reduce weight and serum lipid levels), increased exercise, and control of hypertension through pharmacological means. A subset of high-risk individuals in Watsonville also received a personalized behavioral change program. A third community (Tracy) acted as a "screening only" control group. Communities were assigned to the treatment and control conditions on a nonrandom basis (i.e., according to convenience in the delivery of mass media messages). In

## TABLE I

### Changes on the Coronary Risk Factors in Community CHD Prevention Programs, According to Treatment

| Study | Sample | Duration (years) | Treatment | N | Results | Cigarette smoking | | Body weight | | Systolic blood pressure | | Serum cholesterol | | Exercise | |
|---|---|---|---|---|---|---|---|---|---|---|---|---|---|---|---|
| | | | | | | 0 | % Change | 0 | % Change | 0 | % Change | 0 | % Change | 0 | % Change |
| Aronow et al. (40) USA | Males and females; aged over 20 yrs; voluntary attendants for community coronary screening survey | 1 | Screening only (947) or screening & health education | 1817 | Prevalence | (% smokers) 32.7 | -.7 | (>20% Overweight) 14.9 | +.2 | (>140/90 mm Hg) 8.6 | +5.5 | (>6.4 mmol/liter) 28.7 | +1.8 | 0 | 0 |
| | | | Screening & health education | 872 | | 32.2 | -.8 | 14.4 | 0 | 3.4 | +7.8 | 29.0 | +1.5 | | |
| Farquhar et al. (1) USA | Males and females; aged 35–59 yrs; voluntary attendants for community coronary screening survey | 2 | Screening & community health education (Town 1) | 423 | Mean change | (number/day) 6.5 | -14 | (Relative weight) 1.22 | -.2 | (mm Hg) 133 | -4.5 | (mmol/liter) 5.46 | -1.5 | | |
| | | | Screening & community health education (Town 2) | 397 | | 6.8 | -5 | 1.24 | -.9 | 132 | -7 | 5.46 | -3 | | |
| | | | Screening only (Town 3) | 384 | | 6.9 | -3 | 1.26 | -.4 | 129 | +.1 | 5.39 | +1 | | |
| Werko (42) Sweden | Males; aged 35–59 yrs; voluntary attendants for high | 4 (interim) | Screening plus medical counseling for high | 7500 | Mean change | (% smokers) -31 | | | | 149 | -2 | 6.36 | 0 | | |

| Study | Yrs | Population | Intervention | N | Change type | Serum cholesterol | Cigarettes (Number/day) | (% smokers) | Weight (Absolute kg) / (Body mass index) | Blood pressure | | | % Exercising > twice/week |
|---|---|---|---|---|---|---|---|---|---|---|---|---|---|
| Abramsom et al. (41) Israel | 5 | Males; aged over 35 yrs; residents of four housing projects in Jerusalem | CHD risk subjects for community screening survey — Screening only | 1000 | | −26 | | | | 149 | +1.3 | 6.36 | +1.6 | |
| | | | Screening, medical counseling, and group meetings | 211 | Mean change (age standardized) | | | 54.4  −12.9 | 70.5  0 | 133.8 | −3.3 | 5.46 | −2.8 | |
| WHO European Collaborative Research Group (4) Poland, Spain, U.K., Italy, Belgium | 4 (interim) | Males, aged 40–59 yrs; industrial employees | Screening only | 709 | | | | | 72.2  0 | 132.4 | −.8 | 5.59 | −.13 | |
| | | | Screening, occupational health education, medical counseling for high CHD risk males | 1148 | Mean net change[a] | 44.6  −6.2 | 11.2  −8.2 | 60  +2. | 76.  −.4 | 137 | −1. | 5.56 | −2.2 | |
| Puska et al (2) Finland | 5 | Males and females; aged 25–59 yrs; randomly selected from Finnish population register | Ongoing coronary risk assessment, health education, environmental change, small group behavioral treatments for dietary and smoking control | Males 2002 | Mean change | | 9.9  −18 | | 25.7  +1.5 | 147 | −2.3 | 6.94 | −3.5 | 37  +16.2 |
| | | | | Females 2121 | | | 1.3  −15 | | 26.3  +1.9 | 149.4 | −3.9 | 5.84 | −1.6 | 36.5  +12.8 |
| | | | Screening only | Males 2918 | | | 8.9  −15 | | 25.6  +1.6 | 145 | +1.3 | 6.71 | +.3 | 3.1  +17.7 |
| | | | | Females 3158 | | | 1.4  −7 | | 26.2  0 | 144.1 | +.9 | 6.68 | −1.6 | 27.6  +30 |

[a] Changes in the treatment group after accounting for changes in the "screening only" control group.

207

each community, a random sample of approximately 600 men and women was selected from the population of persons, aged 35–59 years, who were found to be free of CHD upon voluntary coronary risk factor screening. These subjects were reassessed for coronary risk at annual intervals. Changes in the risk factor at the completion of the mass media campaign (after 2 years) were reported in terms of mean percentage change over baseline levels. Relevant to the present discussion are the findings for the entire cohort of subjects in Tracy (control) and Gilroy (screening and health education), and for all subjects in Watsonville who received screening and health education only (i.e., excluding high-risk persons who received individualized behavioral instruction) (see Table I). Daily cigarette intake, based on self-reported smoking levels, was markedly reduced in one of the health education towns, moderately reduced in the other, and showed the smallest decrease in the control group. Systolic blood pressure showed a significant mean reduction (of 5–7%) in the intervention towns and negligible change in the control group. The greater decreases in the former were attributed to more widespread usage of antihypertensive medication. A slight (2–3%) decrease in serum cholesterol levels occurred in the health education cohorts, which compared favorably with the minor (1%) increase in the control condition. The two health education towns, like the control group, demonstrated no change in either weight or level of physical activity at follow-up. Methodological flaws, such as reliance on self-reported change in cigarette smoking (which are notoriously unreliable), failure to take into account the high drop-out rate, and the selective attrition of persons who were initially at higher CHD risk, limit the conclusions which can be drawn regarding the effectiveness of the screening–health education program in the Stanford Study.

In the CHAD program, screening and health education procedures were incorporated into the local medical care system in a small community in Jerusalem (41). Intervention was directed at all adults, (i.e., including those with established disease) living in four adjacent housing projects. The primary aim of the study was to assess the impact of such changes on CHD morbidity and mortality rates. Family physicians and nurses conducted group health education meetings in addition to providing individualized treatment. The latter included recommendations for coronary risk factor screening and other examinations, drug treatment of hypertension, counseling on lifestyle change (i.e., smoking cessation, increased exercise, dietary modification) and ongoing surveillance of coronary risk factor status. Changes in the coronary risk factors in the CHAD community over a 5-year period were compared with those in an adjacent neighborhood which was not exposed to intervention. Results are available only for males aged over 35 years, 80% of whom attended the scheduled coronary risk assessments. Baseline and follow-up data were presented in terms of age-standardized mean values. The intervention group demonstrated improvements in blood pressure and serum cholesterol levels which were slightly (2.5%) greater than those for the control cohort. The proportion of men who smoked cigarettes, based on self-reported smoking patterns, decreased at follow-up in both groups. This change was greater in the CHAD population, where the age standardized prevalence of smoking dropped by almost 13%. Self-appraisals of physical activity revealed no change in the intervention group and a trend toward decreased activity in the control cohort. Body weight remained largely unchanged in both groups after 5 years.

The World Health Organization is currently coordinating a large-scale, randomized, controlled, CHD prevention trial which involves centers in Belgium, Italy, Spain, Poland, and the United Kingdom (3,44–46). Assessment of the extent to which the coronary risk factors can be modified using primarily a health education approach is a secondary objective, the major aim being to determine the impact of coronary risk factor change on CHD incidence. Intervention is centered on the workplace and evaluation involves all male employees, aged 40–59 years, regardless of their initial status on the coronary risk factors. Eighty-eight large industrial groups (mainly factories), paired according to type of industry and area, have been allocated at random to receive either an intervention program or "screening only." Intervention involves coronary risk factor screening, followed by an occupational health education campaign (including posters, brochures, personal letters, progress charts, and group discussions) aimed at lowering body weight and serum cholesterol levels through dietary change, increasing leisure physical activity, and reducing cigarette smoking. High-risk men, in addition to the general propaganda, receive individual counseling from the occupational physician. In the intervention cohort, a random (5%) sample of the entire cohort, plus all initially "high-risk" males, are being assessed on the coronary risk factors at annual intervals. In the control factories, a random sample (10%) of men was screened initially and the same subjects are invited for rescreening after 2, 4, and 6 years.

Final (6-year) data are available only for the United Kingdom cohort, where screening commenced in 1971 (44). Interim (4-year) risk factor changes for almost the entire WHO sample (i.e., except for seven factory pairs in Poland) have been reported and will constitute the basis of the present discussion (3). The pooled data are presented in terms of "net" mean changes on the coronary risk factors in the health education group, and thus take into account changes reported in the "screening only" factories (i.e., changes attributable to sensitization to "high-risk" status and general trends in the population) (see Table I). The 4-year findings for cigarette smoking, based solely on self-reported smoking levels, are somewhat inconsistent. Relative to changes in the control group, mean daily cigarette consumption decreased markedly (by 8%), while the prevalence of smoking showed a slight (2%) increase after 4 years in the intervention cohort. On average, both systolic blood pressure and serum cholesterol levels showed a minor (2%) net improvement as a result of intervention after 4 years. However, there was considerable variability between countries in terms of mean "net" changes on these risk factors. Negligible improvements in body weight were reported for all countries after 4 years. Fitness levels were not assessed.

Finally, a randomized, controlled CHD intervention study which involves all male residents of a Swedish city (Gothenburg) who were aged 47 to 54 years ($N = 30,000$) when the study commenced (42) is evaluating the effectiveness of a screening and health education approach in improving the coronary risk factors. The primary aim of the study is to assess the impact of such changes on CHD morbidity and mortality rates. The latter data are being obtained for all subjects from the National Health Register. Subjects have been randomly assigned either to intervention (Group A), or to one of two control groups (Groups B and C). Persons in the treatment group were initially provided with information on CHD and the coronary risk factors, and invited to attend a free coronary screening program. Approximately 25% ($N = 2543$) failed to attend the initial screening. Data obtained over the first 5 years of the study revealed these "non attenders" to be less healthy than participants, the former having a three times greater mortality rate and two times greater incidence of CHD over this period. Subjects who attended the initial assessment and who were found to have hypertension, hyperlipidaemia, or to smoke cigarettes were referred to outpatient clinics which were conducted by the same medical personnel as the screening program. Treatment in the hypertension clinic centered on antihypertensive medication, while intervention for hyperlipidaemia involved dietary advice and drug treatment. The smoking cessation program involved small group meetings which provided information on the health effects of smoking, and social support for smoking cessation. In addition, chewing gum containing nicotine was provided as a substitute for smoking. Subjects in the intervention group were invited to attend a follow-up coronary screening survey after 4 years. Mean change in the intervention group after 4 years were compared with those reported for a random subsample (of 10%) of males in one of the control groups (group B) (see Table I). Interim results reveal a slight mean decrease (2%) in systolic blood pressure in the intervention group, which was attributed to an increase in the number of persons taking antihypertensive medication. On average, systolic blood pressure for control subjects increased slightly (by 1.3%) at follow-up. Mean serum cholesterol levels in the intervention cohort remained unchanged after 4 years, while a slight (1.6%) increase occurred in the control group. Self-reported smoking patterns indicated a marked reduction (of 31%) in the proportion of current cigarette smokers in the intervention group, and an insignificantly smaller decrease in the control cohort. Questionnaire data revealed that the level of physical activity had actually declined in both the control and treatment groups over the 4-year follow-up period.

In summary, community based CHD prevention programs which have centered on coronary risk factor screening and health education procedures have generally proved disappointing in terms of their impact on the coronary factors. Cigarette consumption, based solely on self-reported smoking levels, is the only risk factor which has been reported to show a dramatic improvement. At best, mean reductions in blood pressure and serum lipid levels which are attributable to intervention (rather than measurement factors) have been modest (2–4%), while improvements in body weight and physical activity levels have generally been negligible.

## B. Behavioral Programs

To date, only one controlled community cardiovascular disease prevention trial, the North Karelia Study, has evaluated intervention which incorporated behavioral procedures. This study (2,47) involved the residents of the North Karelia County in Eastern Finland ($N = 180,000$), with treatment being aimed at improving the detection and control of hypertension, smoking reduction, and dietary change (i.e., the adoption of diets which were lower in saturated fats and higher in vegetables and low-fat food products). In addition to a detailed health education program (involving mass media, community groups, and local health personnel), intervention involved a number of environmental changes aimed at promoting behavioral change. These included the restriction of smoking in public places, greater availability of low-fat products, and the reorganization of health services and training of health personnel to provide ongoing coronary risk factor assessment and feedback. Small group behavioral treatment programs for smoking cessation and dietary modification were also conducted. Changes in the coronary risk factors in North Karelia were compared with those observed over a similar period of time (i.e., 5 years) in a neighboring county (Kuopio) in which no formal intervention program was conducted. The baseline and follow-up (5-year) coronary risk surveys involved independent samples of 6.6% of men and women aged 25–59 years, randomly selected from the National Population Register. The level of attendance at the baseline and follow-up assessments was consistently high (i.e., above 90%). Data for each group were presented in terms of mean changes on the coronary risk factors at follow-up, according to sex (see Table I).

Reduction in self-reported daily cigarette intake in North Karelia after 5 years averaged 18% in males and 15% in females. The control group demonstrated a marked, though significantly lesser improvement in level of smoking. Similarly, the smoking cessation rate in the intervention county after 5 years of 9% in males and 3% in females was higher than for Kuopia. These figures may underestimate the differences between the two groups since serum thiocyanate determinations at follow-up suggested that the control subjects underreported their level of smoking compared to the North Karelia sample. On average, serum lipid and blood pressure levels were slightly improved (by 3%) in the intervention cohort and remained largely unchanged in the control county. Of particular note were the reductions in the prevalence of these risk factors after 5 years. The occurrence of elevated serum cholesterol values (>6.9 mmol/liter) was reduced by 9% in males and 4.5% in females in North Karelia, and remained unchanged in the control group. The prevalence of hypertension (>175 and/or 100 mm Hg) decreased by 7% in males in the intervention group whereas the reference sample showed a 4% increase. The trend for women was similar, with a 12% reduction in North Karelia and no change in the control cohort. Mean body weight and the prevalence of overweight (Body Mass Index > 29) showed a slight increase in both groups at follow-up. The questionnaire responses revealed that in terms of the number of persons who exercised more than twice per week, the two conditions showed a similar, marked improvement. No attempt was made to validate these data through objective assessment of physical fitness levels.

The design of the North Karelia project does not permit a definitive assessment of the contribution to the reported improvements in the coronary risk factors of traditional health education and screening procedures on the one hand and behavioral procedures (e.g., environmental changes, small group behavioral treatments for smoking and diet) on the other. Furthermore, it is difficult to resolve this issue by comparing the findings for the North Karelia cohort with those obtained in community studies which have involved only nonbehavioral procedures (outlined above), due to methodological differences. The former can be expected to provide a more accurate assessment of coronary risk factor change in the community by virtue of its randomly selected, cross-sectional sample, the high level of attendance at the initial and follow-up assessments, and the use of objective outcome measures (e.g., serum thiocyanate levels). By contrast, studies evaluating nonbehavioral procedures have involved longitudinal samples, usually drawn from the population of voluntary attendants at coronary screening surveys, with levels of attrition at follow-up invariably being high. Hence, they can be expected to exaggerate the beneficial impact of intervention in the community (21). Despite the more rigorous approach to evaluation in North Karelia, the behavioral intervention program in this study resulted in comparable, and often greater mean improvements in serum cholesterol, cigarette smoking, and blood pressure levels than was the case in trials in which intervention has centered on screening and health education alone. Thus, it is probable that behavioral procedures, at the environmental level (e.g., smoking restrictions, greater availability of low-fat foodstuffs, community support for behavioral change, provision of ongoing coronary risk factor assessment services) and/or in the form of small group behavioral treatments for smoking and dietary change, contributed to the lasting improvements in the coronary risk factors which were observed in North Karelia.

## IV.  CLINIC-BASED STUDIES

Like community trials, intervention in the majority of "clinic-based" studies has typically centered on screening and health education procedures. The most popular individual approach has involved identifying persons who are at increased risk of CHD through community screening programs, and referring such persons to medical personnel for treatment. Large-scale intervention along these lines has been evaluated in two randomized controlled studies (4,48), one nonrandomized, controlled trial (49,50), and an uncontrolled study (51). Only two large studies have included behavioral procedures in their intervention programs (3,53).

### A.  Screening–Health Education Programs

The initial randomized, controlled trial evaluating a screening-referral approach was conducted in Oslo, Norway, from 1971–1976 (48,52). Subjects were 1232 normotensive men, aged 40–49 years, who were identified at a voluntary screening programme to be at high risk (yet free of clinical evidence) of CHD. All were willing to participate in a 5-year preventive trial. Men assigned to the intervention group received personalized advice from health professionals (e.g., medical personnel, dietitians) aimed at dietary change and smoking cessation, and underwent repeated coronary risk factor assessment (at 6-monthly intervals). Subjects in the control condition underwent screening at annual intervals over the 5-year study period. The level of attendance at the final (5-year) follow-up was very high, with only 12 subjects being unavailable for reassessment. Significant improvements in the coronary risk factors which were the major targets of intervention, namely cigarette smoking and serum cholesterol, occurred in the intervention group after 5 years (see Table II). At baseline, almost 80% of the men in both groups were smokers. After 5 years, the prevalence of smoking in the intervention and control groups was reduced by 35 and 15%, respectively. Self-reported daily cigarette consumption was reduced by almost one-half in the intervention group, which compared favorably with the 25% decrease reported in the control cohort. When serum thiocyanate levels were used as an indicator of smoking, the difference between the two groups was "slightly" less (data were not provided). After accounting for measurement factors (i.e., regression toward the population mean), the intervention cohort demonstrated a dramatic (13%) reduction in serum cholesterol after 5 years, as compared with no change in the control cohort. Body weight showed a slight mean decrease (of 2.5%) in the intervention group and remained unchanged in the control subjects. On average, changes in diastolic blood pressure and physical activity levels did not differ between the groups after 5 years.

**TABLE II**

Changes on the Coronary Risk Factors in Clinic-Based CHD Prevention Trials, According to Treatment

| Study | Sample | Duration (years) | Results | Condition | N | Cigarette smoking 0 | % Change | Body weight 0 | % Change | Systolic blood pressure 0 | % Change | Serum cholesterol 0 | % Change | Exercise 0 | % Change |
|---|---|---|---|---|---|---|---|---|---|---|---|---|---|---|---|
| Hjermann (52) Norway | Males, aged 40–49 yrs, normotensive, free of CHD initially, prepared to participate in 5 year trial | 5–6 | Mean change | Medical counseling; biannual coronary screening | 604 | (Number/day) 13 (% Smokers) 80 | -46 -35 | Absolute kg 77.3 | -2.0 | | | 8.3 | -13 | | |
| | | | | Annual coronary screening | 628 | (Number/day) 12.5 (% Smokers) 80 | -25 -15 | 78.2 | .5 | | | 8.3 | 0 | | |
| WHO European Collaborative Research Group (4) Poland, Spain, U.K., Italy, Belgium | Males, aged 40–59 yrs, industrial employees | 4 (interim) | Mean net change | Occupation health education campaign; medical counseling; annual coronary screening | 2634 | (Number/day) 17.3 (% Smokers) 82 | -13.9 -5.5 | 77 | -.6 | 151 | -3 | 6.6 | -4.9 | | |
| Simons and Jones (50) Australia | Males and females, aged < 60 years, initially free of CHD | 3 | Mean change | Screening and medical treatment | 157 | | | 75.2 (N = 157) | -2.6 | 167 (N = 80) | -13.7 | 7.2 (N = 127) | -5.5 | | |
| | | | | Screening only | 68 | | | 75.8 (N = 37) | +.5 | 168 (N = 34) | -10.7 | 6.9 (N = 39) | +1 | | |
| Meyer and Henderson | Males, aged 35–55 yrs, from shared work environment, free of CHD | .5 | Mean change | Screening; health education; behavioral training; group | 12 | (Number/day) | -13 | | | | | | | Physical activity | |

| Study | Population | Yrs | | Intervention | N | Smoking | Weight | | | | Leisure activity score |
|---|---|---|---|---|---|---|---|---|---|---|---|
| (53) USA | initially | | | meetings | | (% Smokers) −20 | −5.8 kg | 6.9 | −16.6 | 6 | score +25 |
| | | | | Screening; health education | 10 | (Number/day) −12 | | | | | |
| | | | | Screening; brief medical counseling | 14 | (% Smokers) −25 | −5.2 kg | 6.7 | −10.6 | 9 | +10 |
| | | | | | | (Number/day) −9 | | | | | |
| Meyer et al. (55) USA | Males and females, aged 35–59 years, initially free of CHD, who attended three annual coronary screening surveys | 3 | Mean change | Screening; community health education; brief (12 week) group behavioral treatment | 67 | (% Smokers) −33 | −2.8 kg Relative weight 1.23 −.04 | 148 | −6.6 6.0 | −3.1 23 | Leisure activity score +8.6 |
| | | | | | | (Number/day) 11.7 −51.6 | | | | | |
| | | | | | | (% Smokers) 59.7 −50 | | | | | |
| | | | | Screening; community health education | | (Number/day) 15.4 −16 | 1.25 −.8 | 148 | −8.9 6.1 | −.2 25.6 | −8.5 |
| | | | | | | (% Smokers) 56.8 0 | | | | | |
| | | | | Screening only | 90 | (Number/day) 14 −21 | 1.29 −.8 | 138 | −2.0 6.0 | +2.3 19.1 | −12.8 |
| | | | | | | (% Smokers) 52.8 −15 | | (Diastolic) | | | |
| Multiple Risk Factor Intervention Trial Research Group (3) USA | Males, aged 35–57 yrs; prepared to participate in 5 year preventive trial, initially free of CHD | 6 | Mean change | Group meetings; training in behavioral techniques; ongoing coronary risk assessment. | | (Number/day) 33.7 −31 | 91 | −11.5 6.5 | −7.2 | | |
| | | | | | | (% Smokers) 59.3 −50 | | | | | |
| | | | | Referral to usual source of medical care; annual coronary risk screening | 6428 | (Number/day) 34.2 | 91 | −8 6.5 | −5 | | |
| | | | | | | (% Smokers) 59 −29 | | | | | |

The largest study evaluating the impact of medical counseling, coupled with screening and health education, on the coronary risk factor status of high CHD risk individuals is the ongoing World Health Organization trial (3). The design of this trial was outlined above, and will not be duplicated here. Males in the intervention (i.e., health education) factories who were found at baseline to be in the top 15–20% of the CHD risk distribution received personalized advice from the occupational physician on repeated occasions. Coronary risk factor status was assessed at annual intervals. High-risk subjects in the control group received no formal intervention program and were assessed for coronary risk on a 2-yearly basis. Interim (4-year) findings for the entire sample of high CHD risk subjects revealed a significant improvement in cigarette smoking as a result of health education, with a mean "net" reduction in self-reported daily cigarette consumption and prevalence of cigarette smoking of 14 and 5%, respectively (see Table II). The overall mean net improvement in systolic blood pressure after 4 years was slight (3%), but varied considerably between countries (i.e., from −6 to +4%). Similarly, the mean net improvement in serum cholesterol varied considerably between countries (from nil to 12%), with an overall average reduction of 5%. Net improvements in body weight were negligible in all countries after 4 years.

In an Australian study (49,50), known as the Sydney Heart Disease Prevention Programme (SHDPP), subjects were selected from over 10,000 volunteers who were found at a community coronary risk factor screening survey to be at high CHD risk. Findings after 3 years for a selective subsample of subjects who reported that they had received treatment from their medical practitioner aimed at reducing their coronary risk were compared with those for a "post hoc" control group ($N = 68$) of persons who initially manifested one or more of the coronary risk factors but whose overall coronary risk profile was deemed insufficiently severe to warrant medical referral. Subjects in the referral group demonstrated a very small improvement in mean body weight and serum cholesterol levels after three years, while the mean values for the control group on these measures actually worsened (see Table II). Significant mean reductions in systolic and diastolic blood pressure were reported in both the treatment group and control group, the improvements in the latter being attributed to measurement factors (i.e., the pressor effect, regression toward the population mean). The slightly greater mean change (of 5/4 mm Hg) in the referral group was attributed to pharmacological intervention. Cigarette smoking and exercise patterns were assessed but not reported.

Leaman, Crawshaw, and Zelis (51) reported the findings of an uncontrolled, retrospective American study evaluating the effects of screening and referral to medical personnel on the health-related living pattern of 117 subjects (73 males, 44 females) determined to be at high CHD risk in a community coronary screening program. Of these subjects, 62% ($N = 70$) were contacted by telephone 2 years after screening. Of the 11 subjects who initially smoked, four claimed to have stopped smoking during the follow-up period. While approximately half ($N = 39$) of the subjects reported that they had changed their diet to reduce their serum lipid levels, none knew whether their serum cholesterol level had changed over the follow-up period. Only one of the subjects reported being on a regular exercise program. Since the follow-up examination was conducted over the telephone, it was not possible to assess changes in blood pressure or serum lipid levels, or to validate self-reported improvements in dietary, drug usage, or exercise patterns.

In summary, while the findings of nonbehavioral, clinic-based trials have been somewhat inconsistent, intervention along these lines has generally been reported to have a significant impact on self-reported smoking levels and prevalence of cigarette smoking, and to result in modest (3–5%) reductions in serum lipid levels. Such programs have consistently failed to achieve lasting improvements in mean body weight and level of physical activity.

## B. Behavioral Programs

To date, only three controlled clinic-based trials evaluating the effectiveness of preventive programs for CHD have incorporated behavioral assessment and treatment procedures. The first was a small trial involving 36 high CHD risk males (who were free of clinical evidence of CHD), aged 35–55 years, which was conducted as a pilot study for the Stanford Heart Disease Prevention Program (53). Subjects were randomly assigned to one of three treatment conditions, referred to as behavior modification, individual counseling, and physician consultation. Intervention was aimed at dietary change, cessation of cigarette smoking, and improved exercise patterns. The behavioral treatment, which involved weekly group meetings over a 3-month period, included detailed health education and the following behavioral procedures: modeling of appropriate behaviors; social support (from the spouse and other group members); contingency management procedures (e.g., a token reward system); and guided practice of desirable behaviors. In the individual counseling treatment, subjects received short (15-minute), personalized counseling from a health educator on a weekly basis for 11 weeks. The final treatment involved a 20-minute consultation with a medical practitioner during which subjects were informed of high CHD risk levels and were advised to modify coronary risk-related living patterns. All subjects underwent rescreening on the coronary risk factors after 3 and 6 months. Data were presented in terms of mean changes on the coronary risk factors at final follow-up (see Table II).

After 6 months, the behavioral treatment demonstrated a slightly greater mean reduction in weight and serum cholesterol levels than the counseling group, while the physician consultation group showed the smallest improvement.

These findings were consistent with self-reported dietary changes in each of the three groups. Smoking cessation rates at 6 months, based on self-reported smoking patterns, were comparable for the three conditions (20–30%) as were the mean improvements in daily cigarette consumption (9–13 cigarettes/day). Level of leisure time physical activity, based on self-reported exercise patterns, showed an increase in both the behavior modification and individual counseling treatments at post-treatment (and no change in the physician consultation group); these improvements were not maintained over the 3-month follow-up period. Changes in blood pressure were not reported. The researchers concluded that the behavioral treatment was the most effective, particularly in improving body weight and serum lipid levels. However, the small sample size, the short follow-up period, and the failure to control across treatments for potentially therapeutic factors which are nonspecific to behavioral treatments (e.g., amount of contact with health professionals, attendance at small group meetings) (56) restrict the conclusions which can be drawn from this study.

The results of the Stanford pilot study were deemed sufficiently encouraging to include a behavioral treatment for subjects in the Stanford Three Community Study found to be at high CHD risk (1,55). The design of the Stanford Study was discussed earlier and will only be summarized here. In addition to receiving the mass media health education material, two-thirds ($N = 112$) of the subjects in one of the communities (Watsonville) who were in the top decile for CHD risk were invited to participate in a behavioral treatment programme (referred to as "intensive instruction") aimed at improving their coronary risk profile. "Intensive instruction" was provided either at group sessions (involving an average of 25 subjects per group) or on an individual basis (i.e., in the subject's own home). The former were conducted by three therapists (a health educator, his/her assistant, and a dietitian) while individual counseling was provided by graduate students in psychology. The intensive instruction treatment involved health education, information on the behavioral changes required to improve coronary risk, training in a variety of behavioral self-management techniques, establishing long-term goals for coronary risk factor change, and modeling of appropriate food preparation skills. Meetings were held on a weekly basis for the first 6 weeks and at less frequent intervals for the subsequent 6 weeks. Six months after the behavioral treatment ended, subjects were offered "maintenance" sessions: level of attendance at these was poor.

Changes in the coronary risk factor status of subjects who received the behavioral treatment were compared with those for high-risk persons in Watsonville who received the mass media health education campaign only, and "no treatment" control subjects (i.e., subjects who underwent screening only) (see Table II). It is important to point out that "dropouts" were excluded from the data analysis in the Stanford study, despite a nonuniform attrition rate across groups (higher attrition in the behavioral treatment) and the higher attrition rate of persons who were initially at higher CHD risk. Thus, reported improvements on the coronary risk factors may exaggerate actual change, particularly in the behavioral treatment. On average, subjects in the behavioral treatment demonstrated a marked improvement in weight at the first follow-up, but returned to their baseline weight thereafter. Subjects in the health education and control conditions similarly demonstrated negligible long-term improvements in mean body weight. Self-reported smoking levels suggested the behavioral treatment to result in a significantly greater reduction than health education, with a smoking cessation rate in the former of 50% after 3 years. Changes in self-reported exercise patterns revealed all three treatments to have had little lasting impact on level of physical activity. While questionnaire data suggested a major improvement in intake of saturated fat (i.e., a mean reduction of 33%) and cholesterol (i.e., a mean reduction of 40%) in the behavior modification cohort, objective assessment of serum cholesterol levels revealed only a slight (3%) mean improvement after 3 years. Subjects in the health education and screening groups demonstrated negligible long-term improvements in mean serum cholesterol levels. Both the behavioral and health education treatments resulted in highly significant improvements in blood pressure after 12 months (averaging 10/5 mm Hg) which were maintained over the subsequent 2-year period. The control condition, which initially had a markedly lower blood pressure level, demonstrated only a minor improvement on this coronary risk factor. Thus, after 3 years, the behavioral treatment resulted in marked improvements in self-reported levels of cigarette smoking and in systolic blood pressure, and a slight mean decrease in serum cholesterol. By comparison, the health education condition demonstrated a considerably lesser reduction in cigarette smoking, comparable improvements in systolic blood pressure, and negligible change in serum cholesterol. The control subjects demonstrated very little change on the risk factors.

The largest and most recent randomized, controlled CHD intervention trial involving behavioral procedures was the Multiple Risk Factor Intervention Trial (MRFIT) (4). The principal aim of the MRFIT was to determine the effects of a program directed at improving the three primary risk factors (i.e., serum lipid levels, blood pressure, and cigarette smoking) on the incidence of CHD in a sample of initially asymptomatic males aged 40–49 years. Almost 13,000 "high-risk" males, recruited from 22 coronary screening centers throughout America, who were prepared to engage in a 5-year intervention study were randomly assigned to one of two groups. The first, referred to as usual care (UC), involved referral of subjects to their usual source of medical care for help in reducing CHD risk, and annual assessment of their coronary risk profile. The second condition, known as special intervention (SI), involved personalized counseling from medical personnel about the subject's unfavorable status on the coronary risk factors, an initial formal 10-week intervention program, and continued therapeutic contact on either a group or an individual basis in an attempt to further improvements in target behaviors thereafter. SI included health education and the use of behavioral procedures to facilitate desirable dietary change, cessation of cigarette smoking, and adherence to antihypertensive medication. Behavioral procedures included self-monitoring, detailed analysis of target behaviors and environmental factors affecting their occurrence, goal setting, contracting, frequent feedback of changes in target behaviors and the coronary risk factors (including weight, blood pressure, and serum cholesterol), social support for favorable behavioral change, contingency management procedures, stimulus control techniques, modeling of desirable health-related behaviors, cognitive strategies (e.g., positive self-statements), and relaxation training. Treatment and maintenance procedures in the SI condition were repeatedly modified throughout the study in an attempt to maximize coronary risk factor change. Subjects in both the SI and the UC conditions were assessed on the coronary risk factors at annual intervals. Level of attendance at scheduled annual assessments was high (above 90%) in both groups throughout the trial.

At randomization, almost 60% of men reported themselves to be current cigarette smokers. At the first and sixth (final) annual assessments, self-reported smoking cessation rates for the SI were 43 and 50% respectively; thiocyanate adjusted quit rates were lower (31 and 46%, respectively; see Table II). Improvements in smoking for UC subjects were markedly less, with thiocyanate adjusted quit rates of 12% after 1 year and 29% after 6 years. Repeated blood pressure assessments were made at baseline to overcome the measurement problems associated with repeated assessment of this risk factor (i.e., regression toward the population mean; the pressor effect). By 12 months, average reductions in diastolic blood pressure were marked (6.5 mm Hg) for SI men and slight (2.5 mm Hg) for UC men. These gains were improved upon in both groups over the remainder of the study, the average reductions after 6 years being greater in the SI group (10.5 mm Hg) than the UC group (7.3 mm Hg). Serum cholesterol at baseline was relatively free of regression toward the population mean since it was not used as an eligibility criterion to select men at high risk. SI consistently proved slightly more effective in reducing serum cholesterol levels than UC, with mean improvements after 6 years of 7 and 5% respectively.

The results of the MRFIT clearly demonstrated the SI condition (which included behavioral assessment and treatment procedures) to be superior to usual medical care in improving the coronary risk factors, particularly in reducing levels of cigarette smoking. Unfortunately, it is not possible to draw firm conclusions regarding the contribution of behavioral change procedures per se to the superior results obtained in the SI condition, for two reasons. First, the behavioral intervention and control groups were not matched for a number of factors which have been demonstrated to have therapeutic influences in a wide variety of interventions (e.g., smoking, weight control, alcohol abuse) and which are non-specific to behavioral treatments (e.g., attendance at group meetings, participation in a formalized intervention program, and involvement of the spouse in the treatment) (54). Second, the behavioral strategies which were used throughout the treatment and maintenance phases in the SI were frequently modified throughout the study to maximize coronary risk factor change.

To summarize the findings of clinic-based trials involving behavioral techniques, a small pilot study (53) comparing the relative effectiveness of a behavioral treatment, personalized health education, and brief medical counseling over a 6-month period reported the first of these to be the most effective in improving body weight and serum lipid levels, while findings for blood pressure and cigarette smoking were inconclusive. Two subsequent, large scale, controlled studies have compared the long-term effectiveness of behavioral and nonbehavioral (health education, medical counseling) approaches in improving coronary risk, namely the Multiple Risk Factor Intervention Trial MRFIT) (3) and the Stanford Three Community Study (55). Both have reported behavioral treatments to be more effective than traditional approaches in reducing cigarette smoking and serum lipid levels. In the MRFIT, findings for cigarette smoking were validated using serum thiocyanate measures. Whereas the Stanford Study reported little difference in blood pressure reduction between the behavioral treatment and a community health education program, the MRFIT found the SI (behavioral) condition to be more effective than usual medical care in improving this risk factor.

While existing studies have consistently demonstrated behavioral treatments to be more effective than traditional, nonbehavioral approaches in improving the coronary risk factors, the former have been somewhat inconsistent in terms of the magnitude of such changes. The long-term improvements for the behavioral (Special Intervention) group in the MRFIT were consistently greater than those for the "intensive instruction" treatment in the Stanford Study, the former achieving a mean decrease in the prevalence of cigarette smoking of almost 50% after 6 years and an average reduction in diastolic blood pressure and serum cholesterol levels of 12 and 7%, respectively. There are two possible explanations for the superior results in the MRFIT. The first lies in differences in the study populations. Participants in the MRFIT were voluntary attenders at a coronary screening program who were willing to undertake further assessment plus a 5-year preventive health program. They were likely to constitute a "health conscious" group who were strongly committed to reducing their CHD risk. Subjects in the Stanford Study may have been less motivated to effect lasting improvements in their unhealthy living patterns since they were required to participate in only a relatively brief (12-week) treatment program. Furthermore, the MRFIT involved only males, whereas the Stanford Study involved both males and females. The greater homogeneity of subjects in the former study may have rendered the modeling and reinforcement of improvements in target behaviors at group meetings more effective. Alternatively, treatment factors may account for the greater improvements in the MRFIT. These may include the greater attention to the individual needs of each participant, greater provision for the maintenance of improvements on the coronary risk factors through long-term therapeutic contact, and ongoing coronary risk factor screening and feedback to reinforce favorable behavioral change in the MRFIT.

## V.  SUMMARY

Coronary risk factor screening and health education programs have constituted the mainstay of intervention in the large-scale community and clinic-based multifactorial CHD intervention trials which have been conducted in recent years. Community-based trials involving intervention along these lines have generally reported significant improvements in self-reported smoking patterns, slight improvements in blood pressure and serum lipid levels, and negligible changes in weight and physical fitness. The findings of controlled clinic-based trials involving nonbehavioral intervention have generally been only slightly more encouraging. Of note are the impressive findings of the Oslo Study (52), in which intervention involving brief personalized counseling and coronary risk factor assessment at 6-monthly intervals resulted in markedly greater improvements in mean serum cholesterol levels (13%) and the prevalence of smoking (15%) than was a case for the "no treatment" control group. The greater improvements in cigarette smoking were validated using serum thiocianate levels. The findings of both the North Karelia project and the MRFIT suggest behavioral intervention to be superior to traditional "exhortative" (i.e., screening; health education; medical counseling) procedures in achieving lasting improvements in the primary coronary risk factors (i.e., blood pressure, serum cholesterol, and cigarette smoking), but to be similarly ineffectual in changing the secondary risk factors (i.e., body weight, physical fitness). The issues of cost effectiveness, and the role of particular behavioral techniques in achieving lasting improvements in target coronary risk-related behaviors remain to be researched.

## VI.  CONCLUDING REMARKS

While existing studies suggest that behavioral procedures may facilitate the attainment and maintenance of favorable changes in coronary risk-related living patterns and the coronary risk factors in both individual and community-based intervention, their role in preventive programs for CHD remains to be definitively assessed. The dearth of psychological research in this area is surprising given the "epidemic" incidence of CHD in the developed nations, and more importantly the limited success of "exhortative" approaches (such as health education and coronary risk factor screening) in achieving significant, lasting improvements in target behaviors. In view of the encouraging results of both the North Karelia project and the Multiple Risk Factor Intervention Programme, it is to be hoped that greater attention will be paid to behavioral principles and procedures in future CHD prevention programs.

## REFERENCES

1. Farquhar, J. W. *et al*. (1977). Community education for cardiovascular health. *Lancet*, **1**, 1192–1995.
2. Puska, P., Tuomilehto, J., Salonen, J., Nissinen, A., Virtamo, J. *et al*. (1981). *Community control of cardiovascular diseases: The North Karelia Project*. Report published on behalf of National Public Health Laboratory of Finland by the Regional Office for Europe. World Health Organization. Copenhagen.
3. Multiple Risk Factor Intervention Trial Research Group. (1982). Multiple risk intervention trial—risk factor changes and mortality results. *Journal of the American Medical Association*, **248**, 1465–1467.
4. World Health Organisation European Collaborative Group (WHO) (1982). Multifactorial trial in the prevention of coronary heart disease: 2. Risk factor changes at two and four years. *European Journal of Cardiology*, **3**, 184–190.
5. World Health Organization (1981). Vital statistics and causes of death. *World Health Statistics Annual*, **1**.
6. Kannel, W. B. (1974). Prevention of coronary heart diseases by control of risk factors (questions and answers). *Journal of the American Medical Association*, **227**, 227–338.
7. Abramson, E. E. (1977). Behavioural approaches to weight control: An updated review. *Behavior Research & Therapy*, **15**, 355–365.
8. Wilson, G. T., & Brownell, K. D. (1980). Behaviour therapy for obesity: An evaluation of treatment outcome. *Advances in Behaviour Research and Therapy*, **3**, 49–86.
9. Bernstein, D. A., & Glasgow, R. E. (1979). In O. F. Pomerleau & J. P. Brady (Eds.), *The modification of smoking behavior*. Baltimore: Williams & Wilkins.
10. Foreyt, J. P., Scott, L. W., Mitchell, R. E., & Gotto, A. M. (1979). Plasma lipid changes in the normal population following behavioural treatment. *Journal of Consulting and Clinical Psychology*, **47**, 440–452.
11. Epstein, L. H., & Wing, R. R. (1980). Aerobic exercise and weight. *Addictive Behaviours*, **5**, 371–388.
12. Reid, E. L. & Morgan, R. W. (1980). Exercise prescription: A clinical trial. *American Journal of Public Health*, **69**, 6.
13. Wysocki, T., Hall, G., Iwata, B., & Riordan, M. (1979). Behavioural management of exercise: Contracting for aerobic points. *Journal of Applied Behavioural Analysis*, **12**, 55–64.
14. Johnston, D. W. (1982). Behavioural treatment in the reduction of coronary risk factors: Type A behaviour and blood pressure. *Journal of Clinical Psychology*, **21**, 281–294.
15. Davidson, P. O., & Davidson, S. M. (Eds.) (1978). *Behavioural medicine: Changing health lifestyles*. New York: Brunner/Mazel.
16. Enelow, A. J., & Henderson, J. B. (Eds.) (1975). *Applying behavioral science to cardiovascular risk*. New York: American Heart Association Publication.

17. Pomerleau, O., Bass, F., & Crown, V. (1975). Role of behaviour modification in preventive medicine. *New England Journal of Medicine, 292,* 1277–1282.
18. Pomerleau, O., & Brady, J. P. (1979). *Behavioral medicine: Theory and practice.* Baltimore: Williams & Wilkins.
19. Rachman, S. (Ed.) (1980). *Contributions to medical psychology.* Oxford: Pergamon.
20. Williams, R. B., & Gentry, W. D. (1977). *Behavioral approaches to medical treatment.* Cambridge. Mass: Ballinger.
21. Syme, S. L. (1978). Lifestyle intervention in clinic-based trials. *American Journal of Epidemiology, 108,* 87–91.
22. Farquhar, J. (1978). The community based model of life style intervention trials. *American Journal of Epidemiology, 108,* 103–111.
23. Veterans Administrative Co-operative Study Group on Antihypertensive Agents. (1967). Effects of treatment on morbidity in hypertension. Results in patients with diastolic blood pressures averaging 115 through 129mmHg. *Journal of the American Medical Association, 202,* 116–122.
24. Veterans Administrative Co-operative Study Group of Treatment on Morbidity in Hypertension. II. (1970). Results in patients with diastolic pressure averaging 90 through 114mmHg. *Journal of the American Medical Association, 213,* 1143–1152.
25. Smith, W. M. (1977). Treatment of mild hypertension: Results of a ten year intervention trial. *Circulation Research, 40,* 98–105.
26. Carlson, L. A., Danielson, M., Ekberg, I. *et al.* (1977). Reduction of myocardial reinfarction by the combined treatments with clofibrate and nicotonic acid. *Atherosclerosis, 28,* 81–86.
27. Oliver, M. F., Heady, J. A., Morris, J. N., & Cooper, J. (1978). A co-operative trial in the primary prevention of CHD using clofibrate: Report from the Committee of principal investigators. *British Heart Journal, 40,* 1069–1118.
28. Borhani, N. O. (1977). Primary prevention of coronary heart disease: A critique. *American Journal of Cardiology, 40,* 251–259.
29. Stamler, J. (1981). Primary prevention of coronary heart disease: The last twenty years. *American Journal of Cardiology, 47,* 722–734.
30. Henderson, J. B., & Enelow, A. J. (1976). The coronary risk factor problem: A behavioural perspective. *Preventive Medicine, 5,* 128–148.
31. Kristein, M., Arnold, G., & Wynder, E. (1977). Health economics and preventive health care. *Science, 195,* 457–462.
32. Becker, M. H., & Maiman, B. A. (1975). Sociobehavioural determinants of compliance with health and medical care recommendations. *Medical Care, 13,* 10–24.
33. Cohen, C. S., & Cohen, E. J. (1978). Health education: Panacea, pernicious or pointless? *New England Journal of Medicine, 299,* 718–720.
34. Haggerty, R. J. (1977). Changing lifestyles to improve health. *Preventive Medicine, 6,* 276–289.
35. Hosay, P. M. (1977). The unfulfilled promise of health education. *New York University Quarterly, 8,* 1602.
36. Knowles, J. H. (Ed.) (1977). *Doing better and feeling worse: Health in the U.S.* New York: Norton.
37. Ubell, E. (1972). Health behaviour change: A political model. *Preventive Medicine, 18,* 209–221.
38. Caplan, R. D., Robinson, E. A., French, J. R., Caldwell, J. R., Shinn, M. *et al.* (1976). Adhering to medical regimens: Pilot experiments in patient education and social support. *Michigan Institute for Social Research.*
39. Zimbardo, P. G., Ebbesen, E. G., & Maslach, C. (1977). *Influencing attitudes and changing behavior* (2nd ed.). Reading, Mass.: Addison-Wesley.

40. Aronow, W., Allen, W., De Christofaro, D., & Ungermann, S. (1975). Follow-up of mass screening for coronary risk factors in 1817 adults. *Circulation*, **51**, 1038–1044.
41. Abramson, J. H., Hopp, C., Gofin, J., Makler, A., Habib, J., & Ronen, L. (1979). A community program for the control of the cardiovascular risk factors. A preliminary evaluation of the effectiveness of the CHAD program in Jerusalem. *Journal of Community Health*, **5**, 3–21.
42. Werko, L. (1979). Prevention of heart attacks. A multifactorial preventive trial in Gothenburg, Sweden. *Annals of Clinical Research*, **11**, 71–79.
43. World Health Organisation European Collaborative Group (WHO) (1974). An international controlled trial in the multifactorial prevention of coronary heart disease. *International Journal of Epidemiology*, **3**, 219–241.
44. Rose, G., Heller, R. F., Pedoe, H. T., & Christie, D. G. S. (1980). Heart disease prevention project: A randomised controlled trial in industry. *British Medical Journal*, **3**, 747–751.
45. Puska, P., Koskela, K., Pakarinen, H., Puumalainen, P., Soininen, V., & Tuomilehto, J. (1976). The North Karelia Project: A programme for community control of cardiovascular diseases. *Journal of the Scandinavian Society of Medicine*, **4**, 57–60.
46. Kornitzer, M., De Bocker, G., Dramair, M., & Thilly, G. (1980). The Belgian heart disease prevention project: Modification of the coronary risk profile of an industrial population. *Circulation* **61**, 18–25.
47. McAlister, A., Puska, P., Salonen, J. T., Tuomilehto, J., & Koskeal, K. (1982). Theory and action for health promotion: Illustrations from the North Karelia Project. *American Journal of Public Health*, **72**, 43–54.
48. Hjermann, I., Holme, I., Velve Byre, K., & Leren, P. (1981). Effect of diet and smoking intervention on the incidence of coronary heart disease. Report from the Oslo Study Group of a randomised trial in healthy men. *Lancet*, 1303–1310.
49. Simons, L. L., & Jones, A. (1978). Coronary risk factor screening and long-term follow-up: Year one of the Sydney Heart Disease Prevention Programme. *Medical Journal of Australia*, **2**, 455–458.
50. Simons, L. L., & Jones, A. S. (1980). Coronary risk factor screening. *Medical Journal of Australia*, **7**, 278–279.
51. Leamon, D. M., Crawshaw, S. L., & Zelis, R. F. (1981). Assessing the value of mass screening for coronary risks. *Pennsylvania Medicine*, **84**, 29–31.
52. Hjermann, I. (1980). Smoking and diet intervention in healthy coronary high risk men. Methods and five year follow-up of risk factors in a randomised trial. The Oslo Study. *Journal of the Oslo City Hospital*, **30**, 3–17.
53. Meyer, A. J., & Henderson, J. B. (1974). Multiple risk factor reduction in the prevention of cardiovascular disease. *Preventive Medicine*, **3**, 225–236.
54. Jacobson, N. S., & Baucom, D. H. (1977). Design and assessment of nonspecific control groups in behaviour modification research. *Behaviour Therapy*, **8**.
55. Meyer, A. J., Nash, J. D., McAllister, A. L., Maccoby, N., & Farquhar, J. W. (1980). Skills training in a cardiovascular health education campaign. *Journal of Consulting Clinical Psychology*, **48**, 129–142.

# INDEX

## A

Absenteeism
 cardiovascular disease, worksite intervention
  and, 163, 171, 176, 188, 190
 chronic asthma and, 124, 155
Abuse, contingent electric shock and, 2
Accountability, contingent electric shock and,
  6, 7, 32
Accreditation Council for Services for Mentally Retarded and Other Developmentally Disabled Persons (ACMRDD), 3,
  4, 13
Activity Measurement, 65
 DSM-I, 41–44, 64
 DSM-II, 44–47, 64
 DSM-III, 48, 62–64
  affective disorders, 50–60
  attention deficit disorder, 48–50
  organic mental disorders, 60–62
 levels of assessment, 36–39
Acute schizophrenic episode, DSM-II and, 46
Adherence
 coronary heart disease and, 203
 health care regimens and, 89–91
  chemotherapy, 93, 94
  diabetes, 92, 93
  oral hygiene, 91, 92
  radiation therapy, 93, 94
Adolescents, behavioral medicine and
 diabetes, 93
 idiopathic scoliosis, 75
 obesity, 97
 smoking prevention, 100
Adrenergic compounds, chronic asthma and,
  27
Affective disorders
 DSM-II and, 44, 45
 DSM-III and, 50–60
Affective reactions, DSM-I and, 41, 42
Aggression, chronic asthma and, 151

Aggression, contingent electric shock and, 2,
  3, 4, 18
 informed consent document and, 22, 23
  justification, 25, 26
  treatment procedures, 23–25, 29, 30
  treatment program, 26–28
  side effects, 28, 29
Alcohol
 cyclothymic disorder and, 56
 dysthymic disorder and, 58
Ammonia, aromatic
 aggression and, 24
 self-injurious behavior and, 24
Angina, DSM-III and, 64
Anorexia nervosa, DSM-III and, 62, 63
Anxiety, chronic asthma and, 149
Anxiety management training, behavioral medicine and, 82, 86, 99
Anxiety reduction, bulimia nervosa and, 79,
  80
Aphasia, behavioral medicine and, 71–73
Arthritis, DSM-III and, 63
Assertive training
 chronic asthma and, 124, 138, 150, 151,
  153
 smoking prevention and, 100
Association for the Advancement of Behavior
  Therapy (AABT)
 behavioral medicine and, 70
 contingent electric shock and, 3, 4, 13
Asthma, 124, 125
 assertive training, 150, 151
 behavior management intervention, 151–153
 behavioral medicine, 69, 80
 biofeedback, 141–149
 epidemiology, 125, 126
 etiology, 126
 measurement, 127
 methodological issues, 153–156
 pharmacological treatment, 127
 relaxation training, 128–141